Unsustainable Transport and Transition in China

This book discusses various transport sustainability issues from the perspective of developing countries, exploring key issues, problems and potential solutions for improving transport sustainability in China. It first reviews the current transport sustainability baselines in the three key dimensions of environmental, economic and social sustainability, via an international comparison encompassing both developed and developing countries in different world regions. Then, with a time frame up to 2030, the study groups 100 major Chinese cities according to their baseline conditions, projected population and economic growth, and common sustainability challenges in passenger transport.

A systematic attempt is made to discuss the characteristics, strengths and weaknesses of various emerging sustainable transport strategies, including the metro systems, bus rapid transit, light rail, bicycles (and e-bicycles), electric vehicles and walking. Based on the different city clusters identified, the study then explores the opportunities and constraints of introducing a range of emerging sustainable transport strategies through both statistical analysis and detailed fieldwork. Future directions and challenges are identified based on official documents, onsite observations and interviews with local people. The study concludes with thoughts on sustainable transport in smart cities, the importance of governance, local participation, internal and external city movements, and towards a holistic sustainable transport plan.

Unsustainable Transport and Transition in China will be of great interest to scholars interested in carbon emissions, climate change, environmental policy, planning, road safety, sustainability, transportation and urban studies, and is relevant to China and other developing countries.

Becky P.Y. Loo is Professor of Geography at the University of Hong Kong. Her research interests include transportation, e-technologies (defined as microelectronics, informatics and telecommunications) and society. In particular, she excels in spatial analysis, surveys, behavioural modelling, transport carbon emissions, regional infrastructure, transit-oriented development, walkable communities and road safety.

Routledge Studies in Transport, Environment and Development

Unsustainable Transport and Transition in China

Becky P.Y. Loo

Routledge
Taylor & Francis Group
LONDON AND NEW YORK

from Routledge

First published 2018 by Routledge

2 Park Square, Milton Park, Abingdon, Oxfordshire OX14 4RN
52 Vanderbilt Avenue, New York, NY 10017

Routledge is an imprint of the Taylor & Francis Group, an informa business

First issued in paperback 2019

© 2018 Becky P.Y. Loo

The right of Becky P.Y. Loo to be identified as author of this work has
been asserted by her in accordance with sections 77 and 78 of the
Copyright, Designs and Patents Act 1988.

All rights reserved. No part of this book may be reprinted or reproduced or
utilised in any form or by any electronic, mechanical, or other means, now
known or hereafter invented, including photocopying and recording, or in
any information storage or retrieval system, without permission in writing
from the publishers.

Trademark notice: Product or corporate names may be trademarks or
registered trademarks, and are used only for identification and explanation
without intent to infringe.

British Library Cataloguing in Publication Data
A catalogue record for this book is available from the British Library

Library of Congress Cataloging in Publication Data
A catalog record for this book has been requested

ISBN: 978-1-138-93451-1 (hbk)
ISBN: 978-0-367-87416-2 (pbk)

Typeset in Times New Roman
by Wearset Ltd, Boldon, Tyne and Wear

Contents

Figures

Tables

Acknowledgements

The findings of this book are based on a contract research entitled 'China Mobility Transition 2030' funded by CBMM. I am extremely gratefully for the generous support of the company, especially in funding the fieldwork of this research not only in China but also in Brazil, Chile, Sweden and the United Kingdom. In particular, I am indebted to the continual support of Mr Rogerio Magalhaes Pastore and his family throughout the study. I would also like to thank Mr Eduardo Ayroza Galvão Ribeiro, Mr Marcus A. Prates Vicenzetto, Ms Renata Duarte Menezes Rocha, Mr Leonardo Magalhaes Silvestre, Ms Mariana Perez de Oliveira, Mr Joes Isildo Vargas, Mr Pablo Salazar and Mr Kao Chian Tou from CBMM. The fruitful exchange of views has widened my perspective on sustainable transport, and the enormous contributions that a mining company can give to make the world a better place for all of us.

In addition, Mr Wang Meng, Zhang Wei and Mr Guo Aimin of CITIC Metal Co. Ltd in Beijing kindly offered assistance with the fieldwork in China. In this project, I am also very happy to have become acquainted with Professor Jurgen Paulus and Professor Aldemir Drummond of Fundação Dom Cabral (FDC). As this book has taken years to complete, amid my many other obligations, many research assistants and my Doctor of Philosophy students (and now graduates) have contributed in various ways. I would like to express my gratitude to all of them here. They are Mr Hong Chan, Ms Yoki Lam, Mr Kelvin Leung, Dr Linna Li, Mr Tony Phuah, Ms Crystal Shum, Mr Ka Ho Tsoi, Ms Tracy Tsoi, Dr Wu Yuhao and Dr Yao Shenjun.

Last but not least, I could not finish this book without the unfailing love and support of my husband, Mr Kim Wai Ng. This book is dedicated to the future generations, including our three children, Ping Shue Wilbert, Ping Wah Fabian and Ping Lam Concordia. It has really been a joy seeing them growing up. As a working mother, my hope is to set a good example for my children and to show other young ladies that loving your own family does not mean that you should not contribute to the society, and strive to realise the true meaning of your own life. Be bold, be innovative!

Becky P.Y. Loo
Hong Kong
July, 2017

Abbreviations

AFV	Alternative fuel vehicles
AI	Artificial intelligence
ANN	Artificial neural network
BCA	Benefit-cost analysis
BRICS	Brazil, Russia, India, China and South Africa
BRT	Bus rapid transit
CBD	Central business district
CCP	Chinese Communist Party
CDA	Comprehensive development area
DPA	Directly productive activities
ESCAPE	European Study of Cohorts for Air Pollution Effects
GDP	Gross Domestic Product
GNI	Gross National Income
GPS	Global Positioning System
HSRs	High-speed railways
ICT	Information and communication technologies
IoT	Internet-of-things
ISS	Injury Severity Score
ITS	Intelligent transport system
ITU	International Telecommunication Union
LDCs	Less-developed countries
LMDI	Logarithmic Mean Divisia Index
LPG	Liquefied gas
LRT	Light rail transit
MDCs	More-developed countries
NHSA	National Highway Safety Administration
OECD	Organisation for Economic Co-operation and Development
PCA	Principal component analysis
POI	Point of interest
PPP	Public-private partnership
PRC	People's Republic of China
RMB	Renminbi
SOC	Social overhead capital

SUVs	Sports utility vans
TEUs	Twenty-foot equivalent units
TOD	Transit-oriented development
UK	United Kingdom
UN	United Nations
USA	United States of America
USSR	Union of Soviet Socialist Republics
WHO	World Health Organization

1 Introduction

Aims and objectives

This book is concerned with the key issues, problems and emerging strategies to address unsustainable transport. The term 'unsustainable transport', used by Banister (2005), summarises the major trends of unsustainable transport in the developed countries, particularly in Europe, very well. In general, transport in the developed countries is unsustainable mainly because it is almost totally dependent on fossil fuels for energy. The car, mostly powered by diesel or petroleum, is 'an icon of the twentieth century' that is fully embedded in almost every aspect of the everyday life of people living in the developed countries, especially in North America, Europe and Australia. Unsurprisingly, automobiles dominate both passenger and freight transport in these countries; and 'it is impossible to make any real change to that situation' in the near future (Banister, 2005, p. 7).

In this book, the classification of countries into the broad groups of developed, transition and developing economies follows the annex of the report of the United Nations (2014) on *World Economic Situation and Prospects 2014*. It is important to clarify at the outset that the use of the term 'developing countries' is intended to suggest neither that there is only one development path (the one that developed countries have gone through) nor that developing countries will follow clear logical stages of economic growth, as suggested by the modernisation paradigm (Rostow, 1990). These broad categories are intended to show basic economic conditions of the countries, versus geography (by world geographical region, for example) or income of a certain year (by Gross National Income (GNI), for example). Through adopting this more general classification, it is hoped that useful lessons based on the unsustainable transport problems and challenges faced by economies with different basic economic conditions can be learnt. The distinction is general and conceptual rather than specific and statistical because the main point is to recognise that developed and developing countries do generally face different types of unsustainable transport challenges and their basic economic conditions will significantly affect the policy goals of governments (with economic growth being one of the major policy goals among developing countries), the transport needs of the society, as well as the resources and technologies available.

Over time, the environmental, economic and social challenges associated with the unrestrained and ubiquitous use of automobiles in developed countries for almost all trips regardless of the trip characteristics (including trip purpose, distance and locations) and other circumstances (such as the availability of alternative transport modes, level of traffic congestion and parking availability) have been intensifying. There is an urgent need for all of us to re-think car use, particularly in light the consumption of non-renewable energy, vehicle exhaust emission, traffic congestion, the use of non-recyclable materials and traffic crashes (Loo & du Verle, 2017; Loo, 2017). Policy-makers, planners, transport professionals and academics alike need to re-examine and re-think the intertwined relationship between transport and society, and find ways to establish a stronger and more supporting role for transport in making the world more sustainable. While Banister (2005) provides an excellent overview of the relevant issues in developed countries, there is a lack of insights on the situations and trends in developing countries so that policy-makers and researchers from around the world can get a better understanding of pertinent transport issues and problems there, and to formulate appropriate and effective policies and strategies to slow down, if not to reverse, many trends of unsustainable transport also happening in many developing countries worldwide.

Geographers fully understand that the experience of one place cannot be directly transferred to another without regard to the local physical and human environment. The primary focus of this book is on China, where most of the documentary research, data analysis and fieldwork were carried out between 2012 and 2015. Where applicable, case studies at the city level were conducted. This is not to ignore that China, as a vast country of 9.6 million square kilometres (km^2), is extremely diverse in terms of its physical geography (notably relief, climate, flora and fauna) and human geography (including population density, ethnic composition, culture, economy and various social issues).

Table 1.1 shows some key statistics of the 31 provinces and provincial-level municipalities in China. Figure 1.1 is the administrative map of China, which shows the provincial units and the provincial capitals, as appropriate. The physical size of these provincial administrative units varies from the smallest of 0.63 km^2 in Shanghai to the largest of 120.22 km^2 in Tibet; and the average altitude ranges from the lowest of 3 m in Tianjin to the highest at 3,658 m in Tibet – a difference of over 1,000 times! The average monthly temperature in winter (January 2013) was as low as −17.3° Celsius in Jilin and as high as 20.5° Celsius in Hainan. In other words, the temperature range for someone travelling to different parts of China can be over 35° Celsius in winter. Similarly, the average summer temperature differs widely, from as cool as 16.0° Celsius in Qinghai to as hot as 29.5° Celsius in Hainan (July 2013).

In relation to human geography, the absolute population size was the highest in Guangdong (107.24 million in 2014) and the lowest in Tibet (3.18 million in 2014) – a difference of more than 30 times! The Gross Domestic Product (GDP) per capita was the highest in Tianjin (105,231 yuan per capita in 2014) and the

Figure 1.1 Administrative map of China.

Source: Compiled by the author.

lowest in Gansu (26,433 yuan per capita in 2014). The number of ethnic groups in China is as high as 56. As each ethnic group tends to have its own spoken language, traditional costumes and culture, the cultural diversity within the country is amazingly rich. Within mainland China (that is, excluding Hong Kong, Macau and Taiwan), the number of local dialects officially recorded is over 80, while most people also speak Mandarin and share a common history which can be traced to Emperor Qin Shi Huang who unified China, that is, the Qin Dynasty (211–206 BC), if not earlier. The use of a common written language, that is, the Chinese characters (simplified Chinese in mainland China, and traditional Chinese in Hong Kong and Taiwan), and the circulation of one common currency, that is, Renminbi (RMB), also help to build the nation despite its vast geographical diversity.

While the focus of this book is on China, the lessons learnt are not only valuable in gaining a deeper understanding of the country alone but also relevant to other developing countries that also share similar unsustainable transport challenges caused by a combination of factors, namely a low-income base and a

Table 1.1 Key statistics of provinces and provincial-level municipalities in China

	Land area (10,000 km²)	Average altitude of the provincial capital/PLM (km)	The highest altitude in the province (km)	Average monthly temperature in January 2013 (Celsius)	Average monthly temperature in July 2013 (Celsius)	Population size in 2014 (million)	GDP per capita (yuan) in 2014
Beijing	1.64	0.030	2.30	-1.5	26.5	21.52	99,995
Tianjin	1.19	0.003	1.08	-1.0	27.0	15.17	105,231
Hebei	18.85	0.080	2.88	-1.4	25.2	73.84	39,984
Shanxi	15.58	0.780	3.06	-6.9	23.5	36.48	35,070
Inner Mongolia	118.30	1.060	3.56	-6.0	22.0	25.05	71,046
Liaoning	14.84	0.090	1.35	-8.9	23.4	43.91	65,201
Jilin	18.74	0.040	2.74	-17.3	22.8	27.52	50,160
Heilongjiang	47.30	0.170	2.04	-16.2	18.0	38.33	39,226
Shanghai	0.63	0.005	0.10	4.2	27.9	24.26	97,370
Jiangsu	10.72	0.009	0.63	3.2	28.0	79.60	81,874
Zhejiang	10.18	0.040	1.93	6.0	26.0	55.08	73,002
Anhui	14.01	0.030	1.87	2.5	28.5	60.83	34,425
Fujian	13.60	0.080	2.16	11.8	27.4	38.06	63,472
Jiangxi	16.69	0.050	2.16	6.0	27.6	45.42	34,674
Shandong	15.71	0.050	1.52	0.0	25.0	97.89	60,879

Henan	16.60	0.110	2.41	0.0	27.5	94.36	37,072
Hubei	18.59	0.020	3.11	3.0	28.0	58.16	47,145
Hunan	21.18	0.050	2.12	6.7	28.9	67.37	40,271
Guangdong	17.97	0.007	1.90	13.3	28.5	107.24	63,469
Guangxi	23.67	0.072	2.14	10.4	28.0	47.54	33,090
Hainan	3.54	0.014	1.87	20.5	29.5	9.03	38,924
Chongqing	8.24	0.260	2.89	6.0	27.5	29.91	47,850
Sichuan	48.60	0.510	7.56	6.6	23.3	81.40	35,128
Guizhou	17.62	1.070	2.90	4.5	23.5	35.08	26,437
Yunnan	39.40	1.890	6.71	7.0	20.5	47.14	27,264
Tibet	120.22	3.660	8.84	-9.6	16.4	3.18	29,252
Shaanxi	20.58	0.400	3.77	0.0	25.3	37.75	46,929
Gansu	45.37	1.520	6.64	-3.7	21.0	25.91	26,433
Qinghai	72.23	2.260	6.86	-7.0	16.0	5.83	39,671
Ningxia	6.64	1.110	3.56	-8.0	20.8	6.62	41,834
Xinjiang	166.00	0.920	8.61	-7.0	23.8	22.98	40,648

Sources: National Bureau of Statistics of China (2014a, 2014b, 2015a, 2015b, 2015c).

large population, but rapid income growth, motorisation and urbanisation in a relatively short time span in history. Taken together, the scale and speed with which unsustainable transport trends have evolved in many developing countries, especially since 1970, are unprecedented and worthy of closer investigation. On the one hand, there are many common trends of unsustainable transport shared by different developing countries. On the other hand, behind these general trends, the local context is always important in understanding the key issues, problems and emerging strategies to tackle unsustainable transport.

In particular, the group of emerging developing economies of Brazil, Russia, India, China and South Africa, nicknamed the BRICS economies, has attracted much international attention due to their remarkable economic performances. Nonetheless, despite the rapid income growth rates in these emerging developing economies, they are still at a low level of wealth as reflected in the GDP per capita, whether measured in current dollars or purchasing power parity (PPP). In 2015, the GDP per capita, PPP (current international $) of Brazil ($15,390.6), Russia ($24,451.4), India ($6,100.7), China ($14,450.2) and South Africa ($13,195.3) was not only less than half (<50 per cent) that of the United States of America (USA) ($56,115.7) but also far behind the other developed countries of Australia ($46,270.8), Germany ($48,041.7), Japan ($40,763.4) and the United Kingdom (UK) ($41,755.9) (World Bank, 2016). The priority on economic growth and the inequality of wealth within these countries are common problems limiting the resources allocated to tackle the unsustainable transport trends on the one hand, and the range of technical and policy options accessible and feasible to them on the other. A recent study by Loo & Banister (2016), however, demonstrates that many of these developing economies have already been making progress towards decoupling economic growth from some most notable negative transport externalities like carbon emissions and traffic fatalities.

Study approach

There are two general approaches to achieving the overarching goal of this book of gaining a better understanding of the unsustainable transport challenges that China and other developing countries face. The first approach is to carry out a historical review of major unsustainable transport trends in developing countries over the last three decades, from 1970 to 2000, roughly the same period as the book covered by Banister (2005). The key advantage will be the completion of a 'world jigsaw puzzle' so that comparisons can be made among world regions for a comparable period of time.

The second approach is to establish the current baseline among the developing countries and then attempt to look into the future. The key advantage here is the relevance of the research work to contemporary policy-makers and researchers. The establishment of a more recent baseline will also give readers a better idea about the current state of affairs and a broader view of the diversity of issues and problems facing developing countries. More importantly, the future-looking methodology will allow readers to start thinking more seriously and deeply about the sustainable transport strategies to tackle various key issues and problems that people living in many developing countries are currently facing. For the above reasons, the second approach is used. It is hoped that this book will be of interest not only to researchers for academic reasons but also to the industry, the public sector, the wider community and the human race as a whole in exploring possible strategies to address unsustainable transport.

The next step is to determine the time frame of the study. In particular, how far should one be looking into the future? The dilemma is that the longer the time from now that one is projecting, the more likely that unforeseen changes will take place, making the current analysis much less relevant, if not invalid. These changes include both physical and human-induced changes. For the former, natural disasters like large-scale drought or flooding, massive earthquakes and even meteorite hits (like the one that hit Russia in 2013) may happen (Anonymous, 2013). For the latter, they include technological breakthroughs (such as fully-autonomous private vehicles), economic and social innovations (such as universal car-sharing), or other events such as terrorist attacks or large-scale armed conflicts. The longer is the period, the higher is the risk of uncertainty and, hence, the setting in of new trends not foreseen or captured in this study.

Moreover, it is recognised that any emerging sustainable transport strategy, together with its associated policies and technical measures, will need to be further examined for many aspects of applicability and feasibility on different fronts within specific geographical settings before it can be successfully implemented. It must be emphasised at the outset that the various emerging sustainable transport strategies covered in this book are by no means ready solutions, and certainly not panacea, for tackling unsustainable transport challenges. Nonetheless, the earlier that these alternative emerging sustainable transport strategies are systematically presented, widely discussed and critically examined for their feasibility and desirability within the specific local and geographical contexts, the higher is the chance that they can be further modified and adapted to become real, practical and effective bundles of policy and technical options in the medium to long term. The situations in many developing countries are deteriorating at such a rapid pace with daily congestion wasting people's time, air pollution causing global climate change and local health problems, and traffic accidents killing and injuring millions of people, that no time should be wasted in slowing down, halting and possibly reversing these unsustainable transport trends.

Every coin has two sides. It is also important to recognise at the outset that transportation has always been an essential part of people's everyday life throughout history and in both developed and developing countries. Table 1.2 summarises some major costs and benefits of a transport system. A more detailed discussion of the substantive issues and contexts is given in Chapter 2. In tackling the unsustainable transport trends, care must be taken not to neglect the enormous benefits of travel, including travelling purely for leisure, recreation and tourism. Without a doubt, there are many costs associated with transport. They range from

Table 1.2 Major costs and benefits of transportation

Costs	Benefits
CO_2 and other greenhouse gas emissions	Access to opportunities
Congestion	Business
Construction costs	Capital assets and infrastructure
Destruction of natural habitat/ecosystem	Employment
Inequalities	Global trade and finance
Local air pollution	Leisure and recreation
Noise pollution	Physical and mental health
Traffic deaths and injuries	Spatial division of labour
Use of non-renewable energy	Social interactions (social capital)
Visual intrusion	Tourism

Source: The author.

the capital investment, operation expenses, maintenance cost and depreciation of infrastructure, to the use of energy and non-recyclable materials, the emissions of greenhouse gases and local pollutants, the inequality associated with car use, the congestion problem, and traffic deaths and injuries, among others.

Nonetheless, there are also enormous benefits of travel. In the first place, the experience of travel satisfies a fundamental human desire to 'conquer' space and to understand distant places. This concept of the value (or utility) of travel is different from the concept of transport as a derived demand, that is, the satisfaction of a trip merely comes from engaging in the activities at the destinations independent of the travel experience. Following the rationale of transport as a derived demand, travel time and cost are minimised as far as possible. Nonetheless, it has been increasingly recognised that physical movements can actually give rise to positive utility or personal satisfaction for travellers and be linked to individual well-being as well (Bergstad *et al.*, 2011; De Vos *et al.*, 2013; Ettema *et al.*, 2011; Jain & Lyons, 2008; Lyons & Urry, 2005; Metz, 2008; Mokhtarian & Salomon, 2011; Mokhtarian, Salomon & Singer, 2015). In addition, there are enormous economic benefits associated with domestic and international tourism in the global economy. The key importance of travelling for leisure, networking, business and trade does not need much elaboration; and the economic benefits of employment opportunities within various transport industries and related sectors such as automobile manufacturing, public transport services and construction also should not be ignored. These economic benefits include both forward and backward economic linkages. Using the automobile industry as an example, backward linkages include the iron and steel (for the car body and engine), rubber (for tyres), glass (for windscreens), textile and leather (for car upholstery), and plastics (for various car compartments) industries, among others. The forward linkages include a whole range of employment and economic opportunities related to automobile marketing and sales, car accessories, car parks (as service providers), gas stations and even the cement industry (for road construction and various associated infrastructure).

Balancing different considerations, a time frame to 2030, that is, about 15 years from the time of the publication of this work, is chosen. While it may be argued that the time frame is too short for any real fundamental change to take place, this actually also underlines the urgency of taking actions and provides a suitable time framework for reviewing whether the emerging sustainable transport strategies are appropriate or not. Projecting directly into 2050 (as in Dadush & Stancil, 2010; Hawksworth, 2006) will be much more speculative. It is hoped that this book with a timeline up to 2030 will provide some useful lessons for the next longer-term look into the future of 2050 and beyond.

Research design and book organisation

The next chapter (Chapter 2) lays out the contexts of the entire research study. Every problem has to be understood and framed within its specific context. For this study, sustainability concerns and the rise of China provide the broad context. Key terms, such as sustainability and mobility, used in this book are explained in Chapter 2. With reference to the movement of people (versus goods), transport is about accessibility and mobility. Transport gives people access to opportunities, including but not exclusively economic ones. Transport provides people with opportunities to exercise, socialise, relax, study and to engage in a wide range of activities that are essential to a healthy lifestyle and overall well-being. As the desire and need for different opportunities and activities vary for different people, individual accessibility is a useful concept that makes a transport system relevant to the life of an individual. Mobility, in contrast, refers to the ease or amount of travel (distance) as people move around places to engage in various types of activities. In this book, the primary focus is on passenger transport within cities and a people-oriented approach is adopted. Some background about the rapid increase in sustainable transport challenges in China after the introduction of the Open Policy in 1979 will also be provided. Major issues, such as data quality and the institutional framework, in China will also be briefly introduced in Chapter 2.

The organisation of the rest of this book follows the research design of this study, as shown in Figure 1.2. Broadly, this study has been conducted in three stages. Stage 1 is international benchmarking (Chapter 3). Stage 2 systematically examines various geographical diversities within the country and explains the justifications and rationale for the formation of city clusters (Chapters 4–7). Stage 3 further develops the idea of tailor-made and evolving local sustainable transport strategies for municipalities in different city clusters towards 2030 and beyond (Chapter 8).

The primary aim of the Stage 1 research is to understand the current state of affairs related to the key issues and challenges of unsustainable transport explained in Chapter 2. Data related to the three sustainability pillars of the environment, economy and society are collected and analysed at the international level. At Stage 1, countries are used as the unit of analysis. Aggregate cross-sectional comparisons of a wide range of indicators in selected developed and

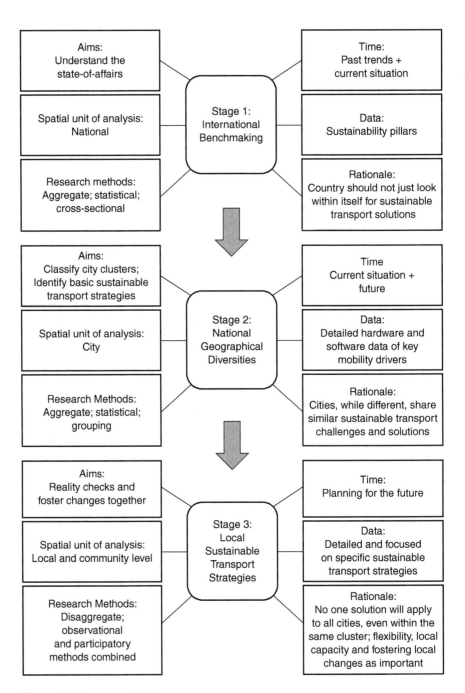

Aims: Understand the state-of-affairs	Stage 1: International Benchmaking	Time: Past trends + current situation
Spatial unit of analysis: National		Data: Sustainability pillars
Research methods: Aggregate; statistical; cross-sectional		Rationale: Country should not just look within itself for sustainable transport solutions

Aims: Classify city clusters; Identify basic sustainable transport strategies	Stage 2: National Geographical Diversities	Time Current situation + future
Spatial unit of analysis: City		Data: Detailed hardware and software data of key mobility drivers
Research Methods: Aggregate; statistical; grouping		Rationale: Cities, while different, share similar sustainable transport challenges and solutions

Aims: Reality checks and foster changes together	Stage 3: Local Sustainable Transport Strategies	Time: Planning for the future
Spatial unit of analysis: Local and community level		Data: Detailed and focused on specific sustainable transport strategies
Research Methods: Disaggregate; observational and participatory methods combined		Rationale: No one solution will apply to all cities, even within the same cluster; flexibility, local capacity and fostering local changes as important

Figure 1.2 The research design.

Source: The author.

developing countries are made to place the situations in China in the broader international light. The statistical analysis not only identifies areas where China is performing poorly but also areas where the country has been performing well. It is important to recognise that a stereotype of blaming the transport systems in developing countries as unsustainable in all aspects and as always less sustainable than developed countries can be the result of a perception bias rather than reality (Loo & Banister, 2016). In addition, the analysis at Stage 1 is also guided by the underlying rationale that a country should not just look within its own territory for potential sustainable transport strategies but also learn from innovative lessons overseas. Through this international benchmarking exercise, the relative strengths and weaknesses of individual countries can come to light. Without *a prior* bias that developed countries are always doing better in sustainability and that developing countries are always creating troubles and lagging behind, a more realistic picture can be obtained. Moreover, apart from the current situation, recent past trends in the last few decades are also outlined.

Stage 2 of this research work aims to classify cities in a country into statistically significant and analytically meaningful city clusters for the purpose of identifying basic sustainable transport strategies. In China, the introduction of the Open Policy in 1979 triggered rapid economic growth and urbanisation on the one hand, but widened income disparity on the other hand (Loo, 1997). These economic changes have fundamental implications on the country's unsustainable transport trends, including the rapidly increasing carbon emissions from passenger transport (Loo & Li, 2012; Li & Loo, 2016). With the rapid motorisation and urbanisation trends in China, cities represent major unsustainable transport challenges that the country must tackle for a transition away from unsustainable transport in 2030 and beyond. The statistical unit of analysis at Stage 2 is therefore changed to the city level. The top 100 cities in terms of projected population by 2025 are studied. The year 2030 is not used directly due to the lack of systematic population projections in China up to that year. In particular, the high concentration and density of population in these largest cities in China will constitute priority areas for addressing the unsustainable transport problems and implementing emerging strategies to redress these unsustainable transport trends.

Based on the largest 100 Chinese cities in 2025 and the local context of China, data related to the ten key drivers of mobility (to be elaborated in Chapter 5) are then identified and systematically analysed by cluster analysis to see whether meaningful city clusters can be identified. The collected data, covering both the current situation and future estimates, are related to the detailed hardware, including infrastructure, and software, such as public transport services, of the key mobility drivers. Once meaningful city clusters are identified, the characteristics of the current unsustainable transport challenges of the different city clusters, their growth potentials and the potential urban transport problems are examined (Chapter 6). The basic rationale is that cities share similar characteristics for meaningful statistical clusters to be identified. Next, the emerging sustainable transport strategies are identified by a systematic review of the international experiences and the local context in China. Initial recommendations for each city cluster are then made (Chapter 7).

Stages 1 and 2 are based on desktop research and will need to be supplemented by empirical fieldwork and be subject to reality checks for real changes to happen. The unit of analysis in Chapter 8 (Stage 3 of the research) zooms in on the local and community levels. The analysis is essentially future-looking with a view of planning for a better future in 2030. The data are mainly primary data based on local fieldwork and specific initial sustainable transport strategies recommended for the respective city clusters in Chapter 7. The rationale is that emerging sustainable transport strategies do need to be critically examined for applicability and feasibility on different fronts within the local geographical contexts. There is a dual focus on observational and participatory survey methods to collect both factual and attitudinal data.

Finally, Chapter 9 concludes this book by highlighting the emerging opportunities and factors for further developing and refining the recommended sustainable transport strategies. Looking forward, there needs to be further efforts (perhaps Stage 4 and beyond) to fine-tune a sustainable transport strategy for each city through involving the citizens in local discussion and consultation, transport professionals for detailed feasibility studies and benefit-cost analysis, and different levels of government to lead the ways through envisioning and proposing bold measures towards sustainable transport. There is also a research agenda to extend the conceptual framework and to apply the methodology to analyse other countries so that more experiences and lessons can be learnt. Some reflections on unsustainable transport globally conclude this book.

References

Anonymous. (2013, February 15). About 1,100 injured as meteorite hits Russia with force of atomic bomb. *Fox News Science*. Retrieved from www.foxnews.com/science/2013/02/15/injuries-reported-after-meteorite-falls-in-russia-ural-mountains.html.

Banister, D. (2005). *Unsustainable Transport: City Transport in the New Century*. Oxon: Routledge.

Bergstad, C.J., Gamble, A., Gärling, T., Hagman, O., Polk, M., Ettema, D., … Olsson, L.E. (2011). Subjective well-being related to satisfaction with daily travel. *Transportation, 38*, 1–15. doi:10.1007/s11116-010-9283-z.

Dadush, U., & Stancil, B. (2010). *The World Order in 2050*. Retrieved from www.carnegieendowment.org/files/World_Order_in_2050.pdf.

De Vos, J., Schwanen, T., Van Acker, V. & Witlox, F. (2013). Travel and subjective well-being: A focus on findings, methods and future research needs. *Transport Reviews, 33*, 421–442. doi:10.1080/01441647.2013.815665.

Ettema, D., Gärling, T., Eriksson, L., Friman, M., Olsson, L.E. & Fujii, S. (2011). Satisfaction with travel and subjective well-being: Development and test of a measurement tool. *Transportation Research Part F: Traffic Psychology and Behaviour, 14*, 167–175. doi:10.1016/j.trf.2010.11.002.

Hawksworth, J. (2006). Projected relative size of economies in 2005 and 2050. In *The World in 2050: How Big Will the Major Emerging Market Economies Get and How*

Can the OECD Compete? Pricewaterhouse Coopers. Retrieved from www.tepav.org.tr/upload/files/haber/1256628344r1748.The_World_in_2050.pdf.

Jain, J., & Lyons, G. (2008). The gift of travel time. *Journal of Transport Geography, 16,* 81–89. doi:10.1016/j.jtrangeo.2007.05.001.

Li, L., & Loo, B.P.Y. (2016). Carbon dioxide emissions from urban transport in China: Geographical characteristics and future challenges. *Geographical Research* (in Chinese), *25,* 1230–1242. Retrieved from www.dlyj.ac.cn/EN/10.11821/dlyj201607002.

Loo, B.P.Y. (1997). Post-reform development in Zhujiang Delta: Growing equality or polarisation? *Asian Geographer, 16,* 115–145. doi:10.1080/10225706.1997.9684028.

Loo, B.P.Y. (2017). Realising car-free developments within compact cities. *Proceedings of the Institution of Civil Engineer – Municipal Engineer.* Advance online publication. doi:10.1680/jmuen.16.00060.

Loo, B.P.Y., & Banister, D. (2016). Decoupling transport from economic growth: Extending the debate to include environmental and social externalities. *Journal of Transport Geography, 57,* 134–144. doi:10.1016/j.jtrangeo.2016.10.006.

Loo, B.P.Y., & du Verle, F. (2017). Transit-oriented development in future cities: Towards a two-level sustainable mobility strategy. *International Journal of Urban Sciences, 21*(Suppl. 1), 54–67. doi:10.1080/12265934.2016.1235488.

Loo, B.P.Y., & Li, L. (2012). Carbon dioxide emissions from passenger transport in China since 1949: Implications for developing sustainable transport. *Energy Policy, 50,* 464–476. doi:10.1016/j.enpol.2012.07.044.

Lyons, G., & Urry, J. (2005). Travel time use in the information age. *Transportation Research Part A: Policy and Practice, 39,* 257–276. doi:10.1016/j.tra.2004.09.004.

Metz, D. (2008). The myth of travel time saving. *Transport Reviews, 28,* 321–336. doi:10.1080/01441640701642348.

Mokhtarian, P.L., & Salomon, I. (2001). How derived is the demand for travel? Some conceptual and measurement considerations. *Transportation Research Part A: Policy and Practice, 35,* 695–719. doi:10.1016/S0965-8564(00)00013-6.

Mokhtarian, P.L., Salomon, I. & Singer, M.E. (2015). What moves us? An interdisciplinary exploration of reasons for traveling. *Transport Reviews, 35,* 250–274. doi:10.1080/01441647.2015.1013076.

National Bureau of Statistics of China (2014a). National Accounts. *China Statistical Yearbook 2014.* Retrieved from www.stats.gov.cn/tjsj/ndsj/2014/indexeh.htm.

National Bureau of Statistics of China (2014b). Population. *China Statistical Yearbook 2014.* Retrieved from www.stats.gov.cn/tjsj/ndsj/2014/indexeh.htm.

National Bureau of Statistics of China. (2015a). National Accounts. *China Statistical Yearbook 2015.* Retrieved from www.stats.gov.cn/tjsj/ndsj/2015/indexeh.htm.

National Bureau of Statistics of China. (2015b). Population. *China Statistical Yearbook 2015.* Retrieved from www.stats.gov.cn/tjsj/ndsj/2015/indexeh.htm.

National Bureau of Statistics of China. (2015c). Resources & Environment. *China Statistical Yearbook 2015.* Retrieved from www.stats.gov.cn/tjsj/ndsj/2015/indexeh.htm.

Rostow, W.W. (1990). *The Stages of Economic Growth: A Non-Communist Manifesto.* Cambridge: Cambridge University Press.

United Nations. (2014). *World Economic Situation and Prospects 2014.* Retrieved from http://unctad.org/en/PublicationsLibrary/wesp2014_en.pdf.

World Bank. (2016). *GDP per capita, PPP (current international $).* Retrieved 6 April 2017 from http://data.worldbank.org/indicator/NY.GDP.PCAP.PP.CD.

2   The context

Sustainability concerns

What is sustainability? In this book, it refers to comprehensive sustainability that encompasses the environmental, economic and social aspects for the current and future generations of human beings. The concept of sustainability is commonly believed to come from the World Conservation Strategy (IUCN, 1980) but was later more fully developed and publicised in the Brundtland Report, *Our Common Future* by the World Commission on Environment and Development (WCED) wherein it is stated that the present generation should develop in such a way that meets their needs 'without jeopardising the ability of future generations to fulfil their needs' (WCED, 1987, p. 43). There is a dual emphasis on fulfilling the 'needs' of the present generation and the 'ability' of future generations to do so. Both concepts are subject to different interpretations depending on society norms over time. In particular, 'ability' is difficult to measure and quantify for informing government policies and inducing changes in the behaviour of the present generation.

Therefore, comprehensive sustainability is a broad concept or vision with shared principles and meanings across the globe, but the specific objectives and plans are often place-based and diverse (Loo, 2002, 2008; Loo & Chow, 2009; Loo & du Verle, 2017). To illustrate the key concept, a diagrammatic representation is presented in Figure 2.1. Comprehensive sustainability aims to balance different needs of the human race in the three major domains of the environment, society and economy. The balance between achieving economic growth and environmental preservation is best described as *sustainable development*. The balance between environmental preservation and social equity is best illustrated by *community liveability*. The balance between economic growth and social equity is crystallised in social and economic *equity*. However, comprehensive sustainability only exists in the small but important overlapping areas of the three domains of environment, economy and society (Loo, 2008).

A radical attempt to stop consuming natural resources and preserving all natural environment at the expense of all forms of economic and urban development is not in accordance with the comprehensive sustainability principle. Similarly, maximising economic growth and efficiency through allocating resources by pure market forces (or economic means) at the expense of social equity is also against the sustainability principle. As comprehensive sustainability is a multi-dimensional concept, it implies that trade-offs and compromises are inevitable. People in a society have to make choices among desirable goals in order to achieve the highest level of comprehensive sustainability, which may not be the highest level achievable when only one of the three dimensions of environmental, economic or social sustainability is the sole or overriding consideration. In other words, 'a sustainable transportation policy is bound to be normative, reflecting the values of the society and the trade-offs that people (in that society) are willing to accept among numerous competing desirable goals like protecting the environment and increased mobility' (Loo, 2008, p. 135).

The original diagram by Preston and O'Connor (2008), however, is inadequate because sustainability is inherently about ensuring that the human race will last, generation after generation. Therefore, the time dimension is important (Figure 2.1). Through time, different kinds of natural and human-made hazards or adverse events have appeared. These hazards can severely disrupt the existing systems and cause various system failures. Developing resilience in this context refers to 'the ability to prepare and plan for, absorb, recover from, and more successfully adapt to adverse events' (The National Academies, 2012, p. 14). With lessons from major natural hazards (such as Hurricane Sandy in the USA in 2012 and the Tohoku earthquake and tsunami in Japan in 2011), resilience is increasingly incorporated in long-term policy and planning. Looking into the future, various types of hazards are expected to appear, possibly with higher frequency and larger impact (especially in relation to the extreme weather and rising sea level caused by climate change) (Sherbinin, Schiller & Pulsipher, 2007). For a

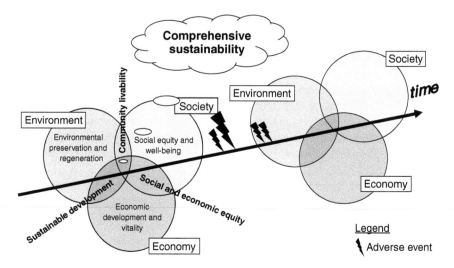

Figure 2.1 The concept of comprehensive sustainability.

Source: Developed from Preston and O'Connor (2008, p. 235).

transport system, these adverse events may be caused by nature (for example, heat stress on railway tracks) (Ferranti *et al.*, 2016; Rogers *et al.*, 2011; Rattanachot *et al.*, 2015) or caused by human beings (including explosions in trains and strikes on main transport arteries) (D'Lima & Medda, 2015; Loo & Leung, 2017). Therefore, key aspects of contingency management (such as prevention, adaptation, mitigation and recovery) need to be fully considered (UNISDR, 2007). As shown in Figure 2.1, resilience essentially lies in the time dimension of sustainability, and in relation to adverse events of different magnitude and nature. In other words, it is not possible to achieve sustainability without resilience; and the latter is an integral part of the former.

Furthermore, comprehensive sustainability has to be supported by technologies and good governance and be acceptable to the local governments and the general public, who should have the ultimate rights and responsibilities of choosing their own destiny. *Technologies* include all different forms of information and communication technologies (ICT) and their applications to enhance people's life. In Loo (2012, p. 3), the e-society essentially refers to a 'style of living whereby e-technologies are so fully integrated into the fabrics of the society that decisions to use them are no longer major household decisions that require long-term or careful ad hoc planning'. *Good governance* encompasses both the political and institutional aspects. Without good governance, well-intended sustainable transport strategies and measures cannot be realised. In particular, many sustainable transport measures require fundamental changes in the transport system and people's behaviour. Hence, they are most likely to require initial capital investment, actual physical infrastructure construction/modifications, new industries and operators, various maintenance and long-term replacement issues. *Local relevancy* needs to be primarily defined by the local community because its members are the ones who use the transport system on a daily basis. Whether a transport system is sustainable depends critically on whether it is preferred and fully integrated in local people's daily life. A transport system not popularly used by the local people will inevitably face many challenges like local opposition (such as complaints of inconvenience, high cost and/or causing congestion, to name just a few), financial loss to the operators (if any), deterioration of the capital assets (including both infrastructure and the rolling stock) and services, and eventual bankruptcy, if private business enterprises are involved, the demolition of supporting infrastructure, and the cancellation of specific sustainable transport schemes/measures. While these issues will be further discussed throughout this book, technologies, governance and local participation are essentially the means for achieving sustainability. Moreover, geographical contexts are always of key importance in defining and understanding 'ability', 'needs' and, in turn, 'sustainability'.

Environmental dimension

Environmentally, emphasis is on environmental preservation and regeneration. The most eminent issues are energy use and air pollution. On energy use, the combustion of non-renewable energy, notably gasoline and other petroleum-related by-products, for fuelling vehicles of all types (notably automobiles, airplanes and ships) is widely considered unsustainable (Loo *et al.*, 2014; Loo & Banister, 2016). In particular, transport is blamed for causing as much as 20–30 per cent of CO_2 emissions at the national level worldwide (IEA, 2013).

Table 2.1 provides an overview of CO_2 emissions from fuel combustion by sector in the world by major region in 2011 (IEA, 2013). The world total CO_2 emissions from fuel combustion have already reached over 31,342.3 million tonnes. The Organisation for Economic Co-operation and Development (OECD) countries, as listed in Table 2.2, roughly contributed more than one-third (39.4 per cent) of the world total. Among the different sectors, 'electricity and heat production' remains the largest contributor, accounting for 41.7 per cent of the world total. However, transport is already the second largest contributor, accounting for 22.3 per cent of the world total. Of the total transport CO_2 emissions by fuel consumption, road transport, primarily automobiles, accounted for nearly 80 per cent (5,172.0 out of 7,001.1 million tonnes). Moreover, wide regional differences exist with the share of transport being the highest in North America (31.01 per cent) and much lower in Asia Oceania (19.79 per cent). The next major contributor of CO_2 emissions is 'manufacturing industries and construction' (6,508.7 million tonnes or 20.8 per cent of the world total), both activities being highly related to the globalisation of the world economy (and the associated growth of the logistics industry) and the rapid urbanisation in developing countries.

The high level of CO_2 from anthropogenic sources is in turn blamed for climate change, and its related impacts of rising sea level and more extreme weather in different parts of the world. Other environmental issues of unsustainable transport are associated with the construction, maintenance and disposal of different elements of the transport system, including rubber tyres, obsolete cars and used concrete, primarily from road re-surfacing. The results of fuel combustion in generating nitrogen oxide, particulate matters (PM) and other harmful gases and materials are also causing major local public health problems, such as pneumonia, for those living near heavy road traffic. Six common air pollutants that have significant adverse effects on health include ozone, PM, carbon monoxide, nitrogen oxides, sulphur dioxide and lead (EPA, 2013).

In particular, the large-scale European Study of Cohorts for Air Pollution Effects (ESCAPE) Project in Europe strongly suggests that vehicular traffic is associated with various respiratory and cardiovascular disease incidences, especially among young children (Beelen *et al.*, 2014; Cesaroni *et al.*, 2014; Eeftens *et al.*, 2012a, 2012b; Gehring *et al.*, 2013; MacIntyre *et al.*, 2014; Raaschou-Nielsen *et al.*, 2013). Vulnerable groups, such as seniors, young children and people with chronic diseases, are susceptible to adverse health impacts by vehicular air pollutants. The longer the duration of exposure to these local air pollutants (notably $PM_{2.5}$), the higher the risk. Hence, apart from home locations, facilities such as schools and playgrounds, where young children spend a substantial period of time, and hospitals, where patients visit regularly or stay for

Table 2.1 An overview of CO_2 emissions from fuel combustion by sector, 2014

	Total CO_2 emissions from fuel combustion*	(I) Electricity and heat production*	(II) Other energy industry own use*#	(III) Manuf. industries and construction*	(IV) Transport*	of which: road*	(V) Other sectors*	of which: residential*	Share of transport in total (%)
World	32,381.0	13,625.0	1,683.1	6,230.1	7,547.3	5,659.8	3,295.5	1,858.8	23.31
Annex I Parties	12,628.4	5,266.6	708.8	1,496.6	3,460.6	2,985.5	1,695.8	989.8	27.40
Annex II Parties	9,933.7	3,856.2	599.8	1,131.0	2,998.9	2,628.3	1,348.0	752.0	30.19
North America	5,731.0	2,222.9	372.5	514.9	1,905.1	1,611.8	715.6	384.9	33.24
Europe	2,609.0	868.1	135.8	338.4	778.7	738.8	488.1	302.9	29.85
Asia Oceania	1,593.6	765.2	91.4	277.7	315.0	277.7	144.3	64.1	19.77
OECD Total	11,855.6	4,732.2	730.9	1,386.7	3,428.5	3,039.5	1,577.3	882.4	28.92

Source: IEA Database (2016).

Notes
* Units are in million tonnes of CO_2.
# Includes emissions from own use in petroleum refining, the manufacture of solid fuels, coal mining, oil and gas extraction and other energy-producing industries.

Table 2.2 Membership of the Organisation for Economic Co-operation and Development (OECD), 2016

Europe	*Outside Europe*
Austria	Australia
Belgium	Canada
Czech Republic	Chile
Denmark	Israel
Estonia	Japan
Finland	Korea
France	Latvia
Germany	Mexico
Greece	New Zealand
Hungry	United States
Iceland	
Italy	
Luxembourg	
Netherlands	
Norway	
Poland	
Portugal	
Slovak Republic	
Slovenia	
Spain	
Sweden	
Switzerland	
Turkey (between eastern Europe and western Asia)	
United Kingdom	

Source: OECD (2016).

treatment, need to be carefully planned. Risk exposure to these transport air pollutants needs to be vigorously assessed.

In addition to air pollution, noise pollution is a huge issue for residents living near airports, train stations and expressways. Increasing evidence suggests that noise nuisance, especially from aircraft but also road traffic, can disturb sleep, increase the risk of cardiovascular disease and lower health-related quality of life (Bell & Galatioto, 2013; Heriter *et al.*, 2014; McGuire *et al.*, 2016).

With globalisation, there is increasingly a spatial dimension to some of these environmental problems, such as the cascading of used cars with lower environmental standards from the developed to the developing countries as well. Many used cars, with much lower fuel efficiency and higher emissions, are exported from the developed to the developing countries causing the environmental burden of polluting vehicles to be disproportionately higher in the latter despite the smaller vehicular fleet.

Economic dimension

Economically, many transport systems are not sustainable, requiring long-term financial subsidies from governments. Most often, financial subsidisation happens in the form of the government directly providing the transport infra-structure, notably roads, major ports and airports, without directly charging for their use. Moreover, it is important to recognise that many public transport service operations are also financially unsustainable requiring long-term and increasing amounts of government subsidies. In some developing countries, like Indonesia, fuel subsidy is provided (Arze del Granado, Coady & Gillingham, 2012; Coady *et al.*, 2006).

Another important economic dimension is the unsustainable trend of worsen-ing traffic congestion, in terms of more roads being affected by congestion, longer hours of congestion during the day, more days for congestion to set in throughout the year and more serious delays at peak hours. For private car drivers, in particular, time wasted in traffic congestion could be more fruitfully spent on other activities, including productive economic activities. This leads to the loss of time and productivity for the entire society. Economists have often attempted to quantify the loss by the value of time.

Moreover, traffic congestion is associated with less efficient fuel consumption and more negative environmental impacts as well. Figure 2.2 summarises the relationship between fuel consumption (g/km) and average speed of Euro 3 diesel and petrol cars (km/hr). Although fuel efficiency is higher for petrol than diesel cars, the most fuel efficient speed occurs at about 70–80 km/hr. Conges-tion, which is often associated with a much lower speed of 15 km/hr or below,

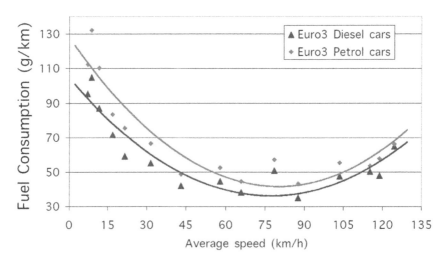

Figure 2.2 Fuel consumption vs. average speed for diesel and petrol cars (ARTEMIS Project).

Source: ECMT (2007, p. 150). Copyright obtained from OECD.

consumes more than double the fuel for the same distance (km) travelled. None-theless, given that the economic loss resulting from rapidly deteriorating traffic congestion is a major concern in many developing countries, the problem of traffic congestion is discussed under the economic dimension.

Social dimension

The social dimension is much less researched in the literature and it relates to the norms and values held by the society and human beings in general. Though traffic safety is an important area in transport research, it is often not directly integrated in the sustainability framework. A transport system cannot be socially sustainable if it persistently takes the life of millions of people and results in several tens of millions injured or even permanently disabled every year. According to the World Health Organization (WHO), there are on average 1.20–1.25 million killed and up to 50 million injured every year on the road worldwide (Peden *et al.*, 2004; WHO, 2015). Table 2.3 shows WHO's projec-tion for the top ten global disease or injury burdens, 2004 and 2030 (WHO, 2008). Road traffic crashes are expected to rise by six places from ninth position in 2004 to third in 2030. Worse still, elderly pedestrians (Loo & Tsui, 2016; Yao, Loo & Lam, 2015), cyclists (Vanlaar *et al.*, 2016), migrants (Chen, Lin & Loo, 2012) and children (DiMaggio, Brady & Li, 2015) were the most vulner-able road users to suffer from the traffic injury burden.

Theoretically, it is possible to capture this social cost by monetising the economic loss and human sufferings associated with traffic crashes. Yet, while traffic crashes do lead to direct economic loss (notably vehicle damage and damage to property) and productivity loss (for example, with hospitalised days and sick leave), the human suffering (for the traffic victims, their fam-ilies and friends) and social implications are so huge that I would consider traffic crashes to be a key problem under the social rather than economic dimension.

Table 2.3 Top ten global disease or injury burdens, 2004 and 2030

Rank	2004	2030
1	Lower respiratory infections	Unipolar depressive disorders
2	Diarrhoeal diseases	Ischaemic heart disease
3	Unipolar depressive disorders	Road traffic accidents
4	Ischaemic heart disease	Cerebrovascular disease
5	HIV/AIDS	Chronic obtrusive pulmonary disease
6	Cerebrovascular disease	Lower respiratory infections
7	Prematurity and low birth weight	Hearing loss, adult onset
8	Birth asphyxia and birth weight	Refractive errors
9	Road traffic accidents	HIV/AIDS
10	Neonatal infections and other	Diabetes Mellitus

Source: WHO (2008).

Another major social issue is transport-induced deprivation. This happens when certain disadvantaged groups are not able to access opportunities (including economic opportunities) and services because of transport-related constraints, such as not owning a car, not having a driving licence, not being able to afford the fuel cost of driving, the lack of available public transport services and/ or poor walking/cycling environment. In particular, children, people with various forms of disability and older people who cannot or do not drive are likely to be transport disadvantaged. The increase in petroleum prices during the peak oil in 2010, for example, has hit many low-income car-dependent rural residents living in the United States (Sipe & Dodson, 2013). When driving is essentially the only means for all kinds of trips, 'filling the gas tanks' even for basic routines like taking children to school, joining social functions and shopping for food and daily necessities can become a heavy financial burden. The lack of affordable, convenient and frequent public transport for low-income people living in suburban or rural areas has now been increasingly recognised (Delbosc & Currie, 2011). Car-dependency can actually limit mobility and, in turn, jeopardises the accessibility of low-income people to many economic opportunities because jobs are still the most abundant and concentrated in downtown areas in most cities (Loo & Chow, 2011). Similarly, without good public transport, these low-income car-dependent household's accessibility to other opportunities like social and recreational opportunities (e.g. going to the beach) is also severely constrained.

Sustainable transport

Comprehensive sustainability is about all three dimensions and about balancing desirable goals in these different dimensions. In developing countries, there is a need to balance, if not to shift, the primary economic concerns to the other two equally important environmental and social dimensions. Referring back to Figure 2.1, comprehensive sustainability refers to the overlapping area of all three circles. Nowadays, related terms such as green transport or low carbon transport are becoming popular, but they are essentially related to the environment only. Sustainable development is concerned with the need to balance environmental concerns with the need for economic vitality and development. Liveable community is concerned with the balance of the environmental dimension and the social dimension. Economic equity is concerned with economic and social balance only. It is important to recognise that none of these concepts can totally replace comprehensive sustainability and these terms should not be used interchangeably. Once again, the importance of technology, good governance and public acceptability in supporting these three sustainability pillars should be recognised. In this book, sustainability refers to comprehensive sustainability and not the more narrowly defined concepts like green or environmentally friendly transport. While comprehensive sustainability is the guiding principle of this book, special emphasis is put on passenger transport in cities and a people-centred approach is adopted.

Elements of transport systems

Traditionally, the elements of transport may be divided into the ways, terminals, energy and vehicles (Hilling, 1996). Figure 2.3 presents these four elements of transport in a diagrammatical manner. *Ways* refers to the routes that connect two or more places, notably the origin and the destination of a trip. For most transport modes, ways need to be constructed and maintained as transport infrastructure. Rail transport, for example, requires dedicated tracks of specific requirements (Ho, 2015). Road transport primarily takes place on surfaced roads and highways. Water transport, especially river transport, often needs additional efforts to maintain the water passage by dredging and constructing seawalls, for example. Although the way for air transport does not need special infrastructure, it involves air rights that need special permission and can significantly affect the air flight routes.

Terminals are the access points for people and goods to use the transport system. Terminals and ways form nodes and links in a transport network that differ in terms of complexity and connectivity. Rail stations, notably terminals and major interchange stations, entail careful planning not only in terms of capacity and safety but also intra- and intermodal integration to facilitate seamless

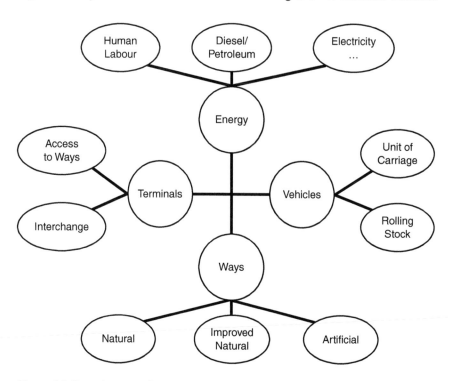

Figure 2.3 Four elements of transport systems.
Source: The author based on Hilling (1996).

transport and enhance passenger experience (Li & Loo, 2016c). Road transport requires terminals notably as car parks at both ends of a trip. Given that a person may engage in different activities over a day, five trips in a day involving six stops can easily mean demand for car parking spaces at six different locations (though they are required only at different specific times of the day). As much as 14 per cent of the Los Angeles County's incorporated land is committed to parking (Chester *et al.*, 2015); and the ratio can be higher in the downtown areas where car parks are more in demand. For heavy vehicles, the large turning radius and required space of manoeuvring mean that multi-storey commercial car parks are seldom built. Water transport requires ferry piers for passenger transport and port facilities for freight transport. Under the international mega-trends of increasingly large containerships and high spatial agglomeration of container traffic, modern container ports are having very specific locational requirements not only on the seaside (for example, with deep sea channels) but also the land-side (for example, with efficient land distribution systems) (Loo & Hook, 2002). These areas along the waterfront are also prime sites for people to enjoy. The terminal requirements for air transport are usually the most demanding and require the highest capital investment. The traditional benefit-cost analysis (BCA) is no longer sufficient for a comprehensive sustainability evaluation of airport construction and expansion projects (Li & Loo, 2016b).

Vehicles are the objects that contain the people and goods to move smoothly in the transport system. They need power to propel or move them along the transport system. Railway locomotives have undergone dramatic technological advancements from using coal engines, steam engines to the electric engines of today. The speed of the vehicles in rail transport also shows substantial variations from trams typically with a speed of 15 km/hr to high-speed railways (HSRs) of up to 320 km/hr (Ho, 2015). Capacity and speed variations are also found: from trams and light rails with much low passenger carrying capacities and speed to the metro systems with much higher capacities and speed. Vehicles used for road transport are typically classified according to vehicle class of different length and mass. In China, the total number of passenger vehicles sold, which includes sales of sedans, sports utility vehicles and multi-purpose vehicles, reached 24.38 million in 2016 (Statista, 2017). Fuel type and oil tank size (cc) are also alternative ways of classifying vehicles on roads. Non-motorised vehicles, such as bicycles, also exist. As for pedestrians, the vehicles are the physical bodies of the individuals. The vehicles for water transport are ferries and ships. Ferry modernisation over the recent decades represents a major challenge in many cities with good river networks and/or protected harbours. Freight ships have changed for the break-bulk and bulk ships to the container ships of Post-Panamax ships with over 12,000 20-foot equivalent units (TEUs) (Loo & Hook, 2002). Vehicles in air transport refers to aircraft. Different types of aircraft have very different fuel consumption, at take-off, taxi, and cruising at different heights. These factors need to be carefully considered for a realistic evaluation of the environmental costs, notably carbon emissions, of air transport (Loo *et al.*, 2014).

Last but not least, *energy* is an essential element of transport. Transport energy can be renewable or non-renewable. The use of fossil fuels (non-renewable) as the primary source of energy for road transport, for example, is one of the reasons for transport being unsustainable worldwide nowadays. With the electrification of railways, its high passenger carrying capacity, railways actually are well placed to contribute to sustainable transport, especially in countries where the electricity is primarily generated from renewable sources like nuclear, wind and water (Givoni, 2007). Road transport, however, has proven to the most persistent in almost depending on petroleum entirely, despite the launch of electric and other alternative fuel vehicles. Vehicles have become more fuel-efficient, that is, achieved higher fuel economy. An often-overlooked energy source in road transport, however, is human energy. Cycling and walking that primarily depends on human energy are increasingly and systematically being promoted for encouraging and supporting sustainable mobility, especially for short trips and connections to and from public transport. These connections have often been called the first and last miles. Based on the primary source of energy, cycling and walking are also called active transport. The wider use of electric bicycles, however, also suggests that bicycles may transform from an active transport mode to a mechanised mode or a combination of both in the future. Water transport, once again, relies quite a lot on petroleum. In a related context, marine bulker oils are known to contain more sulphur, which is more damaging to people's health. The use of fuel in air transport also requires special attention and research. In some cities, where shipping activities are close to population concentrations, legislations for the use of low-sulphur bulker fuel (sulphur content not exceeding 0.5 per cent by weight) while parked can be made. This has been done, for example, in Hong Kong, with effect from 1 July 2015 (Environmental Protection Department, 2017). Similarly, aviation fuel has mainly been diesel-based and has long been exempted from country tax. The fuel efficiency and the emission levels also differ widely based on the aircraft type, the airport operations and load factors in particular (Loo *et al.*, 2014).

This system approach essentially views transportation from a macroscopic point of view and, hence, is not directly addressing people's everyday life and the problems that they face every day. Yet, it is very useful in identifying possible loopholes and potential strategies to address transport problems because most government institutions are structured in this manner, with government branches responsible for transport, major civil works, energy and the environment in a relatively independent manner. In China, the government branches responsible for transport, major civil works, energy and the environment are the Ministry of Transport, Ministry of Civil Affairs, National Energy Administration and the Ministry of Environmental Protection (State Commission Office for Public Sector, 2013). It is apparent that the framework is not directly relevant in identifying and understanding transport problems from a holistic perspective. Yet, it will be valuable for the implementation of any sustainable transport strategy. Hence, I shall return to this subject in the final chapter.

Accessibility, individual accessibility and mobility

To people, transport is about accessibility and mobility. Transport gives people access to different opportunities, including but not exclusively economic ones. Opportunities of socialisation, leisure, study, shopping and gymnasium use, among others, are increasingly important for a healthy lifestyle. As the desire and need for various types of opportunities and activities differ for different people, individual accessibility is a useful concept that makes transport relevant to people's daily life in a non-uniform manner. For instance, for school children and their parents, the most important accessibility is probably to (good) schools. To the unemployed, accessibility to jobs is the most relevant. To be relevant, access has to be not just to any employment opportunity but to jobs that fit the individual's specific knowledge, skills and experience. The availability of a Chief Executive Officer position is not relevant to a fresh university graduate without job experience. The availability of vacancies in law is irrelevant to a fresh graduate of medicine. When accessibility is defined accordingly to relevant opportunities, it becomes a useful basic concept directly relevant to people. There are many useful and interesting studies giving us insights on individual accessibility problems (see, for example, Lam & Loo, 2014). Nonetheless, a major drawback of the accessibility concept is that it is so individually specific that it is difficult to use it as a relevant policy tool for policy-makers and researchers interested in a board range of issues faced by people of all walks of life in a society, and the need to balance different stakeholders at the society level. Data about individual accessibility are always costly to obtain and so specific that they are non-transferable without major assumptions. Changes over time are particularly challenging to capture as individuals are actually going through their own life cycles. Hence, the concept of mobility, which is grounded or built upon the concept of accessibility, is particularly useful in understanding sustainability issues at the society level.

Mobility refers to the ease or amount of travel (distance) conducted as people move around places to engage in different activities. The concept explicitly puts locations or places back in the analysis, which by itself is comforting to geographers. People go to places of interest (hence, the points of interest or POI in online maps). Many places/buildings that are highly relevant or even critical may seem irrelevant to an individual's daily life, but providing easy access to these places is still important. Some notable examples are police stations and hospitals. Although one may not be using these two facilities in a year or even longer, it is crucial that easy access is provided when necessary (often in an emergency). Hence, providing people mobility and ease of getting around by different means of sustainable transport reflects the people-centred philosophy on the one hand and allows macroscopic policies to be made, targets to be set (for example, that all people should be able to reach a public library with 30 minutes), and planning to be conducted on the other. It is against this background that the concept of sustainable mobility is framed. When mobility is achieved with environmental, economic and social sustainability, the state can be described as sustainable mobility. Given that sustainability is an evolving concept, it is used as a guiding concept, rather than as a list of specific objectives. When specific objectives are to be set, the local contexts are always important. Yet, the sustainable mobility concept is helpful in providing the general directions and broad common principles.

Transport challenges in China since 1979

Ever since the introduction of the Open Policy, dramatic changes have taken place in China. From 1980 to 2015, the country's real GDP per capita (in current PPP dollars) dramatically increased, by more than 50 times, from \$306.8 to \$14,107.4 (IMF, 2016). When the USA's GDP per capita (at current PPP dollars) is used as the base for comparison (USA = 100), China's GDP per capita has increased by nearly tenfold from 3.5 in 1980 to 34.5 in 2015 (that is, increasing from only about 3.5 per cent to about 35 per cent of the USA). Furthermore, the share of China's urban population and the share of labour working in manufacturing industries have reached 54 per cent and 30 per cent, respectively (World Bank, 2016). While China's economic miracle has been widely discussed, there are also many sustainability concerns and debates on the worrying trends observed.

Worldwide environmental concerns

In 2011, China had already become the largest CO_2 emitter in the world but its real GDP per capita suggests that it is still a developing country. This 'tipping point', of China being the world largest CO_2 emitter, occurred much earlier than its projected rise to be the largest economy in the world in 2030; and this has raised much concern, especially in light of the sustainability concerns (Garnaut, Jotzo & Howes, 2008). Moreover, the worries are fuelled by the lack of understanding and in some cases the lack of reliable and internationally comparable statistics for a sound opinion to be formed about this third physically largest country (after Russia and Canada) in the world. Typically, national CO_2 emissions are estimated using the fuel combustion data only (IEA, 2013). Neither breakdowns of CO_2 emissions by passenger and freight nor by mode are available. In particular, it was only recently that the CO_2 emissions from passenger transport in the country (since 1949) have been systematically estimated and analysed by Loo and Li (2012) and later updated in Li and Loo (2016a). Using the distance-based approach, Loo and Li (2012) estimated that the CO_2 emissions of passenger transport in China increased from a range of 4–34 million tonnes in 1980 to 187–496 million tonnes in 2009. Their fuel-based approach estimated that the transport CO_2 emission rose from 3.1 million tonnes in 1980 to 270.9 million tonnes in 2009. The estimates were very close to the average of the distance-based approach. On a per capita basis, this suggests a rise from 3.14 tonnes per 1,000 population in 1980 to about 203 tonnes per 1,000 population in 2009. This represents a huge increase, of over 66 times in less than three decades from passenger transport sources alone. Subsequently, Li and Loo (2016a) further extended the estimation of total passenger transport CO_2 emissions using the fuel-based approach. The results show that the absolute volume of passenger transport CO_2 emissions has continued to rise rapidly from 270.9 million in 2009 to 494.0 million in 2012.

Two other findings are noteworthy. First, with the detailed decomposition methodology, Loo and Li (2012) have also been able to identify the contributions of different transport modes to the total CO_2 emissions of passenger transport. Figure 2.4 shows the modal split of passenger transport CO_2 emissions in China. Based on the Kaya Identity and the Logarithmic Mean Divisia Index (LMDI) approach, Figure 2.5 suggests that most of the CO_2 emissions increases came from road transport and the rapid motorisation of the country. The reason, as is evident from both the additive and multiplicative decomposition results (Figure 2.5), is primarily income growth. In this light, this is arguably what all developing countries are expected to undergo – economic growth, if not economic development. Despite the theoretical possibility of decoupling economic growth from transport CO_2 emissions, the empirical evidence suggests that absolute decoupling has not yet been achieved widely and persistently in Europe (Tapio *et al.*, 2007). Nonetheless, as shown in Loo and Banister (2016), when the carbon intensity of transport of the same country in the 1990–1995 period and the 2010–2012 period is compared, decarbonisation of the transport sector (that is, lower carbon intensity of transport) has already happened in Australia, China, Canada, France, Germany, Mexico, Russia, the UK and the USA, at least in terms of their national carbon emissions (a discussion on the carbon emissions not captured in the national statistics will be provided below). The best record was achieved in Germany; the country has achieved a 43.8 per cent reduction in its carbon intensity of transport from 1995 to 2012.

Second, the increase in passenger transport CO_2 emissions in China was not caused so much by the increasing number of trips made by individuals but by *how* these trips were made. In China, many people have been shifting from the more environmentally friendly mode of railways to roads. The numbers of private cars, in particular, have increased dramatically. Furthermore, the lower fuel efficiency of private cars over time is worth mentioning. Substantial technological advancement has happened in airplanes to reduce the CO_2 emissions per passenger km by air over time. Private cars, however, have become less efficient in terms of CO_2 emissions per passenger, with more solo driving and more options like air conditioning and luxury items like hi-fi systems and mini-refrigerators, making the automobiles heavier and less fuel efficient. The use of stronger materials (often heavier) and installation of safety features (such as air bags), which improve the safety of the car's occupants, have also contributed to the heavier weight of automobiles. Recently, the popular trends for using sports utility vans (SUVs) and larger and heavier American cars (versus the more compact Japanese cars) in China has also contributed to the rise in passenger transport CO_2 emissions (Anonymous, 2015; Yang *et al.*, 2017).

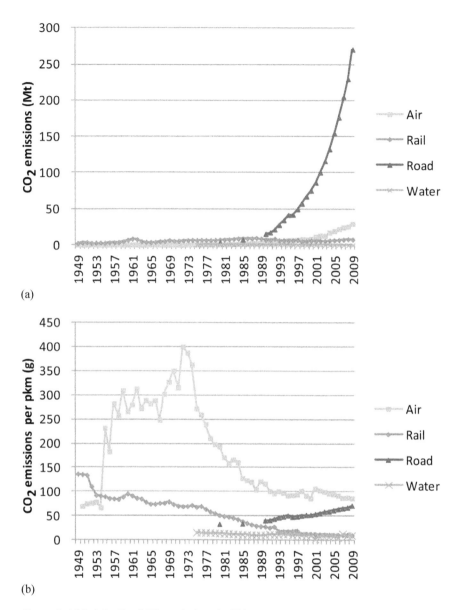

(a)

(b)

Figure 2.4 Modal split of CO$_2$ emissions in China, 1949–2009.

Source: Loo and Li (2012, p. 469). Copyright obtained from Elsevier.

Notes

a CO$_2$ emissions from passenger travel based on fuel consumption.

b CO$_2$ emissions per pkm from passenger transport based on fuel consumption.

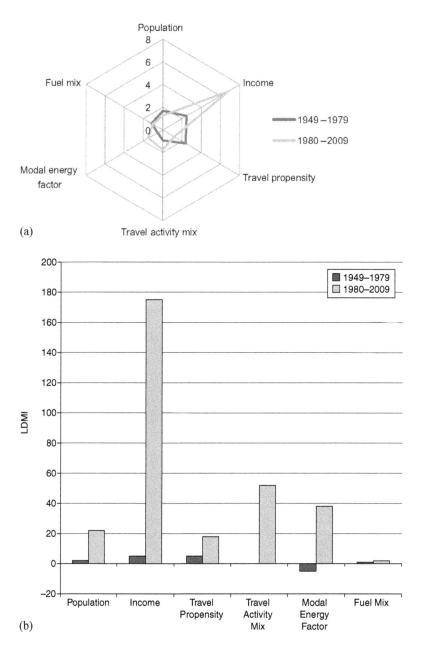

(a)

(b)

Figure 2.5 Contributions to increasing passenger transport CO$_2$ emissions in China.

Source: Loo and Li (2012, p. 472). Copyright obtained from Elsevier.

Notes
a LDMI multiplicative decomposition.
b LDMI addictive decomposition.

Heavy economic burden of traffic congestion

In the economic dimension, the rising traffic congestion needs no further elaboration. It was causing residents in Beijing and Shanghai an average of about 52 minutes and 48 minutes to commute to work in 2011, respectively (Banister, 2012). The increase in commuting time over time was due not only to the increase in commuting distance (related to urban form) but also worsening traffic congestion (related to increasing car ownership and usage). It is recognised that not all travel time is 'wasteful'. For instance, travel time spent on commuting a long distance may be associated with good feelings (utility) of having a larger living space in a suburban environment and a clear separation of work and home, especially if the commuting route is scenic. Yet, given any specific commuting distance, congestion (defined generally as travelling below the free flow speed) is undesirable and 'wasteful' that does not generate any positive utility (see EMCT, 2007 for a more elaborate discussion on traffic congestion). The average travel speed by car in the city proper of Beijing and Shanghai was only 10 km/hr and 18 km/hr, respectively in 2005 (Woetzel *et al.*, 2009, p. 139). In Hong Kong, a recent report by the Transport Advisory Committee has shown that the average travelling speed of many strategic roads in Central CBD has fallen below 15 km/ hour over the last five years (Transport Advisory Committee, 2014). The amount of time savings associated with reducing congestion can generate substantial benefits in terms of a general improvement in people's quality of life and productivity gain for the work force.

While the above are broad-brush estimates, the huge geographical variations in China should not be ignored. Given that the most serious traffic congestion always happens in cities (especially large metropolitan cities) where people's value of time also tends to be higher, the resultant economic loss caused by traffic congestion is enormous. For metropolitan cities with a huge population, the metro or underground railways are often viewed as the most efficient and environmentally feasible solution. Nonetheless, it is not the case when the economic and financial dimensions are also considered. Loo and Cheng (2010) reviewed over 100 metro systems across the world and suggested that the metro systems are mostly making financial losses and requiring persistent government subsidies. Similarly, the analysis of Chinese metro systems by Loo and Li (2006) reveals both opportunities and constraints. While the population and income growth in cities made metro systems potentially the best candidates for solving traffic congestion, the technology, financing and affordability gaps remained in many Chinese cities, especially those located inland. In addition, common problems were often associated with the long lead time of building metro systems (often seven years or more), the huge investment (ranging from US$47.4 million to US$0.3 billion per km in Hong Kong), complex financing models (with a need to build in depreciation and the ability to set fares or derive alternative sources of income) and the lack of efficient and safe management (the software) (Loo & Cheng, 2010). These problems have made the metro option a difficult, if not unfeasible, for many Chinese cities with a smaller population, a weaker economy and a low level of foreign investment for sustainable transport. For instance, Loo and Cheng (2010) found that the average population of Asian cities was as high as 5.7 million when the first metro line was built.

Enormous social costs associated with traffic injury

Socially, China's road safety records have also been worrying. Loo, Cheung and Yao (2011) analysed China's road safety records from 1949 to 2011 against the light of its rapid motorisation and urbanisation, especially in the more developed coastal region. In 2012, 57,227 people were killed on Chinese roads and another 210,554 were injured (National Bureau of Statistics of China, 2013). In China, the Ministry of Public Security defines a road death as death in a road crash or within seven days of the crash (Ministry of Public Security, 2005). Yet, the international standard of the Convention of Road Traffic in 1968 states that 'a road death is deemed to have occurred when an injured person dies within 30 days of the crash as a result of that crash' (United Nations Economic Commission for Europe, 1993). Hence, an upward adjustment factor of 1.08 should be applied before one can really understand the real burden of road fatalities in China (Jacobs, Aeron-Thomas & Astrop, 2000). Note that this adjustment does not take into account underreporting, which tends to be more stable in high-income countries (Loo & Tsui, 2007) but much more serious in developing countries (WHO, 2015)

Within China, the traffic injury burden is unevenly distributed spatially, as exemplified in Figure 2.6. It is clear that some road safety policies and measures have already been put in place to tackle the serious public health issues, resulting in a noticeable reduction in road casualties after 2005. Moreover, the increase in road fatalities has to be understood in the context of the rapidly growing car ownership rate in China. From 1970 to 2008, the number of vehicles in China skyrocketed from just 0.4 million to over 154.2 million. Taking the absolute vehicle fleet size into consideration, the number of traffic crashes has actually dropped dramatically from 132.0 per 1,000 vehicles in 1970 to 1.7 per 1,000 vehicles in 2008 (Loo, Cheung & Yao, 2011). Nonetheless, the levels of road casualties in China remain alarmingly high. In 2012, the traffic fatality and relevant exposure figures suggest 0.04 and 0.52 deaths per 1,000 population and per 1,000 vehicles, respectively (National Bureau of Statistics of China, 2013).

After a board overview of the existing literature and in brief terms, the unsustainable transport challenges that China has been facing since its economic take-off have primarily been associated with the huge increase in the volume of trips made by people, the places where these trips were made (increasingly in cities) and the ways that these trips are made (on what modes). Many of the unsustainable transport trends, especially those associated with the widespread use of automobiles, observed in Europe by Banister (2005), are not confined to OECD countries. Yet, these trends have been caused by a combination of factors which can only be better appreciated and understood with respect to the economic growth and changing circumstances in China, especially after since the Open Policy in 1979.

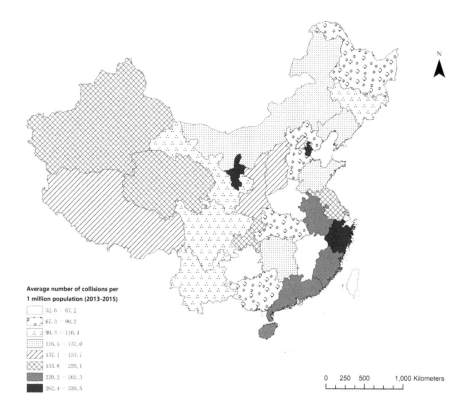

Average number of collisions per
1 million population (2013-2015)

- 32.6 – 67.2
- 67.3 – 90.2
- 90.3 – 116.4
- 116.5 – 137.0
- 137.1 – 153.7
- 153.8 – 220.1
- 220.2 – 262.3
- 262.4 – 339.5

0   250   500   1,000 Kilometers

Figure 2.6 Spatial distribution of traffic fatality burden in China, 2013–2015.

Source: Compiled by the author based on Ministry of Public Security of the People's Republic of China (Various Years).

References

Anonymous. (2015). *The Chinese Automotive Fuel Economy Policy*. Retrieved 10 January 2016 from www.globalfueleconomy.org/transport/gfei/autotool/case_studies/apacific/china/CHINA%20CASE%20STUDY.pdf.

Arze del Granado, F.J., Coady, D. & Gillingham, R. (2012). The unequal benefits of fuel subsides: A review of evidence for developing countries. *World Development, 40*, 2234–2248. doi:10.1016/j.worlddev.2012.05.005.

Banister, D. (2005). *Unsustainable Transport: City Transport in the New Century*. Oxon: Routledge.

Banister, D. (2012). Viewpoint: Assessing the reality. Transport and land use planning to achieve sustainability. *Journal of Transport and Land Use, 5*(3), 1–14. doi:10.5198/jtlu.v5i3.388.

Beelen, R., Raaschou-Nielsen, O., Stafoggia, M., Andersen, Z.J., Weinmayr, G., Hoffmann, B., … Hoek, G. (2014). Effects of long-term exposure to air pollution on natural-cause mortality: An analysis of 22 European cohorts within the multicentre ESCAPE project. *Lancet, 383*, 785–795. doi:10.1016/S0140-6736(13)62158-3.

Bell, M.C. & Galatioto, F. (2013). Novel wireless pervasive sensor network to improve the understanding of noise in street canyons. *Applied Acoustics, 74,* 169–180. doi:10.1016/j.apacoust.2012.07.007.

Cesaroni, G., Forastiere, F., Stafoggia, M., Andersen, Z.J., Badaloni, C., Beelen, R., … Peters, A. (2014). Long term exposure to ambient air pollution and incidence of acute coronary events: Prospective cohort study and meta-analysis in 11 European cohorts from the ESCAPE project. *BMJ, 348,* f7412. doi:10.1136/bmj.f7412.

Chen, C., Lin, H. & Loo, B.P.Y. (2012). Exploring the impacts of safety culture on immigrants' vulnerability in non-motorised crashes: A cross-sectional study. *Journal of Urban Health, 89,* 138–152. doi:10.1007/s11524-011-9629-7.

Chester, M., Fraser, A., Matute, J., Flower, C. & Pendyala, R. (2015). Parking infrastructure: A constraint on or opportunity for urban redevelopment? A study of Los Angeles County parking supply and growth. *Journal of the American Planning Association, 81,* 268–286. doi:10.1080/01944363.2015.1092879.

Coady, D., El-Said, M., Gillingham, R., Kpodar, K., Medas, M. & Newhouse, D. (2006). *The Magnitude and Distribution of Fuel Subsidies: Evidence from Bolivia, Ghana, Jordan, Mali, and Sri Lanka* (IMF Working Paper No. 06/247). Washington, D.C.: International Monetary Fund. doi:10.5089/9781451865073.001.

D'Lima, M., & Medda, F. (2015). A new measure of resilience: An application to the London Underground. *Transportation Research Part A, Policy and Practice, 81,* 35–46. doi:10.1016/j.tra.2015.05.017.

Delbosc, A., & Currie, G. (2011). Exploring the relative influences of transport disadvantage and social exclusion on well-being. *Transport Policy, 18,* 555–562. doi:10.1016/j.tranpol.2011.01.011.

DiMaggio, C., Brady, J. & Li, G. (2015). Association of the safe routes to school program with school-age pedestrian and bicyclist injury risk in Texas. *Injury Epidemiology, 2,* 15. doi:10.1186/s40621-015-0038-3.

Eeftens, M., Beelen, R., de Hoogh, K., Bellander, T., Cesaroni, G., Cirach, M., … Hoek, G. (2012a). Development of land use regression models for PM2.5, PM2.5 absorbance, PM10 and PMcoarse in 20 European study areas: Results of the ESCAPE project. *Environmental Science & Technology, 46,* 11195–11205. doi:10.1021/es301948k.

Eeftens, M., Tsai, M.-Y., Ampe, C., Anwander, B., Beelen, R., Bellander, T., … Hoek, G. (2012b). Spatial variation of PM2.5, PM10, PM2.5 absorbance and PMcoarse concentrations between and within 20 European study areas and the relationship with NO2: Results of the ESCAPE project. *Atmospheric Environment, 62,* 303–317. doi:10.1016/j.atmosenv.2012.08.038.

Environmental Protection Agency (EPA), United States Government. (2013). *Criteria Air Pollutants*. Retrieved from www.epa.gov/criteria-air-pollutants.

Environmental Protection Department, Hong Kong SAR Government. (2017). *Air Pollution Control (Ocean Going Vessels)(Fuel at Berth) Regulation (the Regulation) Frequently Asked Questions*. Retrieved from www.epd.gov.hk/epd/english/environmentinhk/air/prob_solutions/frequently-asked-questions.html.

European Conference of Ministers of Transport (ECMT). (2007). *Managing Urban Traffic Congestion*. Paris: OECD.

Ferranti, E., Chapman, L., Lowe, C., McCulloch, S., Jaroszweski, D. & Quinn, A. (2016). Heat-related failures on Southeast England's railway network: Insights and implications for heat risk management. *Weather, Climate, and Society, 8,* 177–191. doi:10.1175/WCAS-D-15-0068.1.

Garnaut, R., Jotzo, F. & Howes, S. (2008). China's rapid emissions growth and global climate change policy. In L. Song & W.T. Woo (Eds.), *China's Dilemma: Economic Growth, the Environment and Climate Change* (pp. 170–189). Washington, DC: Brookings Institution Press.

Gehring, U., Gruzieva, O., Agius, R.M., Beelen, R., Custovic, A., Cyrys, J., ... Brunekreef, B. (2013). Air pollution exposure and lung function in children: The ESCAPE project. *Environmental Health Perspectives, 121,* 1357–1364. doi:10.1289/ehp. 1306770.

Givoni, M. (2007). Environmental benefits from mode substitution: Comparison of the environmental impact from aircraft and high-speed train operations. *International Journal of Sustainable Transport, 1,* 209–230. doi:10.1080/15568310601060044.

Heritier, H., Vienneau, D., Frei, P., Eze, I.C., Brink, M., Probst-Hensch, N. & Röösli, M. (2014). The association between road traffic noise exposure, annoyance and health-related quality of life (HRQOL). *International Journal of Environmental Research and Public Health, 11,* 1652–1667. doi:10.3390/ijerph111212652.

Hilling, D. (1996). *Transport and Developing Countries.* London and New York: Routledge.

Ho, T.K. (2015). Exporting railway technologies. In B.P.Y. Loo & C. Comtois (Eds.), *Sustainable Railway Futures: Issues and Challenges* (pp. 185–200). Surrey: Ashgate.

International Energy Agency (IEA). (2013). *CO2 Emissions from Fuel Combustion 2013 Highlights.* Retrieved from www.oecd-ilibrary.org/docserver/download/6113251e.pdf?expires=1499768144&id=id&accname=ocid194359&checksum=0B45F579E113032 99DD41129CACE5194.

International Energy Agency (IEA). (2016). *CO2 Emissions from Fuel Combustion 2016 Highlights.* Retrieved from www.iea.org/publications/freepublications/publication/CO2EmissionsfromFuelCombustion_Highlights_2016.pdf.

International Monetary Fund (IMF). (2016). *World Economics Outlook Databases.* Retrieved from www.imf.org/external/ns/cs.aspx?id=28.

International Union for Conservation of Nature and Natural Resources (IUCN). (1980). *World Conservation Strategy.* Gland, Switzerland: International Union for Conservation of Nature and Natural Resources.

Jacobs, G., Aeron-Thomas, A. & Astrop, A. (2000). *Estimating Global Road Fatalities* (TRL REPORT 445). Berkshire: Transport Research Laboratory.

Lam, W.W.Y., & Loo, B.P.Y. (2014). Does neighbourhood count in affecting children's journeys to schools? *Children Geographies, 13,* 89–113. doi:10.1080/14733285.2013.8 28450.

Li, L., & Loo, B.P.Y. (2016a). Carbon dioxide emissions from urban transport in China: Geographical characteristics and future challenges. *Geographical Research* (in Chinese), *25,* 1230–1242. Retrieved from www.dlyj.ac.cn/EN/10.11821/dlyj201607002.

Li, L., & Loo, B.P.Y. (2016b). Impact analysis of airport infrastructure within a sustainability framework: Case studies on the Hong Kong International Airport. *International Journal of Sustainable Transportation, 10,* 781–793. doi:10.1080/15568318.2016.11 49647.

Li, L., & Loo, B.P.Y. (2016c). Towards people-centered integrated transport: A case study of Shanghai Hongqiao Comprehensive Transport Hub. *Cities, 58,* 50–58. doi:10.1016/j.cities.2016.05.003.

Loo, B.P.Y. (2002). Role of stated preference methods in planning for sustainable urban transportation: State of practice and future prospects. *Journal of Urban Planning and Development, 128,* 210–224. doi:10.1061/(ASCE)0733-9488(2002)128:4(210).

Loo, B.P.Y. (2008). Editorial. *International Journal of Sustainable Transportation, 2*, 135–137. doi:10.1080/15568310701517232.

Loo, B.P.Y. (2012). *The E-society.* New York, NY: Nova Science.

Loo, B.P.Y., & Banister, D. (2016). Decoupling transport from economic growth: Extending the debate to include environmental and social externalities. *Journal of Transport Geography, 57*, 134–144. doi:10.1016/j.jtrangeo.2016.10.006.

Loo, B.P.Y., & Cheng, A.C.H. (2010). Are there useful yardsticks of population size and income level for building metro systems? Some worldwide evidence. *Cities, 27*, 299–306. doi:10.1016/j.cities.2010.02.003.

Loo, B.P.Y., & Chow, A.S.Y. (2009). The relevance of transport-development strategies to understanding travel behaviour and transport sustainability in Hong Kong. *Asian Geographer, 26*, 67–82. doi:10.1080/10225706.2009.9684144.

Loo, B.P.Y., & Chow, A.S.Y. (2011). Jobs-housing balance in an era of population decentralisation: An analytical framework and a case study. *Journal of Transport Geography, 19*, 552–562. doi:10.1016/j.jtrangeo.2010.06.004.

Loo, B.P.Y., & du Verle, F. (2017). Transit-oriented development in future cities: Towards a two-level sustainable mobility strategy. *International Journal of Urban Sciences, 21*(Suppl. 1), 54–67. doi:10.1080/12265934.2016.1235488.

Loo, B.P.Y., & Hook, B. (2002). Interplay of international, national and local factors in shaping container port development: A case study of Hong Kong. *Transport Reviews, 22*, 219–245. doi:10.1080/01441640110091486.

Loo, B.P.Y., & Leung, K.Y.K. (2017). Transport resilience: The Occupy Central Movement in Hong Kong from another perspective. *Transportation Research Part A: Policy and Practice*, 106, 100–115. doi: 10.1016/j.tra.2017.09.003.

Loo, B.P.Y., & Li, D.Y.N. (2006). Developing metro systems in the People's Republic of China: Policy and gaps. *Transportation, 33*, 115–132. doi:10.1007/s11116-005-3046-2.

Loo, B.P.Y., & Li, L. (2012). Carbon dioxide emissions from passenger transport in China since 1949: Implications for developing sustainable transport. *Energy Policy, 50*, 464–476. doi:10.1016/j.enpol.2012.07.044.

Loo, B.P.Y., & Tsui, K.L. (2007). Factors affecting the likelihood of reporting road crashes resulting in medical treatment to the police. *Injury Prevention, 13*, 186–189. doi:10.1136/ip. 2006.013458.

Loo, B.P.Y., & Tsui, K.L. (2016). Contributory factors to critically wrong road-crossing judgments among older people: An integrated research study. *Hong Kong Journal of Emergency Medicine, 23*, 13–24.

Loo, B.P.Y., Cheung, W.S. & Yao, S. (2011). The rural-urban divide in road safety: The case of China. *The Open Transportation Journal, 5*, 9–20. doi:10.2174/187444780110 5010009.

Loo, B.P.Y., Li, L., Psaraki, V., & Pagoni, I. (2014). CO_2 emissions associated with hubbing activities in air transport: An international comparison. *Journal of Transport Geography, 34*, 185–193. doi:10.1016/j.jtrangeo.2013.12.006.

McGuire, S., Muller, U., Elmenhorst, E.-M. & Banser, M. (2016). Inter-individual differences in the effects of aircraft noise on sleep fragmentation. *Sleep, 39*, 1107–1110. doi:10.5665/sleep. 5764.

MacIntyre, E.A., Gehring, U., Mölter, A., Fuertes, E., Klümper, C., Krämer, U., … Heinrich, J. (2014). Air pollution and respiratory infections during early childhood: An analysis of 10 European birth cohorts within the ESCAPE project. *Environmental Health Perspective, 122*, 107–113. doi:10.1289/ehp. 1306755.

Ministry of Public Security, PRC Government. (various years). *Quan guo dao lu jiao tong shi gu tong ji zi liao hui bian* (China's road crashes statistical book). Beijing: Qun Zhong Chu Ban She.

National Bureau of Statistics of China. (2013). *Census Yearbook 2013*. Retrieved from www.stats.gov.cn/tjsj/ndsj/2013/indexch.htm.

Organisation for Economic Co-operation and Development (OECD). (2016). List of OECD Member countries – Ratification of the Convention on the OECD. Retrieved from www.oecd.org/about/membersandpartners/list-oecd-member-countries.htm.

Peden, M., Scurfield, R., Sleet, D., Mohan, D., Hyder, A.A., Jarawan, E. & Mathers, C. (Eds.) (2004). *World Report on Road Traffic Injury Prevention*. Geneva: World Health Organization.

Preston J., & O'Connor, K. (2008). Revitalised transport geographies. In R. Knowles, J. Shaw & I. Docherty (Eds.), *Transport Geographies: Mobilities, Flows and Spaces* (pp. 227–237). Malden, MA: Blackwell.

Raaschou-Nielsen, O., Andersen, Z.J., Beelen, R., Samoli, E., Stafoggia, M., Weinmayr, G., … Hoek, G. (2013). Air pollution and lung cancer incidence in 17 European cohorts: Prospective analyses from the European Study of Cohorts for Air Pollution Effects (ESCAPE). *Lancet Oncology, 14*, 813–822. doi:10.1016/S1470-2045(13)70279-1.

Rattanachot, W., Wang, Y., Chong, D. & Suwansawas, S. (2015). Adaptation strategies of transport infrastructures to global climate change. *Transport Policy, 41*, 159–166. doi:10.1016/j.tranpol.2015.03.001.

Rogers, C.D.F., Bouch, C.J., Williams, S., Barber, A.R.G., Baker, C.J., Bryson, J.R., … Quinn, A.D. (2011). Resistance and resilience: Paradigms for critical local infrastructure. *Proceedings of the Institute of Civil Engineers: Mechanical Engineering, 165*, 73–83. doi:10.1680/muen.11.00030.

Sherbinin, A., Schiller, A. & Pulsipher, A. (2007). The vulnerability of global cities to climate hazards. *Environment and Urbanisation, 19*, 39–64. doi:10.1177/0956247807076725.

Sipe, N., & Dodson, J. (2013). Oil vulnerability in the American city. In J.L. Renne, & B. Fields (Eds.), *Transport Beyond Oil-Policy Choices for a Multimodal Future* (pp. 31–50). Washington, D.C.: Island Press.

State Commission Office for Public Sector. (2013). *Government Organisation in China*. Beijing: State Commission Office for Public Sector.

Statista. (2017). *Automotive Industry in China: Sales – Statistics & Facts*. Retrieved 6 March 2017 from www.statista.com/topics/1100/automobile-sales-in-china/.

Tapio, P., Banister, D., Luukkanen, J., Vehmas, J. & Willamo, R. (2007). Energy and transport in comparison: Immaterialisation, dematerialisation and decarbonisation in the EU15 between 1970 and 2000. *Energy Policy, 35*, 433–451. doi:10.1016/j.enpol.2005.11.031.

The National Academies. (2012). *Disaster Resilience: A National Imperative*. Washington, D.C.: National Academies Press.

Transport Advisory Committee. (2014). *Report on Study of Road Traffic Congestion in Hong Kong*. Hong Kong: Hong Kong SAR Government.

United Nations Economic Commission for Europe. (1993). *Convention on Road Traffic*. Retrieved from www.unece.org/fileadmin/DAM/trans/conventn/Conv_road_traffic_EN.pdf.

United Nations Office for Disaster Risk Reduction (UNISDR). (2007). *Terminology*. Retrieved from www.unisdr.org/we/inform/terminology.

Vanlaar, W., Hing, M.M., Brown, S., McAteer, H., Crain, J. & McFaull, S. (2016). Fatal and serious injuries related to vulnerable road users in Canada. *Journal of Safety Research*, *58*, 67–77. doi:10.1016/j.jsr.2016.07.001.

Woetzel, J., Mendonca, L., Devan, J., Negri, S., Hu, Y., Jordan, L., … Yu, F. (2009). *Preparing for China's Urban Billion*. New York, NY: McKinsey & Company.

World Bank. (2016). *Urban Population (% of Total)*. Retrieved 19 May 2016 from http://data.worldbank.org/indicator/SP.URB.TOTL.IN.ZS.

World Commission on Environment and Development (WCED). (1987). *Report of the World Commission on Environment and Development: Our Common Future*. Retrieved from www.un-documents.net/our-common-future.pdf.

World Health Organization. (2008). *The Global Burden of Disease: 2004 Update*. Geneva: World Health Organization.

World Health Organization. (2015). *Global Status Report on Road Safety 2015*. Retrieved from www.who.int/entity/violence_injury_prevention/road_safety_status/2015/GSRRS 2015_Summary_EN_final2.pdf.

Yang, X., Jin, W., Jiang, H., Xie, Q., Shen, W. and Han, W. (2017). Car ownership policies in China: Preferences of residents and influence on the choice of electric cars. *Transport Policy*, *58*, 62–71. doi:10.1016/j.tranpol.2017.04.010.

Yao, S., Loo, B.P.Y. & Lam, W.W.Y. (2015). Measures of pedestrian activity-based exposure to the risk of vehicle-pedestrian collisions: Space-time path vs potential path tree methods. *Accident Analysis and Prevention*, *75*, 320–332. doi:10.1016/j.aap.2014.12.005.

3 Benchmarking at the international level

Benchmarking around 2010

With a projected timeline to 2030, 2014 is chosen as the benchmark year for putting the existing situation in context. Arguably, the analysis should benchmark all dimensions that are relevant to sustainable transport. Nonetheless, a non-discriminatory benchmarking exercise of all available data and information will not be very useful in generating insights about the current unsustainable transport trends and in facilitating the subsequent analysis on future sustainable transport strategies. Nowadays, with the abundance of data (especially big data collected from the internet-of-things (IoT), involving an enormous range of e-sensors, digital information transmitted on the internet, and stored in cloud or local servers), an intellectual line of enquiry is particularly valuable and important in guiding meaningful social science research. Following the conceptual framework of comprehensive sustainability (see Chapter 2), key variables related to the economic, environmental and social dimensions of sustainable transport are therefore selected for the cross-country analysis in this chapter.

Notes about international comparisons

Before the data analysis, it is worthwhile to emphasise once again that the aim of international comparisons is to put the case of China in the international arena to see where the country is doing better and where it is lagging. At this stage (Stage 1 in Figure 1.1), the aim is primarily to describe, rather than to explain. The reasons for differences in the performance of a specific indicator across different countries may reflect very deep-seated historical, cultural and other actors that can only be revealed with detailed country and case study analysis. For instance, the cycling culture in the Netherlands long existed before the sustainability concerns were raised at a global level in *The Brundtland Report* (WCED, 1987). Moreover, international comparisons are bound to be affected by differences in statistical definition, compilation and quality across different countries. China's highly fluctuating and inconsistent export values from different sources (namely the Chinese National Customs and the Ministry of Foreign Trade and Economic Co-operation), for instance, once triggered much concern about the data quality or even doubts regarding the falsification of data in China (Loo, 2004). Nonetheless, when one looks closely into the statistical definitions and the institutional framework for collecting export values in China over time, these differences were mostly due to statistical definitions and specific purposes of data collection by different institutions in China (Loo, 2004). Moreover, in some cases, national figures can mask huge geographical diversity within countries, especially for a large country like China. Reports of worsening road safety may co-exist with a reduction in the number of road fatalities per passenger-km at the national level. Successful stories of improvements in air quality may co-exist with a deterioration in nationwide air pollution indices in this chapter. Some of the enormous geographical variability of the physical and human geography in the country have been discussed in Chapter 1. Therefore, one should always interpret the results of international comparisons with care.

Economic indicators

First and most fundamental, how are people and goods circulating in the country now? Quantifiable data in relation to traffic volumes are valuable in answering the above question. Some key guiding questions that help to give insights about the current transport systems of a country are:

1   What are the volumes of passenger (in passenger-kilometres, pkm) and freight (in tonne-kilometres, tkm) traffic?
2   What have the trends been over time?
3   Are there any obvious changes in the ways people and goods have been moving in the country in terms of the use of different traffic modes?

Environmental indicators

Second, recognising that CO_2 emissions are one of the most important environmental impacts of transportation, they are examined for getting a useful picture of the current environmental problems arising from the passenger and freight transport systems of countries in different parts of the world. The key research questions are:

1   What is the volume of CO_2 emissions from transportation (in million metric tonnes)?
2   What recent trends are notable?
3   How did transport CO_2 emissions compare to the total volume generated from other economic sectors?
4   What is the CO_2 emissions efficiency in terms of population, the economy, and the passenger and freight traffic volumes?

Social indicators

Finally, the road safety situation is compared in an attempt to reflect the social dimension of the current sustainable transport challenges. The key research questions in relation to the road traffic injury burden are:

1 How serious is the road safety problem in terms of fatalities and casualties?
2 What were the identifiable trends?
3 How have these trends been related to the growth of population, the economy, and the passenger and freight traffic volumes in respective countries over time?

Choice of countries

In fact, compiling the above data and trends within China is a daunting task by itself. China is the third largest country in terms of physical size with a vast territory of 9.6 million km². Its 2014 year-end population reached 1.37 billion (National Bureau of Statistics of China, 2016). Nonetheless, fully appreciating the scale and the urgency of the opportunities and problems in China's transport sector would not be possible without some international comparisons. To make the international comparison meaningful, only countries that are also of relatively large territorial size and population are chosen. Data availability is also a concern. Finally, seven countries are chosen in this benchmarking exercise. They include three developing countries – Brazil, India and Russia – and four developed countries – France, Germany, UK and USA. A map showing the countries included in the international comparisons is shown in Figure 3.1. Given the sample bias and various limitations about international data and comparisons mentioned above, no attempt is made to analyse the sustainability

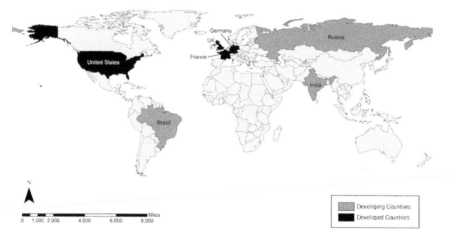

Figure 3.1 The seven selected countries for international comparisons.
Source: The author.

performances of the developed and developing economies statistically as two separate groups.

Furthermore, an attempt to generalise about developed versus developing economies can easily fall into the conceptual pitfall of the modernisation paradigm that developing economies are only/inevitably repeating the steps of the developed economies and are inferior in all sustainability aspects. This study recognises that developing economies can learn good lessons from developed economies, and vice versa. Hence, countries rather than blocks of countries (like developed versus developing economies) are our focus. Empirically, Loo and Banister (2016) also clearly demonstrate that the sustainability and transport performances of countries in neither the developed nor developing economies are uniformly high or low. No country, whether in the developed or developing category, excels in all aspects of transport sustainability. Most countries have done well in certain aspects but not others. Hence, while the distinction of developed and developing economies is still helpful in understanding the results and mapping the way forward (as the latter do have a much lower economic capacity to address unsustainable transport problems, for example), the main statistical analysis will use country as the unit of analysis.

A variety of data sources are used in this chapter. Transport performance and other data are gathered from individual countries' official statistical and transport authorities, including the National Bureau of Statistics of China (2011a, 2011b, 2011c, 2011d, 2011e, 2011f), the Russian Federation Federal State Statistics Service (2011a, 2011b), France's National Institute of Statistics and Economic Studies (2010), German Federal Statistical Office (2012), UK's Department for Transport (2011a, 2011b), the Federal Highway Administration, US Department of Transportation (2010) and the USA's Bureau of Transportation Statistics (2012a, 2012b). The road fatality data were compiled from the European Commission (2012), German Federal Statistical Office (2012), India's Ministry of Road Transport and Highways (2012a, 2012b, 2012c, 2012d), China's Ministry of Public Security (2011), National Bureau of Statistics of China (2011a, 2011b, 2011c, 2011d, 2011e, 2011f), Pan American Health Organisation (2012), Russian Federation Federal State Statistics Service (2012), UK's Department for Transport (2011a, 2011b) and the USA's National Highway Traffic Safety Administration (NHTSA) (2012).

Despite substantial efforts, not all seven comparison countries can be included in every sustainability dimension discussed below because comparable data are sometimes not available or just too piecemeal to make a systematic comparison possible. Moreover, in cases where international data for 2014 are not available, the closest year is used.

Traffic volume baselines

Arguably, passenger-kilometres (pkm) and tonne-kilometres (tkm) are the two most important summary indicators of the performance of a society in transporting people and goods. Figure 3.2a shows the passenger turnover in pkm in China and the comparison countries (which have comparable data) from 1995 to 2014. The linear, rather than the log, scale is used to allow readers to appreciate the huge mobility gap between the USA and the other countries, including China, Russia, the UK, Germany and France. To identify the trends over time, Figure 3.2b uses 1995 as the base year for comparison.

For passenger transport, China has had the second highest passenger transport volume among the six selected countries throughout the period (Figure 3.2a). However, China was very far behind the USA in absolute terms. In 2010, the total passenger volume in China and the USA were 2,789.43 billion pkm and

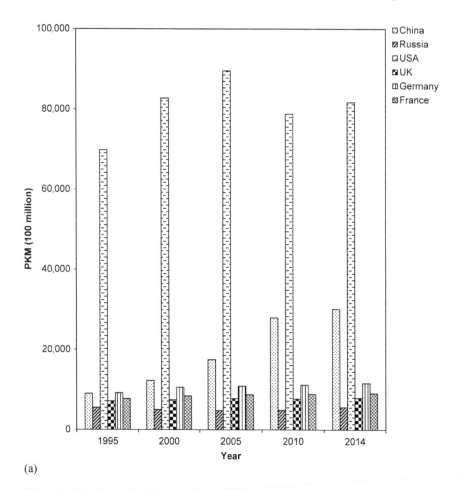

(a)

Figure 3.2 An international comparison of passenger transport.

Source: Compiled by the author.

Notes
a Total passenger turnover in pkm.
b Change of passenger turnover compared to 1995.

continued

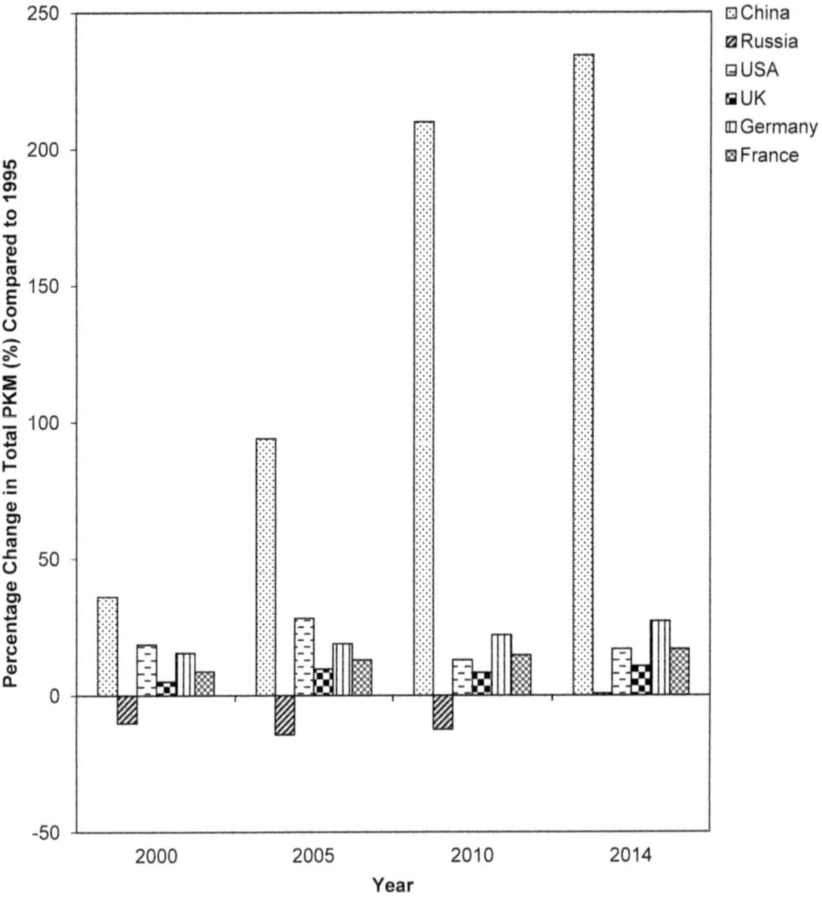

(b)

Figure 3.2 Continued

7,881.36 billion pkm respectively. While the territorial extent of both countries is vast, the USA (population of 309.35 million) was much less populated than China (population of 1,337.71 million) in the same year. Taking 2010 as an example, if people's mobility in China (2,085 thousand pkm per 1,000 population) were to increase to the level of the USA (25,477 thousand pkm per 1,000 population), the total passenger volume in China would increase by 12.2 times (or 1,220 per cent) to 34,084.51 billion pkm! In 2014, the total passenger volumes in China and the USA were 3,009.74 billion pkm and 8,168.67 billion pkm respectively, showing that the absolute growth of pkm in China (7.90 per cent) was higher than that in USA (3.65 per cent) between 2010 and 2014. In China, an efficient transport network for transporting people around cities and across long distances is therefore vital. As China's economy further develops, the rapid increase in passenger transport can pose a severe threat to the sustainability of its transport system.

From Figure 3.2b, one sees that the percentage increase of passenger turnover in China has not only been positive but also steadily rising throughout the 2000s. From 1995 to 2000, the passenger turnover volume in China increased by 36.21 per cent. By 2010, the figure had risen by more than 209.87 per cent compared to 1995. Growth was still observed in 2014, when China grew by 234.35% compared to 1995. The drop in passenger turnover in Russia during the 2000s was also noteworthy. A preliminary analysis suggests that it was partly due to the changing levels of subsidy provided by the Russian government on passenger travel. With the government subsidy, in 2000 long-distance passengers and commuter train passengers paid only 55 per cent and 15 per cent of the cost respectively (Russian Federation Federal State Statistics Service, 2009). By 2006, the corresponding figures were raised to 80 per cent and 50 per cent respectively (Russian Federation Federal State Statistics Service, 2009). The reduction in subsidy has meant an increase in passenger fares in Russia after 2000. The passenger turnover on the Russian railway network dropped by 45 per cent from 1992 to 2010 (Russian Federation Federal State Statistics Service, 2014). More recently, the financial crisis of 2008 has further hit the Russian economy and reduced passenger travel (Russia CEIC Database Team, 2011). In 2014, there was a recovery of pkm by 14.92 per cent to 556.2 million in Russia when compared to 2010, and it reached a level similar to 1990 (552,300 million).

For freight transport, the respective sets of data for freight turnover are shown in Figures 3.3a and 3.3b respectively. Figure 3.3a reveals that by 2010 China had already surpassed the USA as the country with the highest freight turnover (in tkm) among the group of selected countries (China, Russia, the USA, the UK, Germany and France). The sharp increase in freight transport in China cannot be separated from the emergence of China as the world's 'factory' and its industrialisation (Loo, 2002, 2004). As shown in Figure 3.3b, China's freight turnover in 2010 had risen by about 295 per cent compared to 1995, while the figures for the other countries were all lower than 70 per cent. Until 2014, the total tkm of China almost quadrupled (418 per cent) compared to 1995. The UK even recorded a decrease in freight volume in both 2010 and 2014. The drop was probably due to both the financial crisis of 2008 and the associated economic slowdown. In particular, the sharp reduction in global trade had a great impact on the UK's manufacturing sector (Office for National Statistics, 2011), which was observed by a decline in freight turnover of 18.5 per cent in 2014 compared to 1995. Both the domestic and international freight handled in the UK dropped noticeably after 2008. In fact, the level of domestic freight in the UK in 2009 was only broadly at the same level as in 1991 (UK Department for Transport, 2011a, 2011b). This huge difference can probably be explained by the discrepancy between China's rapidly growing economy and industrialisation, and the UK's more stabilised, industrialised and mature economy.

In addition, many transport facilities built in the developed economies, notably the expressway system in the USA, have already become congested and

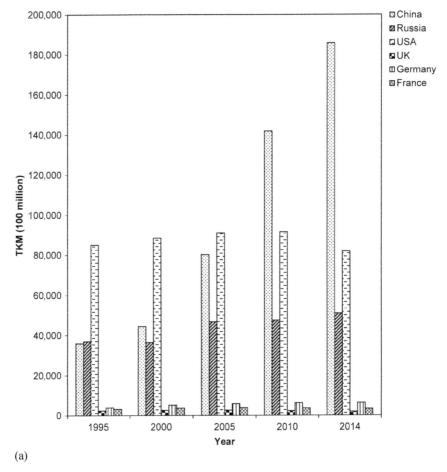

(a)

Figure 3.3 An international comparison of freight transport.

Source: Compiled by the author.

Notes
a Total tonne-kilometre (tkm).
b Change compared to 1995.

in need of repair, maintenance and upgrades. The room to cater for further growth in traffic volume is limited without major new transport infrastructural projects. On the contrary, China, as a developing country, is still at a stage of rapid economic growth and large-scale infrastructural development. The total length of paved roads in China, for example, increased by more than four times from 0.9 million km in 1980 to 4.0 million km in 2010. Meanwhile, the total length of American paved roads remained relatively stable at 6.5 million km in the same period. In 2014, the total length of paved roads in China was

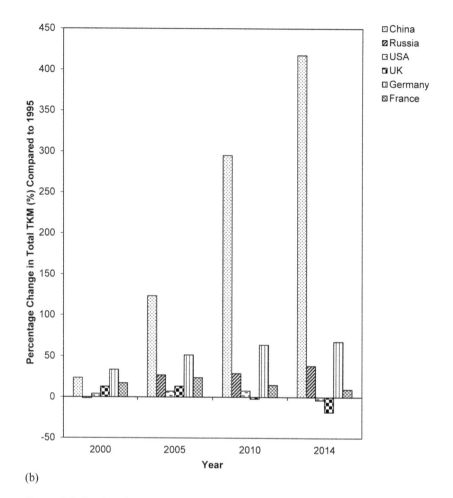

(b)

Figure 3.3 Continued

4.5 million km. The availability of more new transport infrastructure in China is likely to further boost its passenger and freight turnovers in the near future.

Modal split of total passenger turnover

Figure 3.4 shows the changing modal split of passenger transport in China, Russia, France, Germany, the UK and the USA. Two points are noteworthy. First, although it is clear that highways have been the major mode of passenger transport in all six countries, France, Germany, the UK and the USA in the developed countries group generally relied more heavily on road than China and Russia in the developing countries group. In France, the UK and the USA, despite the relatively small decline in importance of highways in the modal share

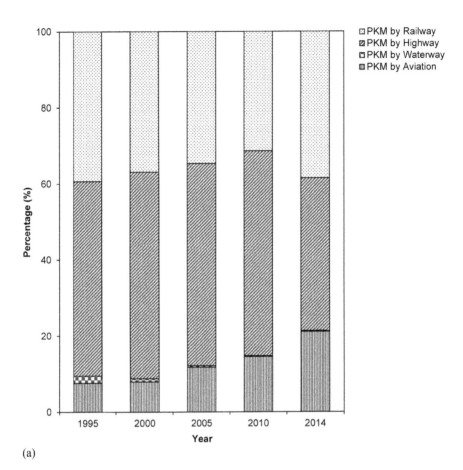

(a)

Figure 3.4 An international comparison of modal split of passenger transport.

Sources: Compiled by the author based on German Federal Statistical Office (2011), Ministry of Road Transport and Highways, Government of India (2010), National Institute of Statistics and Economic Studies, Government of France (2011) and Russian Federation Federal State Statistics Service (2010).

Notes
a China.
b Russia.
c France.
d Germany.
e UK.
f USA.

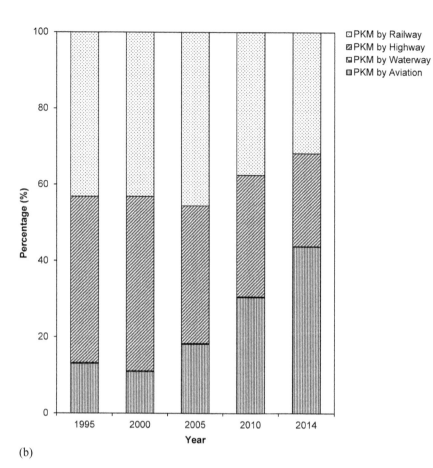

(b)

Figure 3.4 Continued

continued

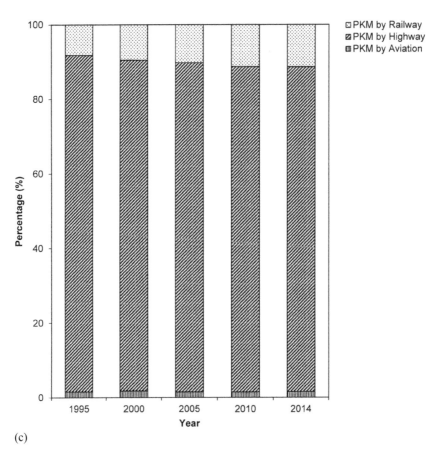

(c)

Figure 3.4 Continued

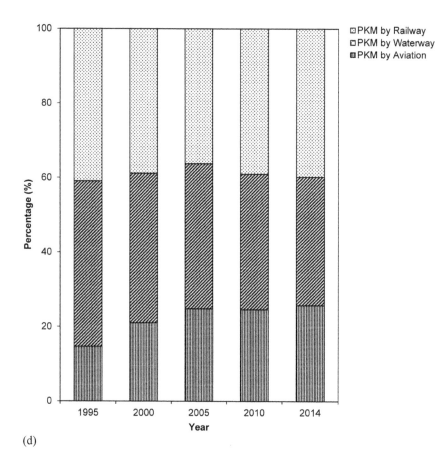

(d)

Figure 3.4 Continued

continued

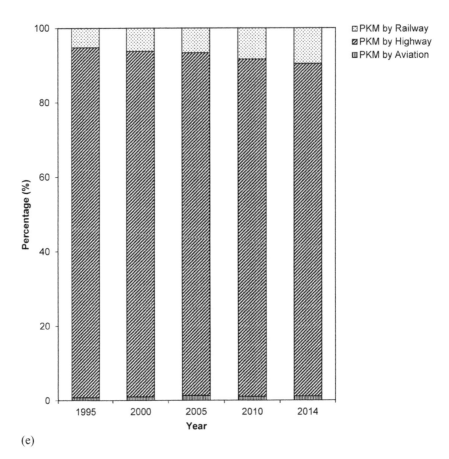

(e)

Figure 3.4 Continued

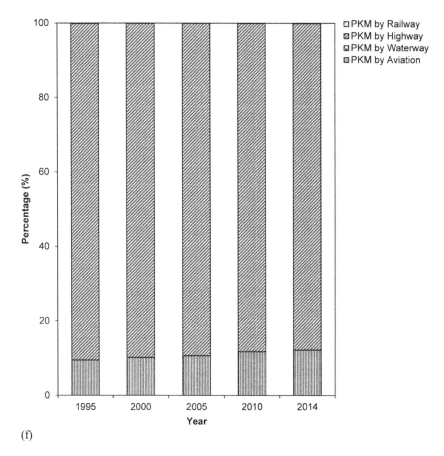

(f)

Figure 3.4 Continued

of passenger transport between 1990 and 2014, highways consistently made up 85–95 per cent of the total passenger turnover. The high percentage share reflects the high automobile dependency of the American, British and French population. In these countries, highways play a vital role of moving people not only within cities (urban transport) but also in connecting major towns and other cities (rural and regional transport). In contrast, railway was a comparatively more important mode of inter-city passenger transport in China and Russia in the 1990s and throughout the 2000s. Up to 2014, railways in both China and Russia still accounted for 39 per cent and 32 per cent of the passenger turnover respectively.

Second, we can see that the modal split among the developed countries of France, Germany, the UK and the USA remained relatively stable over the entire study period; yet, the situation in the developing countries of China and Russia has been changing much more dramatically. In particular, there has been a consistent drop in railway passenger transport and a persistent increase in aviation passenger transport in China. More recently, China has undergone an increase in railway passenger transport again, from 2010 to 2014, mainly due to the rapid development of high-speed railways. With the technological advancement and increasing interactions of China with rest of the world under globalisation and the significant growth of tourism, the role of civil aviation has become increasingly important in China (and also Russia). Both China and Russia recorded a growth in aviation passenger transport from 1990 to 2014 by 280 per cent and 340 per cent respectively. Though not yet constituting the majority share in total passenger turnover, there has been an ostensible increase in its modal share in both China and Russia. Generally, it seems that the composition of total passenger turnover in the developing economies has been much more dynamic. Changes in France, the UK and the USA have been relatively minor, and the modal split of passenger transport has been relatively stable, despite the huge absolute volume and steady growth.

Modal split of total freight turnover

Figure 3.5 shows the changing situation of total freight turnover in the six selected countries. Again, some striking contrasts are worth mentioning. First, in contrast to the heavy reliance on highways for moving goods in France, Germany and the UK, China relied more heavily on waterways during the entire study period (48.2–61.9 per cent). The high share of waterways in freight transport can partly be attributable to the huge capacities of China's river systems (especially Changjiang/Yangtze and Huang He/Yellow River) and the large number of cities built along these river systems. Huang He is commonly regarded as the cradle of the Chinese civilisation. Table 3.1 shows some major cities along Changjiang and Huang He rivers in China. Some great cities, both as huge population centres and economic activities, like Xining in Qinghai, Lanzhou in Gansu, Yinchuan in Ningxia, Xian in Shanxi, Zhengzhou in Henan and Jinan in Shandong are along Huang He. Similarly, Changjiang flows across the major cities of Chongqing, Wuhan in Jiangxi, Nanjing in Jiangsu, and Shanghai (Figure 3.6). Chongqing and Shanghai are two provincial-level municipalities of high political significance as well. But more recently, a rapid increase in highway freight transport in China was also recorded, especially between 2005 and 2009. Putting the situation in an international perspective, the shares of waterways of China and the UK were 61.9 per cent and 23.7 per cent respectively in 2005. By 2010, the respective shares had dropped to 48.2 per cent and 18.9 per cent in China and the UK respectively. In 2014, Chinese waterway freight turnover increased slightly to 49.9 per cent, and the corresponding share in the UK further decreased to 14.6 per cent.

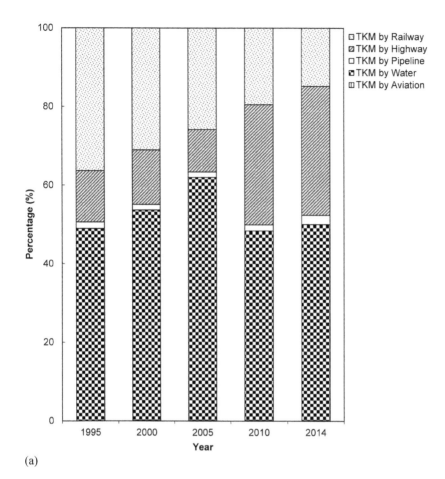

(a)

Figure 3.5 An international comparison of modal split in freight transport.

Sources: Compiled by the author based on German Federal Statistical Office (2011), Ministry of Road Transport and Highways, Government of India (2010), National Institute of Statistics and Economic Studies, Government of France (2011) and Russian Federation Federal State Statistics Service (2010).

Notes
a China.
b Russia.
c France.
d Germany.
e UK.
f USA.

continued

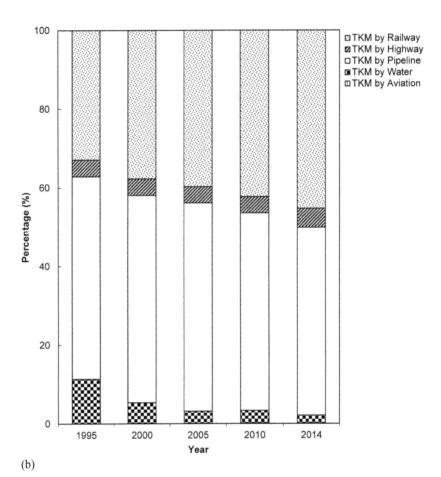

(b)

Figure 3.5 Continued

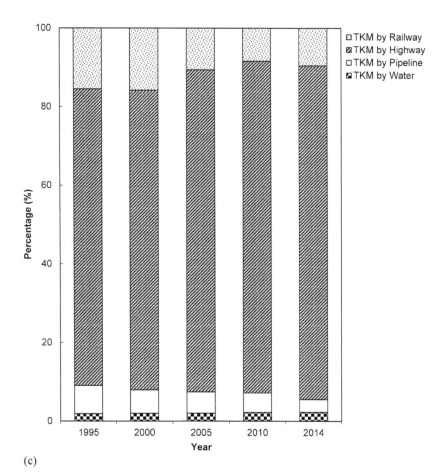

(c)

Figure 3.5 Continued

continued

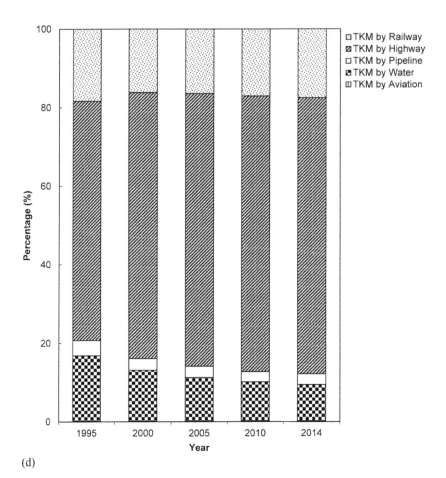

(d)

Figure 3.5 Continued

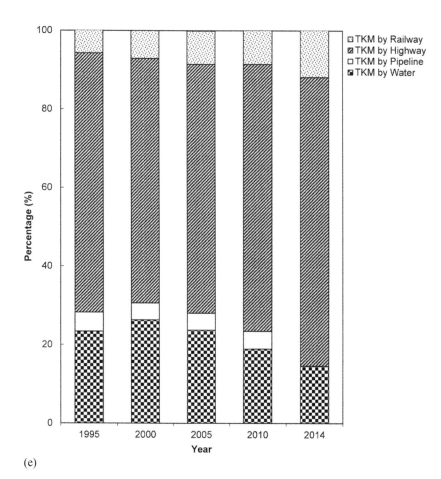

(e)

Figure 3.5 Continued

continued

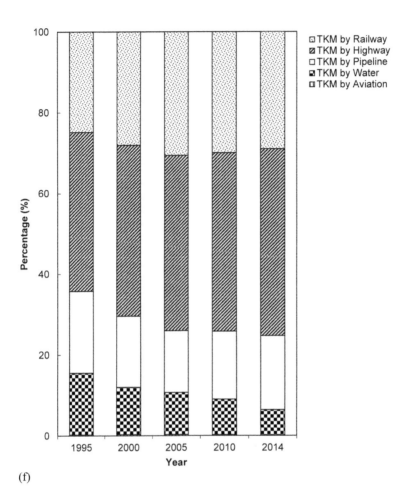

(f)

Figure 3.5 Continued

Table 3.1 Economic and demographic characteristics of cities along major rivers in China

Provincial-level municipalities	City name	Population size in 2013 (10,000 persons)	GDP in 2013 (10,000 yuan)	GDP per capita in 2013 (yuan)	Share of manufacturing sector in GDP in 2013 (%)	Share of manufacturing sector in GDP in 2013 (%)
(a) Changjiang/Yangtze River						
Shanghai	Shanghai	1,432.3	216,021,200	150,853	37.16	62.24
Jiangsu	Suzhou	653.8	130,157,000	199,017	52.63	45.73
	Wuxi	472.2	80,701,800	170,978	52.14	46.02
	Changzhou	365.9	43,609,347	119,151	51.61	45.22
	Nanjing	643.1	80,117,800	124,600	43.07	54.38
	Yangzhou	459.8	32,520,078	70,696	52.08	41.02
	Zhenjiang	271.8	29,272,800	107,621	52.93	42.66
	Nantong	766.5	50,388,916	65,696	52.07	41.08
	Taizhou	507.8	30,069,100	59,191	52.35	40.80
Anhui	Wuhu	384.5	20,995,271	54,533	66.12	27.75
	Anqing	621.7	14,182,282	22,801	53.14	32.61
	Maanshan	228.4	12,928,032	56,702	64.52	29.34
	Tongling	74.2	6,806,000	91,973	72.14	26.10
	Chizhou	161.9	4,622,452	28,534	48.80	36.62
Jiangxi	Jiujiang	508.1	16,017,317	31,530	56.08	35.80
Hubei	Wuhan	822.1	90,512,700	110,113	48.57	47.72
	Jinzhou	661.0	13,349,300	20,196	44.66	31.44
	Ezhou	109.8	6,309,400	57,358	59.45	28.11
	Huangshi	262.3	11,420,300	43,589	61.22	30.44
	Huangang	750.2	13,325,500	17,767	39.12	34.11
	Yichang	400.1	28,180,700	70,452	60.10	27.97
	Xianning	300.5	8,721,100	28,974	48.51	32.81
	Shiyan	346.7	10,805,900	31,141	50.62	36.14

continued

Table 3.1 Continued

Provincial-level municipalities	City name	Population size in 2013 (10,000 persons)	GDP in 2013 (10,000 yuan)	GDP per capita in 2013 (yuan)	Share of manufacturing sector in GDP in 2013 (%)	Share of manufacturing sector in GDP in 2013 (%)
Hunan	Yueyang	808.3	11,300,386	13,986	54.98	33.90
Chongqing	Chongqing	3,358.4	126,566,900	37,691	50.55	41.53
Sichuan	Luzhou	508.4	11,404,815	22,450	60.01	26.35
	Yibin	550.4	13,428,937	24,416	60.65	24.56
	Panzhihua	112.0	8,008,832	71,507	74.57	21.95
(b) Huang He/Yellow River						
Shandong	Dongying	187.0	32,502,000	173,807	69.49	26.91
	Jinan	613.3	52,301,948	85,321	39.26	55.30
	Heze	957.5	20,500,100	21,421	54.32	33.24
	Binzhou	381.6	21,557,271	56,433	51.31	38.90
	Jining	847.8	35,015,400	41,292	51.11	36.92
Henan	Zhengzhou	919.1	62,019,000	67,485	55.96	41.67
	Luoyang	692.3	31,407,596	45,387	57.74	34.34
	Sanmenxia	226.8	11,920,868	52,515	65.90	25.74
	Kaifeng	553.1	13,635,447	24,657	44.71	34.73

Shanxi	Xi-an	806.9	48,841,300	60,522	43.36	52.18
	Yan-an	237.8	13,541,350	56,896	72.23	19.84
	Yulin	377.0	28,467,500	75,511	69.75	25.35
Shanxi-coal	Lvliang	393.9	12,286,015	31,183	70.60	24.13
	Yuncheng	522.4	11,401,151	21,841	44.35	38.47
Inner Mongolia	Baotou	225.0	35,030,200	155,690	51.63	45.52
	Bayannur	253.2	8,348,900	45,622	56.23	24.33
	Wuhai	55.3	5,701,293	103,660	65.94	33.15
Ningxia	Yinchuan	172.6	12,890,199	74,510	53.42	42.28
	Wuzhong	143.7	3,519,276	24,439	54.29	31.58
	Shizuishan	76.6	4,464,393	57,979	64.38	30.39
	Zhongwei	121.5	2,868,250	23,705	44.69	39.15
Gansu	Lanzhou	368.6	17,762,823	48,138	46.19	51.05
	Baiyin	177.0	4,633,061	26,175	54.63	33.86
Qinghai	Xining	226.8	9,785,314	43,107	52.53	32.00

Sources: National Bureau of Statistics of China (2014a, 2014b, 2014c).

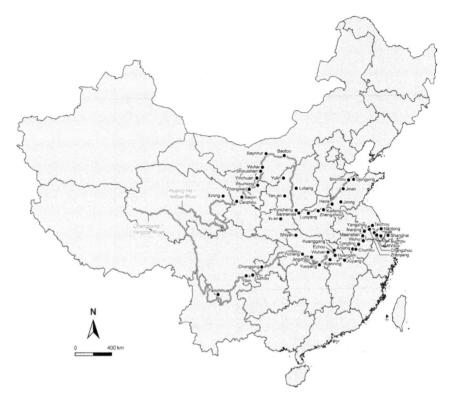

Figure 3.6 Geographical locations of cities along major rivers in China.
Source: Compiled by the author.

Transport carbon emissions

Following the Kyoto Protocol, there has been increasing awareness of the negative environmental impact of CO_2; and a consensus on a reduction of CO_2 emissions from anthropogenic sources as a goal for both developed and developing countries. More recently, the United Nations Conference on Climate Change 2015 was held in Paris, France. The first universal climate agreement for mitigating climate change was adopted by 195 countries at COP21 (21st Yearly Session of the Conference of the Parties, 2015). All eight countries included in this analysis are signatory nations.

Before the data analysis, we need to recognise that the World Bank transport CO_2 emissions figures are not comprehensive and only include domestic aviation, domestic navigation, road, rail and pipeline transport (World Bank, 2015). In other words, CO_2 emissions from international shipping and international aviation are not attributed to specific countries. For international travel, there are complex problems of attribution and allocation (Loo *et al.*, 2014; Aall, 2014).

Using the example of international air flights, should the CO_2 emissions of an international flight from country A to country B be attributed solely to the originating country A, destination country B or all countries along the flight path? Should the nationalities of the passengers or freight (if possibly identified) be considered? The problems of international aviation CO_2 emissions attribution and accounting are complex, depending also on the airport congestion level and the aircraft types used. Loo *et al.* (2014), for example, have examined the issue at great depth at different spatial scales of the airport, air space and entire atmosphere. For small countries with much international air travel like Norway, international civil aviation could amount to a 20 per cent addition to the official CO_2 emissions figures (Aall, 2014). The relative importance of international and domestic civil aviation depends on many factors, including the territorial size of the country and the population distribution. For international marine bunkers, should the CO_2 emissions be attributed to the country(ies) producing the oil, the countries owning the vessels using the bunker fuels, the countries producing or consuming the goods on the international vessels, or those providing the port facilities, which may be different from the producing or consuming countries? Recognising the limitations of transport CO_2 emissions data by country, the issues of CO_2 emissions from international marine bunkers and international aviation have been addressed separately in a concerted effort to decarbonise the transport sector globally (IEA/OECD, 2009). The percentage change in CO_2 emissions from fuel combustion of international marine bunkers and aviation bunkers reached as high as 68.5 per cent and 94.9 per cent respectively from 1990 to 2014 (IEA, 2016). Hence, decarbonising international marine bunkers and international aviation deserve serious efforts at the global level.

With the above understanding, Figure 3.7 shows the average annual CO_2 emissions from the transport sector at the national level in China, Brazil, India, Russia, the UK, the USA, Germany and France in five periods: 1991–1995, 1996–2000, 2001–2005, 2006–2010 and 2011–2014. It is clear that the USA had consistently much higher transport CO_2 emissions than all other countries for all periods. While the average annual transport CO_2 emissions of Brazil, France, Germany, India, Russia and the UK have been relatively steady, the situation in China has changed notably. The average annual transport CO_2 emissions in China increased by approximately four times from the 1991–1995 period to the 2006–2010 period, and 5.5 times from the 1991–1995 period to the 2011–2014 period. Among the four developing countries analysed, China has already surpassed Russia and has been emitting the largest volume of CO_2 in the transport sector since the 1996–2000 period. Nonetheless, the absolute level of transport CO_2 emissions in China was still much lower than the USA in the 2006–2010 period. The gap between China and the USA in transport CO_2 emissions has significantly narrowed in the 2011–2014 period, where China's was 72 per cent lower than the USA's in the period 2006–2010 and 58 per cent lower in the period 2011–2014. In fact, when the total CO_2 emissions from all domestic sources are considered, China has already surpassed the USA as the world's largest carbon emitter (Netherlands Environmental Assessment Agency, 2007).

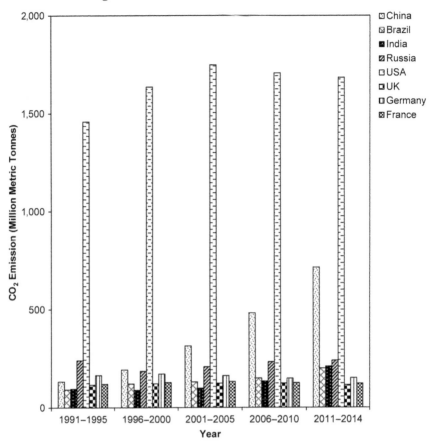

Figure 3.7 An international comparison of average transport CO_2 emissions.

Source: Compiled by the author.

Figure 3.8 shows the percentage share of the transport sector in the total CO_2 emissions of the respective country. Among the eight countries analysed, the transport sector contributed from less than 5 per cent to over 40 per cent of the total CO_2 emissions during the study period from 1990 to 2014. Developed countries generally show higher percentages than developing countries, indicating that the former have a more polluting or carbon-based transport sector. In 2014, France and the UK even reached the highest percentage of transport's share in national total CO_2 emissions after 1990. The findings underpin the urgency to reduce transport-related pollution in moving towards low-carbon economies in developed countries, as advocated by Banister (2005). The case of Brazil is also worth discussing because its energy sector is relying heavily on renewable and non-polluting sources, such as hydroelectricity. And worldwide, electricity and heat production represents the largest source (about 41.69 per cent) of CO_2 emissions from fuel combustion (see Table 2.1). As over

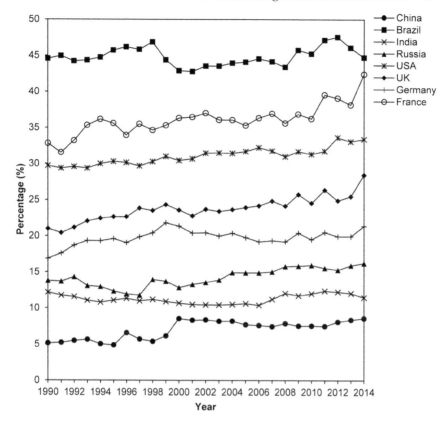

Figure 3.8 An international comparison of transport's share in national total CO$_2$ emissions.

Source: Compiled by the author.

three-quarters of Brazil's electric power came from hydro power, the share of the transport sector in the total CO$_2$ emissions of the country is exceptionally high (US Energy Information Administration, 2016). The situation actually raises the challenge that the transport sector (with heavy reliance on fossil fuels and the internal combustion engine) has been particularly unresponsive to shifting to low carbon technologies such as solar or hydro power, and, hence, needs special attention in the entire initiatives to reduce CO$_2$ emissions from human sources.

Throughout the study period, China consistently showed the lowest percentage in the share of the transport sector in total CO$_2$ emissions among the four developing countries of Brazil, China, India and Russia. The range was between 4 per cent and 9 per cent in all years. The low share reflects, on the one hand, the heavy reliance of the Chinese economy on coal in both electricity generation and other energy consumption, and, on the other hand, the country's relatively low passenger volume (Figure 3.2) and non-road-based travel patterns of people and waterway-dependent freight transport up to the late 2000s (Figures 3.4 and 3.5). Putting the picture together, the potential challenges of increasing CO_2 emissions from the transport sector, if the current trends of rapid motorisation, urbanisation and economic growth continue or even accelerate in China, can be alarming. Actions must be taken to tackle these trends of unsustainable transport in the country to facilitate a sustainable transport transition by 2030.

Transport carbon emission per million population

Figures 3.9a and b show the CO_2 emissions from the transport sector per million population (million metric tonnes per million people) in linear and log scales

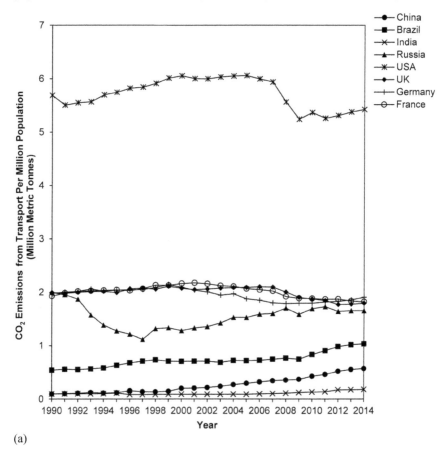

(a)

Figure 3.9 An international comparison of transport sector CO_2 emissions per million population.

Source: Compiled by the author.

Notes
a Linear scale.
b Log scale.

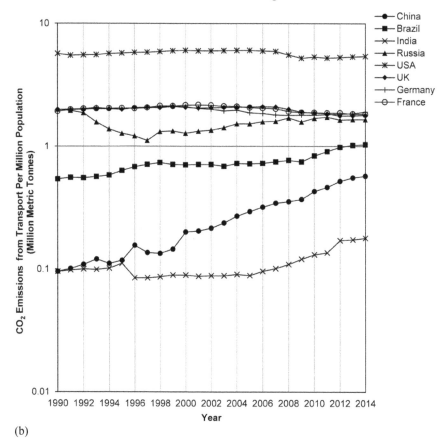

(b)

Figure 3.9 Continued

among the eight selected countries. The huge gap between the USA and the other seven countries once again demonstrates the environmentally unsustainable automobile-dependent lifestyle of the Americans during the study period. Figure 3.9a reveals that the figure in the USA was far above that of all the other countries, including the other developed countries like France, Germany and the UK. In 2014, the CO_2 emissions from the transport sector per million population in the USA was still 2.8 times higher than the other three developed nations, despite the salient reduction observed in 2006.

Despite China's large population base, the country did not have the lowest average transport CO_2 emissions rate per million population. Instead, India had the best performance. While China's level was the second lowest among all eight countries, it has shown a worrying upward trend, especially after the mid-1990s (particularly evident in Figure 3.9b). The figures were 0.43 in 2010 and 0.57 in 2014, indicating an increase by a factor of 3.6 and 4.8 when compared to 1995 respectively. In contrast, Brazil, which was the third lowest, showed a relatively stable level of transport CO_2 emissions per million population throughout the 1990s and 2000s. One of the reasons was due to the wide use of alternative fuel vehicles, particularly methane, in Brazil with the country's rich natural endowment and a good infrastructure for supporting both methane and petroleum stations throughout the country. Methane, in turn, emits much less CO_2 than petroleum when used in an internal combustion engine.

Transport carbon emissions and economic development

According to Tapio *et al.* (2007), a low transport intensity of the economy suggests a process called immaterialisation, which refers to a decoupling of material production and consumption (in this case, transport activities) from economic production (represented by GDP). A lower carbon intensity of transport can be described as dematerialisation, referring specifically to the decoupling of environmental harm (in this case, CO_2) from material production (in this case, transport activities). Ideally, countries can delink environmental harm from economic production by increasing the latter without a proportionate increase in the former – a process called decarbonisation. In reality, Tapio *et al.* (2007), however, found that neither the transport intensity of the economy (pkm/GDP and tkm/GDP) nor the carbon intensity of transport (CO_2/pkm and CO_2/tkm) had reduced in Europe in the 1970–2000 period.

With a different time period (1990–2009) and a different group of countries, Figure 3.10 suggests that transport decarbonisation (that is, lower transport CO_2 per capita/GDP per capita) seems to be happening gradually over time from 1990 to 2010 with all eight countries of Brazil, China, France, Germany, India, Russia, UK and USA. The time-series data of each country have all demonstrated a downward-sloping curve. By 2007, all countries were noted with transport CO_2 emissions per million GDP less than 200 tonnes. Within the same country, the CO_2 emissions generated by transport activities associated with the production of one dollar of GDP have become lower over time. The sharper the decline, the faster is transport decarbonisation happening in the country. Notably, while transport decarbonisation has happened in all eight countries, the process was the slowest in the USA in the study period of 1990 to 2010. Notably, the figures of all countries were lower than 120 tonnes of transport CO_2 emissions per million GDP in 2014.

Yet, despite the overall improvement over time, there is still a notable positive relationship between economic growth and transport CO_2 emissions across all different countries at different points in time. Figure 3.11 shows the correlation between economic development and transport CO_2 emissions of the group of eight countries in 1990 and 2010. There is a positive relationship between the two variables of GDP per capita (current US dollars) and transport CO_2 emissions per million population (million metric tonnes). The R^2 is about 0.5 ($p < 0.00$). Considering that there are not many cases and there is only one variable in the regression model, about 50 per cent of the variability of the transport CO_2 emissions per million population can be accounted for by the variability of the GDP per capita.

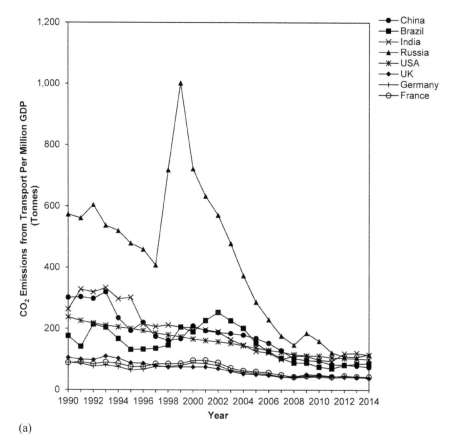

(a)

Figure 3.10 Transport sector CO_2 emissions per million GDP.

Source: Compiled by the author.

Notes
a Linear scale.
b Log scale.

continued

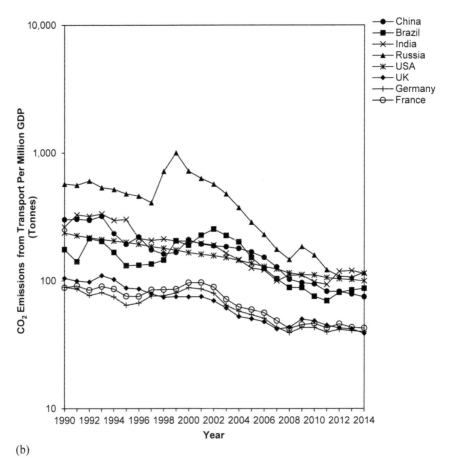

(b)

Figure 3.10 Continued

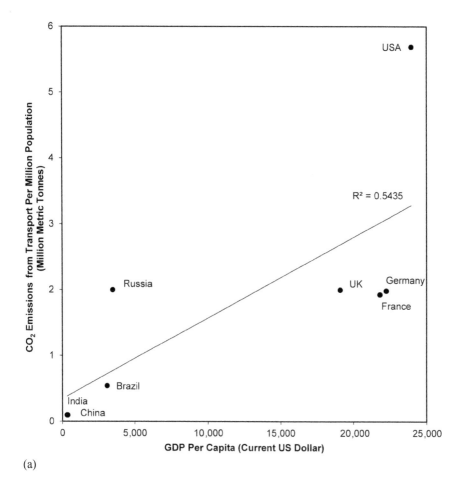

(a)

Figure 3.11 Correlation of economic development and CO_2 emissions from transport per million population.

Source: Compiled by the author.

Notes
a 1990.
b 2010.

continued

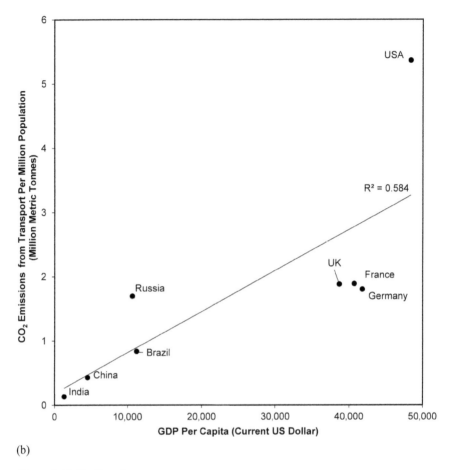

(b)

Figure 3.11 Continued

The above relationship only reflects a historical pattern based on the situations in the countries from 1990 to 2010. If there are emerging solutions of achieving sustainable transport, the relationship may not necessary apply in the future. Yet, for the moment, it does seem that an absolute decoupling of transport CO_2 emissions from economic growth has not been happening at an international scale. The cross-sectional analysis suggests that for a country with a higher GDP per capita increase (x-axis), its transport CO_2 emissions per million population (y-axis) is also higher. To the developing countries, it seems that an improvement in GDP per capita will still lead to more transport CO_2 emissions per capita – an environmental cost that has to be paid for its economic development.

Transport carbon emissions and traffic volumes

Figure 3.12a shows the average transport CO_2 emissions per total traffic volume of the society. It shows how well the developing and developed countries have been doing in reducing air pollution while developing the transport sector and enhancing traffic performance. Converting tkm to pkm by the formula of 1 tkm = 10 pkm (European Commission, 2009), we can see that the four developed countries showed much higher CO_2 emissions for the same level of 'transport output' that they are delivering. When this freight-to-passenger turnover conversion formula is

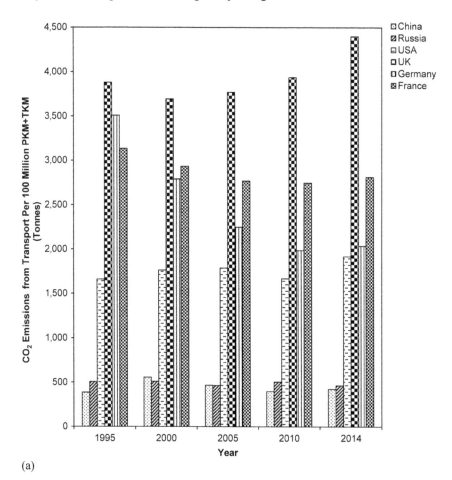

(a)

Figure 3.12 An international comparison of transport CO_2 emissions per transport volume.

Source: Compiled by the author.

Notes
a CO_2 emissions per transport turnover.
b Change over time.

continued

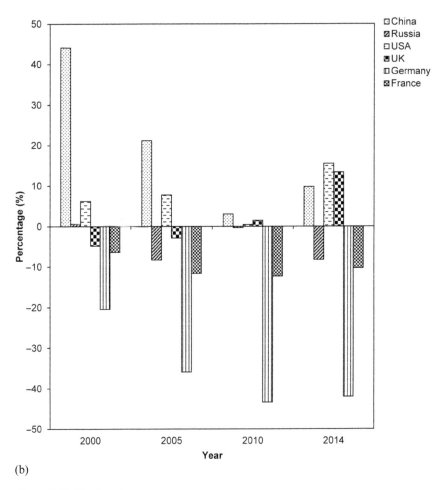

(b)

Figure 3.12 Continued

changed, the results will also change (Loo & Banister, 2016). Generally, a higher conversion factor (1 tkm = more than 10 pkm) will make countries with a larger freight sector look more favourable in generating lower transport CO_2 emissions per unit of traffic volume, and vice versa. Overall, the performances of the developing countries have not been uniformly poor. Should a higher freight-to-passenger turnover conversion factor be used, a developing country undergoing rapid industrialisation like China will have even better transport CO_2 emissions efficiency. The major freight transport modes in China and Russia being the waterways and pipelines respectively has greatly contributed to the higher CO_2 emissions efficiency of the two developing countries during the study period from 1995 to 2010.

Figure 3.12b shows the percentage change in transport CO_2 emissions per traffic volume compared to 1995. If the process of transport dematerialisation had been happening, the percentage change would have been negative. A closer look at Figure 3.12b shows that most of the changes are indeed negative. The results are encouraging, especially in 2010, when France and Germany achieved a significant transport dematerialisation and other remaining countries obtained a minimal increase or a slight decrease in transport CO_2 emissions per total traffic volume. In particular, Germany is a very good example, demonstrating a persistent trend of transport dematerialisation. In 2010 and 2014, there was a 43.4 per cent and 42 per cent decline of transport CO_2 emissions per traffic volume when compared to 1995 respectively. A combination of transport, land use and taxation policies in Germany have contributed to the lower environmental harm, in this case CO_2, per transport output. These factors include the use of more fuel efficient vehicles, reduced automobile usage for short trips, increased public transport patronage and the rise of walking and cycling as alternative transport modes (Buehler & Pucher, 2009). In some notably successful sustainable towns, car-free developments have been implemented. These innovations have demonstrated a culture of being environmentally sensitive when using automobiles and in providing an environment in which people can be supported for a high level of mobility without relying on private cars (Loo, 2017). These case studies are worthy of closer examination. Though it is encouraging to notice that most countries have dematerialised the transport sector to a certain extent, it is noteworthy that some developed countries such as the USA and the UK had higher transport CO_2 emissions per traffic volume in 2014 when compared to 1995.

Road fatalities

Road safety is one of the key issues in sustainable transport and it is undoubtedly a great challenge faced by China given the country's rapidly increasing vehicle fleet. In international comparisons, the number of road fatalities is by far the most important single indicator of road safety in a country. First, the definition of serious injury differs widely among countries using different yardsticks, including the length of stay at hospital (as in Hong Kong) and the Injury Severity Score (ISS). A simple formula of direct conversion between injury severity (as recorded more accurately in hospitals by ISS) and hospitalisation (as marked by police officers in traffic crash records) is often impossible without much error (Tsui *et al.*, 2009). Second, when slight injury and property-damage-only traffic crashes are considered, the issues and variability of under-reporting will also become much more serious (Loo & Tsui, 2007). For instance, Loo and Tsui (2007) show that while the average underreporting was generally around 40–45 per cent in Hong Kong and elsewhere, the underreporting rates for minor injuries (based on hospital data) can be over 70 per cent, especially for vulnerable groups like children, cyclists and senior citizens. Third, the outcome of fatality is much more definite, that is, dead or alive. It is only the time scale and the cause that may differ in various administrations. Following the definition of the International Road Federation (2010), a road fatality refers to any immediate deaths or death within 30 days as a result of a road accident. Standard adjustment factors can be applied if a country uses a different time period, such as seven days in China, in defining road fatalities (Jacobs, Aeron-Thomas & Astrop, 2000).

Figure 3.13 shows the number of road fatalities in China, France, Germany, India, the UK and the USA in linear and log scales. India has gone through a dramatic increase in road fatalities since the 2000s. Clearly, this consistently increasing road traffic injury burden in India should be seriously looked into and properly addressed (Parsekar *et al.*, 2015). In 2010, the total number of road deaths in India reached 134,513. Among the developing countries, the respective figures in Brazil, Russia and China were 43,531, 26,600 and 65,225 respectively. In 2014, India and Russia experienced a growth in road fatalities to 139,671 and 27,000 respectively. Notably, China went through a different temporal trajectory

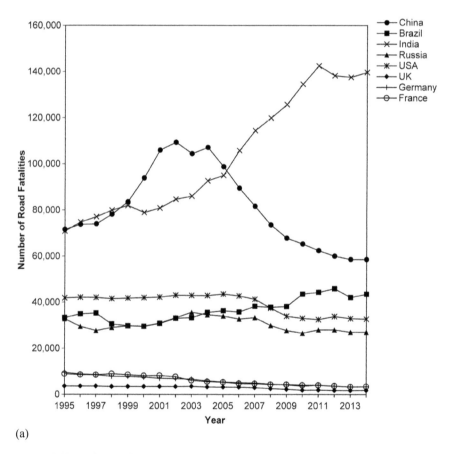

(a)

Figure 3.13 An international comparison of road fatalities.

Source: Compiled by the author.

Notes
a Linear scale.
b Log scale.

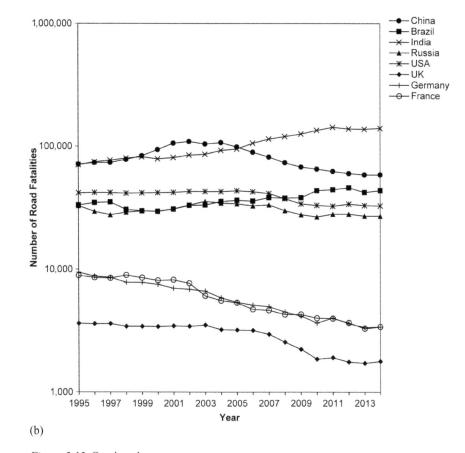

(b)

Figure 3.13 Continued

during the study period with its road fatality number first increasing dramatically after 1995 but then taking a sharp downward turn in 2004. The 'Law of the People's Republic of China on Road Traffic Safety', which came into effect on 1 May 2004, was considered instrumental in improving road safety conditions in the country (National People's Congress, 2003). The Law was the first national law on road traffic safety in the country ever since its establishment in 1949. On the contrary, France, Germany, the UK and the USA have managed to reduce the road fatality number consistently up to 2010. The trend was more variable thereafter. Nonetheless, by 2014, the absolute number of road deaths in the USA (32,675) still stayed at a notably higher level than in the other developed countries of France (3,384), Germany (3,377) and the UK (1,775). Overall, all developed countries and China demonstrated a decline in the total road fatalities in 2014 when compared to 1995.

Road fatalities per million population

Figure 3.14 shows the fatality rate per million population. Among the countries studied, the discrepancy remains large by 2010. Variations in the number of deaths per million population are particularly great among the developing countries, with 48.8 in China, 109.8 in India, 186.2 in Russia and 219.2 in Brazil. Yet, the developed countries group shows great variations also, with the number of road deaths per million population at 29.5 in the UK, 44.6 in Germany, 61.4 in France and 106.7 in the USA. In 2014, all countries except Brazil and India managed to reduce their fatality rates per million population when compared to 1995, and India has replaced the USA for the third highest fatality rate per million population since 2010. In general, the developing countries have poorer road safety performance per million population, except for China. The developed countries show better road safety performance per million population, except for the USA.

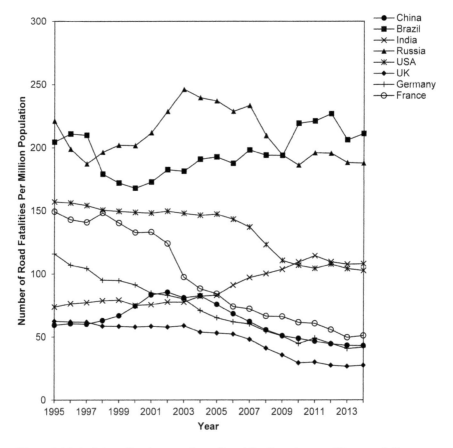

Figure 3.14 An international comparison of road fatality rate per million population.

Source: Compiled by the author.

Obviously, there are many other factors determining the road fatality rate, such as the modal split, government's effectiveness in improving road conditions and people's road safety awareness (Loo *et al.*, 2005, 2007). In cities like Hong Kong, people's heavy reliance on non-road-based transport modes, like the metro system, will mean a dramatic reduction in exposure to road hazards (Loo *et al.*, 2005). Hence, these factors need to be considered when more in-depth analysis is to be conducted.

Road fatalities per 100 million pkm by road

Road fatalities per million population are only one of the indicators used to understand road safety in a country. Figure 3.15 shows the road fatality data in terms of 100 million road pkm. This indicator reflects the concept of exposure in

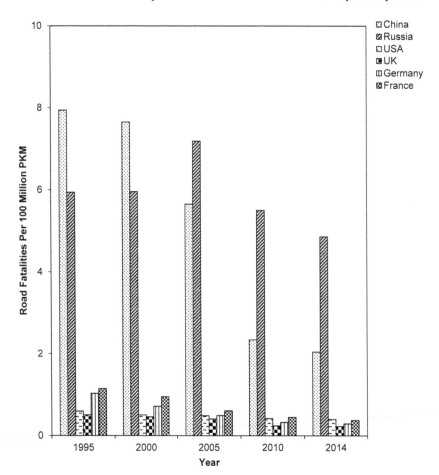

Figure 3.15 An international comparison of road fatalities per 100 million road pkm.
Source: Compiled by the author.

road safety (Loo & Anderson, 2016). When this indicator is considered, China and Russia consistently showed much higher fatality rates than France, Germany, the UK and USA. This finding may be explained by the relatively poor road conditions, transport facilities, vehicle quality and enforcement of safety regulations in developing countries. Over time, China has greatly reduced its road fatality rate from around eight per 100 million pkm in 1995 to lower than three in 2010. In other words, this road death per 100 million pkm indicator has reduced to only one-third of its level in less than one-and-a-half decades. In contrast, Russia has not demonstrated significant improvements as such. The difference reveals that the Chinese government has been successful in reducing road fatality despite a dramatic increase in traffic volume as its economy develops. The enormous efforts spent in improving China's road safety should be recognised; and the useful lessons should be properly studied and shared.

Road fatalities per billion GDP (current US dollars)

Last but not least, Figure 3.16 shows the road fatalities per billion GDP in linear and log scales. From 1995 to 2010, both developing countries and developed countries achieved significant improvements in road fatalities per billion GDP, as evidenced from the declining trend. The overall declining trend was sustained towards 2014, as the figures for all countries in this year were the lowest since 1990. Moreover, the developed and the developing countries quite clearly separate into two groups, with the former being able to achieve lower levels of road fatalities per billion GDP than the latter. Among the developed countries, the road fatalities per billion GDP in 2010 ranged from 0.76 in the UK to 2.21 in the USA. The figures in France and Germany were 1.51 and 1.07 respectively. Among the developing countries, the road fatalities per billion GDP in 2010 ranged from 10.69 in China to 81.20 in India. The figures in Brazil and Russia were 19.71 and 17.44 respectively. Focusing on the case of China, it has achieved significant reduction in the fatality rate over the years and recorded the lowest figure among the four developing countries by 2010. China hit a record low of 5.58 in 2014. Yet, the gap with the developed countries remained.

Summary

Results of the international benchmarking (Stage 1 analysis in Figure 1.1) demonstrate that China has neither always the worst nor the best performance in terms of comprehensive sustainability. Nonetheless, it has consistently exhibited characteristics closer to the group of developing countries included in this analysis. There is much room for improvement and the absolute scale of the unsustainable transport problems (including the high volumes of passenger and freight turnovers, the total volume of transport CO_2 emissions and the total number of road fatalities) is enormous, even among the other large countries included in this analysis.

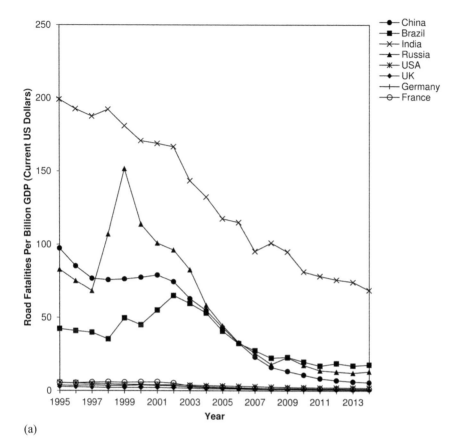

(a)

Figure 3.16 An international comparison of road fatalities per billion GDP, 1995–2014.

Source: Compiled by the author.

Notes
a Linear scale.
b Log scale.

continued

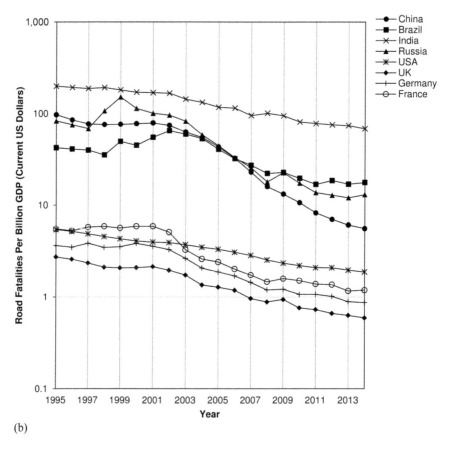

Figure 3.16 Continued

References

21st Yearly Session of the Conference of the Parties (COP21). (2015). *2015 United Nations Climate Change Conference*. Paris: United Nations Framework Convention on Climate Change.

Aall, C. (2014). Sustainable tourism in practice: Promoting or perverting the quest for a sustainable development? *Sustainability, 6*, 2562–2583. doi:10.3390/su6052562.

Banister, D. (2005). *Unsustainable Transport: City Transport in the New Century*. Oxon: Routledge.

Buehler, R., & Pucher, J. (2009). Sustainable transport that works: Lessons from Germany. *World Transport Policy and Practice, 15*(1), 13–46.

Bureau of Transportation Statistics, United States Government. (2012a). *Ton-Miles of Freight (BTS Special Tabulation)*. Retrieved from www.rita.dot.gov/bts/sites/rita. dot.gov.bts/files/publications/national_transportation_statistics/html/table_01_50. html.

Bureau of Transportation Statistics, United States Government. (2012b). *U.S. Passenger-Miles*. Retrieved from www.rita.dot.gov/bts/sites/rita.dot.gov.bts/files/publications/national_transportation_statistics/html/table_01_40.html.

European Commission. (2009). The Future of Transport, Focus Groups' Report, 20th February 2009. Retrieved October 15, 2015 from http://ec.europa.eu/transport/themes/strategies/doc/2009_future_of_transport/2009_the_future_of_transport.pdf Accessed 7th June 2015.

European Commission. (2012). *Road Safety Evolution in EU*. Retrieved 21 September 2012 from https://ec.europa.eu/transport/road_safety/sites/roadsafety/files/pdf/observatory/historical_evol.pdf.

Federal Highway Administration, United States Department of Transportation. (2010). Public road mileage – VMT – lane miles 1920–2010. *Highway Statistics 2010*. Retrieved from www.fhwa.dot.gov/policyinformation/statistics/2010/vmt421.cfm.

German Federal Statistical Office. (2011). Traffic: Key indicators by comparison. *Statistical Yearbook 2011* (p. 415). Wiesbaden, Germany: German Federal Statistical Office.

German Federal Statistical Office. (2012). Accidents and casualties covered (from 1950). *Facts and Figures: Transport (Road Traffic Accidents)*. Retrieved 20 September 2012 from www.destatis.de/EN/FactsFigures/EconomicSectors/TransportTraffic/TrafficAccidents/Tables_/RoadTrafficAccidents.html.

International Energy Agency (IEA). (2016). *CO_2 Emissions from Fuel Combustion: 2016 Edition*. Paris: OECD/IA.

International Energy Agency (IEA/OECD). (2009). *Transport, Energy and CO_2: Moving Toward Sustainability*. Paris: OECD/IEA.

International Road Federation. (2010). Sections presentation: Definitions & specifications. *World Road Statistics 2010* (p. v). Washington, D.C.: International Road Federation.

Jacobs, G., Aeron-Thomas, A. & Astrop, A. (2000). *Estimating Global Road Fatalities* (TRL REPORT 445). Berkshire: Transport Research Laboratory.

Loo, B.P.Y. (2002). The textile and clothing industries under the Fifth Kondratieff Wave: Some insights from the case of Hong Kong. *World Development, 30*, 847–872. doi:10.1016/S0305-750X(02)00005-0.

Loo, B.P.Y. (2004). Export expansion in the People's Republic of China since 1978: A case study of the Pearl River Delta. *The China Quarterly, 177*, 133–154. doi:10.1017/S0305741004000086.

Loo, B.P.Y. (2017). Realising car-free developments within compact cities. *Proceedings of the Institution of Civil Engineer – Municipal Engineer*. Advance online publication. doi:10.1680/jmuen.16.00060.

Loo, B.P.Y., & Anderson, T.K. (2016). *Spatial Analysis Methods of Road Traffic Collisions*. Boca Raton, FL: CRC Press.

Loo, B.P.Y., & Banister, D. (2016). Decoupling transport from economic growth: Extending the debate to include environmental and social externalities. *Journal of Transport Geography, 57*, 134–144. doi:10.1016/j.jtrangeo.2016.10.006.

Loo, B.P.Y., & Tsui, K.L. (2007). Factors affecting the likelihood of reporting road crashes resulting in medical treatment to the police. *Injury Prevention, 13*, 186–189. doi:10.1136/ip. 2006.013458.

Loo, B.P.Y., Hung, W.T., Lo, H.K. & Wong, S.C. (2005). Road safety strategies: A comparative framework and case studies. *Transport Reviews, 25*, 613–639. doi:10.1080/01441640500115892.

Loo, B.P.Y., Li, L., Psaraki, V. & Pagoni, I. (2014). CO_2 emissions associated with hubbing activities in air transport: An international comparison. *Journal of Transport Geography, 34,* 185–193. doi:10.1016/j.jtrangeo.2013.12.006.

Loo, B.P.Y., Wong, S.C., Hung W.T. & Lo, H.K. (2007). A review of the road safety strategy in Hong Kong. *Journal of Advanced Transportation, 41,* 3–37. doi:10.1002/ atr.5670410103.

Ministry of Public Security, Traffic Management Bureau, PRC Government. (2011). *Statistical Yearbook on Road Traffic Accidents in P.R.C. 2010* (pp. 17–42). Wuxi: Ministry of Public Security – Traffic Management Bureau.

Ministry of Road Transport and Highways, Government of India. (2010). Road accidents, persons killed and injured: 1970–2009. *Road Accidents in India 2009.* Retrieved from http://morth.nic.in/showfile.asp?lid=419.

Ministry of Road Transport and Highways, Government of India. (2012a). Freight movement by road transport & railways: 1999–2000 to 2010–11. *Road Transport Year Book (2009–10 & 2010–11).* Retrieved from http://morth.nic.in/showfile.asp?lid=838.

Ministry of Road Transport and Highways, Government of India. (2012b). Passenger movement by road transport & railways: 1999–2000 to 2010–11. *Road Transport Year Book (2009–10 & 2010–11).* Retrieved from http://morth.nic.in/showfile.asp? lid=838.

Ministry of Road Transport and Highways, Government of India. (2012c). Road accidents, persons killed and injured: 1970–2011. *Road Accidents in India 2011.* Retrieved from http://morth.nic.in/showfile.asp?lid=835.

Ministry of Road Transport and Highways, Government of India. (2012d). Total Number of registered motor vehicles in India: 1951–2011. *Road Transport Year Book (2009–10 & 2010–11).* Retrieved from www.morth.nic.in/showfile.asp?lid=838.

National Bureau of Statistics of China – Department of Urban Socio-economic Surveys. (2011a). *China City Statistical Yearbook 2011.* Beijing: China Statistics Press.

National Bureau of Statistics of China – Department of Urban Socio-economic Surveys. (2011b). *China Urban Life and Price Yearbook 2011* (pp. 97–101). Beijing: China Statistics Press.

National Bureau of Statistics of China – Department of Urban Socio-economic Surveys. (2011c). *China Statistical Yearbook for Regional Economy* (pp. 359–368). Beijing: China Statistics Press.

National Bureau of Statistics of China (2014a). National Accounts. *China Statistical Yearbook 2014.* Retrieved from www.stats.gov.cn/tjsj/ndsj/2014/indexeh.htm.

National Bureau of Statistics of China (2014b). Population. *China Statistical Yearbook 2014.* Retrieved from www.stats.gov.cn/tjsj/ndsj/2014/indexeh.htm.

National Bureau of Statistics of China (2014c). Industry. *China Statistical Yearbook 2014.* Retrieved from www.stats.gov.cn/tjsj/ndsj/2014/indexeh.htm.

National Bureau of Statistics of China. (2011d) Transport, postal and telecommunications. *China Statistical Yearbook 2011.* Retrieved from www.stats.gov.cn/tjsj/ndsj/.

National Bureau of Statistics of China. (2011e). Household consumption expenditure. *China Statistical Yearbook 2011.* Retrieved from www.stats.gov.cn/tjsj/ndsj/.

National Bureau of Statistics of China. (2011f). *China Energy Statistical Yearbook 2010.* Beijing: China Statistics Press.

National Bureau of Statistics of China. (2016). *2015 Nian Guo Min Jing Ji He She Hui Fa Zhan Tong Ji Gong Bao* (Year 2015 national economic and social development statistical bulletin). Retrieved from www.stats.gov.cn/tjsj/zxfb/201602/t20160229_ 1323991.html.

National Highway Traffic Safety Administration, United States Government. (2012). Fatalities and fatality rates, 1994–2010 – state: USA. *Fatality Analysis Reporting System (FARS) Encyclopedia*. Retrieved from www.governing.com/gov-data/fatality-analysis-reporting-system-state-data.htmlhttp://www-fars.nhtsa.dot.gov/Trends/TrendsGeneral.aspx.

National Institute of Statistics and Economic Studies, Government of France. (2010). Terrestrial inland transport of goods by mode in 2010. *Services – Tourism – Transport*. Retrieved from https://web.archive.org/web/20131202175858/www.insee.fr:80/fr/themes/tableau.asp?reg_id=0&ref_id=NATTEF13634.

National Institute of Statistics and Economic Studies, Government of France. (2011). Passenger transportation. *France in Figures 2011*. Retrieved from https://web.archive.org/web/20151206111230/www.insee.fr/en/publications-et-services/default.asp?page=collections-nationales/france-en-bref/services.htm.

National People's Congress. (2003). *Law of the People's Republic of China on Road Traffic Safety*. Retrieved from www.npc.gov.cn/englishnpc/Law/2007-2/05/content_1381965.htm.

Netherlands Environmental Assessment Agency. (2007). *China Now No. 1 in CO_2 Emissions; USA in Second Position*. Retrieved from www.pbl.nl/en/dossiers/Climatechange/Chinanowno1inCO2emissionsUSAinsecondposition.

Office for National Statistics. (2011). 2011 Census data. *2011 Census*. Retrieved from www.ons.gov.uk/census/2011census.

Pan American Health Organisation. (2012). Mortality rate from transport accidents. *Regional Core Health Data Initiative: Table Generator System*. Retrieved 24 September 2012 from https://web-beta.archive.org/web/20121029072826/www.paho.org:80/English/SHA/coredata/tabulator/newTabulator.htm.

Parsekar, S.S, Singh, M.M., Venkatesh, B.T. & Nair, S.N. (2015). Road safety in India: A public health concern. *Indian Journal of Community Health*, 27, 191–196.

Russia CEIC Database Team. (2011). Russia's unemployment rate drops to 6.1% in August. *CEIC DATA BLOG*. Retrieved from https://web-beta.archive.org/web/20120622111854/http://blog.securities.com:80/2011/10/russias-unemployment-rate-drops-august/.

Russian Federation Federal State Statistics Service. (2009). *Section 2.20: Financial Results of Freight and Passenger Rail Public Transport*. Retrieved from www.gks.ru/bgd/regl/B09_55/IssWWW.exe/Stg/02-0.htm.

Russian Federation Federal State Statistics Service. (2010). The length of roads. *Basic Indicators of Transport Performances in Russia*. Retrieved from www.gks.ru:80/wps/wcm/connect/rosstat/rosstatsite/main/publishing/catalog/statisticCollections/doc_1136985163781.

Russian Federation Federal State Statistics Service. (2011a). Freight turnover by transport mode. *Russia in Figures – 2011*. Retrieved from www.gks.ru/bgd/regl/b11_12/IssWWW.exe/stg/d01/18-2.htm.

Russian Federation Federal State Statistics Service. (2011b). Passenger turnover by public transport mode. *Russia in Figures – 2011*. Retrieved from www.gks.ru/bgd/regl/b11_12/IssWWW.exe/stg/d01/18-6.htm.

Russian Federation Federal State Statistics Service. (2012). Number of accidents and persons suffered in rolling stock accidents. *Russia in Figures – 2011*. Retrieved from www.gks.ru/bgd/regl/b11_12/IssWWW.exe/stg/d01/18-0.htm.

Russian Federation Federal State Statistics Service. (2014). *Passenger Turnover by Public Transport Mode in Russia*. Retrieved 19 February 2014 from www.quandl.com/RFSS/TRPASS-Passenger-Turnover-by-Public-Transport-Mode.

Tapio, P., Banister, D., Luukkanen, J., Vehmas, J. & Willamo, R. (2007). Energy and transport in comparison: Immaterialisation, dematerialisation and decarbonisation in the EU15 between 1970 and 2000. *Energy Policy, 35*, 433–451. doi:10.1016/j.enpol. 2005.11.031.

Tsui, K.L., So, F.L., Sze, N.N., Wong, S.C. & Leung, T.F. (2009). Misclassification of injury severity among road casualties in police reports. *Accident Analysis and Prevention, 41*, 84–89. doi:10.1016/j.aap. 2008.09.005.

United Kingdom Department for Transport. (2011a). Domestic freight transport by mode: 1953 onwards. *Transport Statistics Great Britain 2011*. Retrieved 5 September 2012 from www.gov.uk/government/uploads/system/uploads/attachment_data/file/575314/ tsgb0401.ods.

United Kingdom Department for Transport. (2011b). Passenger transport by mode: Annual from 1952. *Transport Statistics Great Britain 2011*. Retrieved 6 September 2012 from www.gov.uk/government/uploads/system/uploads/attachment_data/file/586 451/tsgb0101.ods.

United States (US) Energy Information Administration. (2016). *International Energy Outlook 2016*. Retrieved from www.eia.gov/outlooks/ieo/pdf/0484(2016).pdf.

World Bank. (2015). *Indicators – Data*. Retrieved 8 June 2015 from http://data.worldbank. org/indicator.

World Commission on Environment and Development (WCED). (1987). *Report of the World Commission on Environment and Development: Our Common Future*. Retrieved from www.un-documents.net/our-common-future.pdf.

4   Looking into the future and the dynamics within the nation

China since 1949

Contemporary studies on society in China cannot ignore the fact that China is (still) a centrally planned economy. On 1 October 1949, the People's Republic of China (PRC) was established in China under the leadership of the Chinese Communist Party (CCP). Since then, the Chinese development path has generally been guided by a series of Five-Year Plans, which outlined the major economic goals with a planning horizon of five years. The First Five-Year Plan of the country covered the period 1953–1957. Following the Soviet model, much emphasis was put on the development of heavy industries (particularly iron and steel), mechanisation and modernisation. In theory, socialist countries have much in common and are organised along an advanced socialist line in accordance with Marx's analysis. However, have there been any systematic similarities in the development of the PRC, the former Union of Soviet Socialist Republics (USSR), and other former or present socialist countries in Eastern Europe and Asia in relation to transportation? Over time, one finds significant changes in the philosophy on the 'ideal' organisation of the socialist society on domestic regional and transport development. In particular, the Chinese central government has taken bold initiatives in guiding the economic and transport development of the country. In the following discussion, a few general socialist principles about transport are discussed first. Then, their evolution and actual changes in China are highlighted to provide a background to better understand the more drastic changes happening after introduction of the Open Policy in 1979.

Transport as a general condition of production

Transport, as a traditional and large sector of the economy, unlike agriculture and industry, did not receive the attention of Marx as a separate chapter in his three volumes of *Capital*. Nonetheless, he explicitly mentioned that 'The revolution in the modes of production of industry and agriculture made necessary a revolution in the general conditions of the social process of production, i.e., in the means of communication and transport' (Marx, 1887, pp. 379–380). In this way, the use of machinery in modern industry, which produced cheap articles on a large scale, and the improved means of transport and communication have furnished the 'weapons' for conquering foreign markets and ruining handicraft production (Marx, 1887, p. 453). In the past, transport improvements have been used by the bourgeoisie to achieve capitalistic goals. Accordingly to Marx (1972, p. 250), 'the bourgeoisie, by the rapid improvement of all instruments of production, by the immensely facilitated means of communication, draws all, even the most barbarian, nations into civilisation'. Nonetheless, he has also conceptualised use of the improved transport (railways) to speed up the formation of a union of the modern proletariat on the eve of socialist revolution (Marx, 1972). As such, transport, though recognised as a material production sector and having a crucial role in speeding up the circulation of commodity and capital (hence, increasing commodity circulation and production), has not been discussed separately and systematically in its own right in Marx's analysis.

The unified transport system concept

The role of transport in socialist development has only been discussed more clearly and elaborated by Soviet writers after the Bolshevik Revolution. Marx's criticisms of the geographical uneven distribution of wealth and the exploitative transport systems of the capitalist countries were contrasted to formulate the socialist patterns of development and transport. Accordingly to Mellor (1975), the capitalist transport system suffers from two major problems. The first is associated with the irrational distribution of the means of transport, which, in turn, has been attributable to the 'irrational' distribution of production in these societies. The second is associated with 'wasteful' competition in the transport industry, which leads to the unnecessary duplication of transport facilities and services. In direct opposition, Lavrishchev (quoted in Mellor, 1975) argues that the socialist transport system can be free from all these defects because

> The systematic, proportional development of socialist economy conditions the rational development and distribution of all forms of transport over the territory of the country. The distribution of the transport in its turn fosters a systematic distribution of production all over the country.

In this way, all the different means of transport would develop 'as a single system of transportation which systematically combines all forms of transport and works in accordance with a plan established by the state'. Wasteful duplications of transport lines and services are, thus, eliminated. In this way, transport in a socialist country should be characterised by a unified transport system, with no 'wasteful' duplication or competition.

Furthermore, transport is considered a production input only. Hence, it should be minimised with the aim of maximising the production of outputs. This socialist rationale for 'minimum input–maximum output' is illustrated most clearly by Mellor (1975, p. 77):

[B]ecause transport is not in a material sense 'productive', it is essential to reduce the effort required to handle these flows to a minimum in order to reduce the input of human and material resources to the lowest possible level within the transport infrastructure so that such resources may be used in more materially productive sectors of the economy.

In order to achieve this ideal, passenger and freight traffic volumes should be 'rationally' minimised and assigned to the most appropriate means of transport and routes. In other words, the negative and passive role of transport in supporting, rather than generating, development has been emphasised. Under central planning, the socialist transport system forms a unitary whole and, hence, is able to develop without crises and its freight turnover can increase continuously.

Transport as a 'servant' of heavy industry

In practice, it has been commonly agreed that the Soviet and Eastern European countries have not been able to achieve a unified transport system (Ambler *et al.*, 1985). In its place, Hunter's (1965) view on the 'Communist approach to transport' has been commonly accepted as the transport development strategy being adopted in these countries (Vetterling & Wagy, 1972; Lyons, 1987). According to this view, transport is basically a servant of heavy industry and 'the transport sector as a whole is a handmaiden, not a prime mover' of development (Lyons, 1987, p. 83). In fact, 'the stress on heavy industrial production means that transport is merely a means to an end' (Hunter, 1965, p. 74). Transport investment was merely a 'passive' component of the overall economic and regional development strategies that has been kept to a minimum under development via the social overhead capital shortage approach (Hunter, 1965, pp. 83–84).

Figure 4.1 illustrates the two different approaches to developing transport infrastructure by Hirschman. In an economy, there needs to be infrastructure or social overhead capital (SOC) (*x*-axis) and directly productive activities (DPA) (*y*-axis). Ideally, a country will achieve economic growth along the diagonal line from the origin, suggesting the best combinations of minimum SOC and minimum DPA for a production level. To some extent, substitution or compensation between SOC and DPA is possible. For instance, the shortage of transport infrastructure (below the optimal level) will result in traffic congestion and a higher cost of economic activities. Yet, economic production is still possible. As the imbalance gets more obvious, the substitution between SOC and DPA will become more difficult. With the trade-offs between SOC and DPA, the production line is convex to the origin, suggesting that the substitution between SOC and DPA becomes more inefficient at the two ends of the curve. Over time, economic growth is manifested in a move from y_1, y_2, y_3, y_4 and so on. The best path is along the diagonal with a proportionate increase in SOC and DPA. However, as a government never knows exactly where its economy is, the growth path/trajectory is usually not a smooth one but reflects the philosophy of growth via SOC shortage (the $y_1, s_1, y_2, s_2, y_3, s_3, y_4$ path) by allowing congestion and other

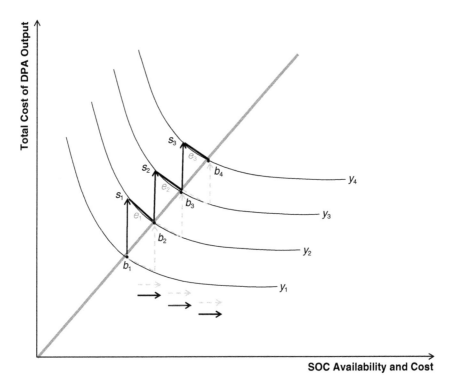

Figure 4.1 Hirschman's schema.

Source: Adapted from Hirschman (1958).

externalities to set in for the shortage of infrastructure until increased economic activity justifies the expansion of the infrastructure, or growth via SOC surplus (the y_1, e_1, y_2, e_2, y_3, e_3, y_4 path) by providing the infrastructure well in advance to attract more economic activities to come later. The 'Communist approach to transport' is much closer to the former as transport infrastructure is considered a 'servant' to (existing) economic activities only. In contrast, investment in directly productive activities, particularly heavy industries, was considered 'productive' and crucial to modernisation.

With limited transport investment funds, there has been a common emphasis on the development of bulk freight transport for the heavy producer industries, notably by railways, at the expense of light consumer industries and passenger transport in China, the former USSR and many former socialist East European countries. Geographically, 'the needs of state industry, centralised in a few locations, take precedence over all other transport claimants' (Hunter, 1965, pp. 83–84). In his work, Hunter has drawn evidence from the former USSR and China to show that 'massive expansion of transport capacity is not *a prior* condition for economic progress' in socialist countries (Hunter, 1965, p. 83).

Instead, it is argued that their experiences have exemplified how frugality in transport investment has indeed successfully supported the industrialisation of these countries. In China, this has become commonly accepted as a general reflection of the transport ideology under the leadership of Mao Zedong (Vetterling & Wagy, 1972; Lyons, 1987), although there were also many differences between the Soviet and Maoist development models as well (Cheng, 1963, 1982; Selden, 1988).

'Socialism with Chinese characteristics'

Ever since the introduction of the Open Policy in China, there has been an increasing literature focusing on changes in the ideological and development paths of China. According to Kernig (1987), the course of the reforms so far shows that China aims neither at a Western model nor at an old-fashioned socialist model of the Soviet-type. The almost universal consensus, even by the Chinese leadership, on the failure and impossibility of the success of the Soviet and Maoist development models has led to the formulation of market socialism or 'socialism with Chinese characteristics' (Estrin & Le Grand, 1989; Peterson, 1995). In brief, market socialism is characterised by state ownership of the majority of the means of production but decisions on consumption and distribution are left to the market mechanisms. In other words, there is a separation of ownership and management to increase economic efficiency in a socialist economy. Market socialism, as cogently argued by Chow (1994) and Hsu (1991), is both feasible and sustainable in China. Such change in the official ideology has led to changes in government policies, most notably in the form of the acceptance of investment from different sources and participation in the international division of labour. The impacts of these changes on the transport–development relationship need to be properly interpreted. In socialist China, these changing philosophies on the 'ideal' socialist organisation of the economy have a particularly important role to play in affecting government transport and regional development policies.

Economic growth

China's prospective economic development can significantly affect the country's priorities and ability to make a transition to transport sustainability. Figure 4.2 shows the GDP of the group of eight countries from 1990 to 2010 in log scales. We see that China's GDP has gone through a consistent yet rapid growth over the past two decades. In 2008, China surpassed Germany and became the country with the second highest GDP among the eight countries.

Furthermore, according to the projections of Dadush and Stancil (2010), Hawksworth (2006), Pricewaterhouse Coopers (2009) and the Carnegie Endowment for International Peace (2010), China will maintain fast GDP growth at around 6 per cent annually up to 2050. Figure 4.3 shows the GDP forecasts of the countries up to 2050. China's projected growth rate is only lower than that of

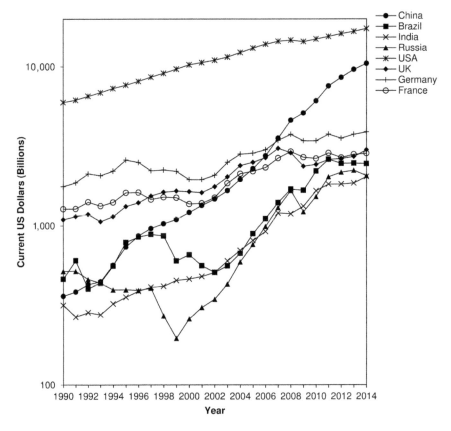

Figure 4.2 China's GDP growth in perspective, 1990–2014.

Source: Compiled by the author.

India and is much higher than the developed countries. By the projection of Pricewaterhouse Coopers (2009), China's GDP will be very close to that of the USA in 2030 and will surpass the latter before 2050.

In terms of economic structure, the Open Policy has been associated with a clear economic restructuring from the primary to the secondary sectors. Looking towards 2030, another major shift towards the tertiary or services sector is expected. Figure 4.4 shows the share of economic output in China by sector, as projected by Haltmaier (2013). From 2011 to 2030, the share of output from the primary sector is expected to drop further from 8 per cent to 3 per cent. The secondary sector output will also drop from 51 per cent to 47 per cent. Correspondingly, the tertiary sector output will increase from 41 per cent to 50 per cent. This forecast is consistent with the current Chinese government policies, especially in encouraging the demand for consumer services, the financial sector, the healthcare system and 'Internet Plus' enterprises (Ehmer, 2011; Valli & Saccone,

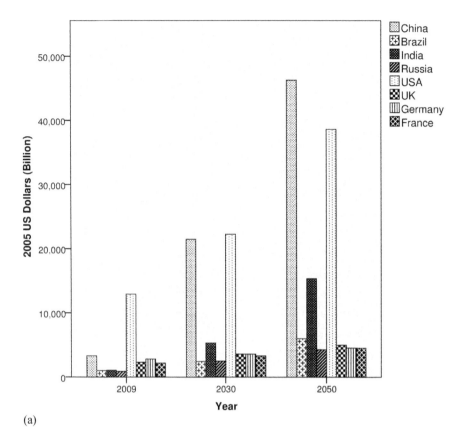

(a)

Figure 4.3 China's GDP growth projection in international perspective, 2009–2050.

Source: Compiled by the author.

Notes
a GDP in billion US dollars.
b GDP growth rate.

continued

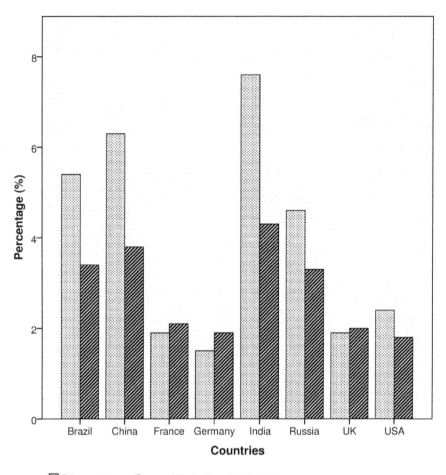

PricewaterhouseCoopers' Projection (2005–2050)

The Carnegie Endowment for International Peace's Projection (2009–2050)

(b)

Figure 4.3 Continued

2009; Wang & Loo, 2017). Nonetheless, it is worth noting that the secondary sector was still expected to be the largest sector of the economy. In other words, China is still likely to remain as the "world's largest factory" with a large labour force employed in the secondary sector. Currently, China is still the world's largest producer of agricultural products, including rice, wheat, potatoes, sorghum, peanuts, tea, millet, barley, cotton, oilseed, pork and fish (Economy Watch, 2013). Moreover, its agricultural employment is substantial, with the sector employing a work force of over 300 million, representing 34.8 per cent of the labour force (Economy Watch, 2013). The smooth transition of the national

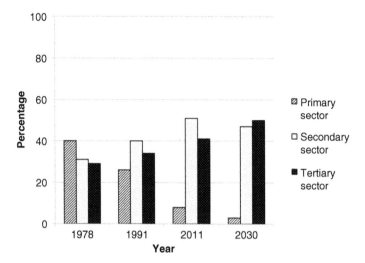

Figure 4.4 Projected changing economic structure in China up to 2030.

Source: Haltmaier (2013).

economy (and its labour force) towards the tertiary sector will remain a major challenge. According to Deutsche Bank Research (2010), the lack of enough demand for consumer goods among broad sections of the Chinese population, especially outside the large metropolitan areas, is one of the stumbling blocks for China to transit to a service economy.

Implications on the sustainable transport transition

Being projected to become the largest economy in the world and still having a large manufacturing sector, China will need to develop a higher capacity to carry out improvements to tackle the three major unsustainable transport issues associated with its economic development, namely CO_2 emissions, traffic congestion and road fatalities. In a positive light, the higher economic power can mean that both the government and citizens can afford more innovations and technologies to move towards sustainable transport.

As stated in both its 12th Five-Year Plan (2011–2015) and 13th Five-Year Plan (2016–2020), the Chinese government will devote efforts and allocate resources to develop relevant technologies in the aspects of automobile manufacturing, railway construction, environmental conservation and traffic safety (Li & Tao, 2011; National People's Congress, 2011; National People's Congress, 2016). For instance, to achieve higher efficiency in reducing air pollution in the road sector, the Chinese government will facilitate the development of advanced internal combustion machines and hybrid electric vehicles. Furthermore, for railways, the government will promote the use of stronger steel and higher efficiency energy control systems (National People's Congress, 2011; National People's Congress, 2016).

Although China will have greater access to relevant technologies due to its rapid national economic growth, it should be noted that the relatively low income level of some regions may constitute barriers to the adoption of those technologies. In particular, many transport-related policies are made at the local level and have to be funded locally. In other words, in order to really understand and to explore the emerging solutions to sustainable transport, the local context becomes pertinent. In the following analysis, the spatial scale will be larger, with the national picture of this chapter as the background.

Urbanisation

Figure 4.5 shows the percentage of urban population in China from 1950 up to 2030. The averages of the less-developed countries (LDCs), the more-developed countries (MDCs) and the world are also presented (United Nations, 2011). Ever since the 1950s, China's urbanisation rate (the share of population living in cities) has been increasing. According to the United Nations (2011), China's

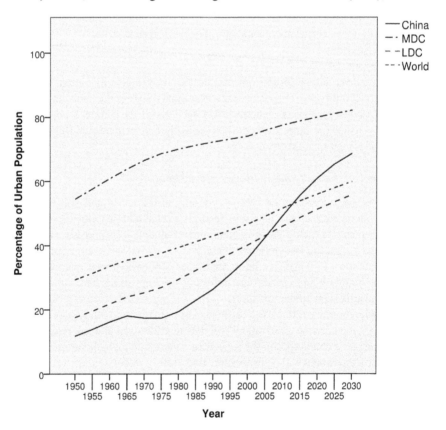

Figure 4.5 Urbanisation in China, 1950–2030.

Source: United Nations (2011).

urbanisation rate caught up with the LDCs average around 2005, and was around the world average around 2010, and is expected to rise even further after 2010. It is also interesting to see the changing urbanisation in China in the light of the world average, which reached 50 per cent in 2008 and is expected to rise to 60 per cent in 2020. With the 2014 World Urbanisation Prospects (United Nations, 2014), China's urbanisation is projected to increase further, from 59 per cent in 2014 to 78 per cent in 2050. Moreover, in absolute numbers, the size of the urban population in the country is expected to increase from 758 million in 2014 to 1,050 million in 2050 (United Nations, 2014). Such a huge urban population size in China is already much larger than the entire population of most countries nowadays, except India.

Implications on the sustainable transport transition

This consistent increase in urban population has and will continue to exert a great pressure on major cities' transport systems since they will have to handle larger volumes of passengers and goods. Air pollution issues will worsen and both traffic congestion and collisions will occur more frequently if the government does not handle the challenges of the resulting urban transportation efficiently and effectively.

In China, the definitions of small, medium, big and mega cities have undergone many changes over time since the introduction of the Open Policy. Table 4.1 summarises some of the major changes. According to the National Bureau of Statistics of China (1985–1992), cities have been classified as small, medium, large and mega based on the size of the urban non-agricultural population. The thresholds used for small, medium, large and mega cities in China were 200,000, 500,000, one million and more than one million respectively. For planning purposes, the State Council of China (1989) considered the urban and suburban non-agricultural population size, and defined small, medium and large cities using the thresholds of 200,000, 500,000 and over 500,000.

Ma and Cui (1987) were among the first scholars to have systematically analysed the various issues associated with the rapidly growing urban phenomenon of 'mega cities' or 'extra-large cities' in China. In 1993, the National Bureau of Statistics of China (1993) further revised the definition of 'mega cities' by using the term 'huge cities' to refer to cities with an urban non-agricultural population of between one million and two million, and reserving 'mega cities' to refer to only those with an urban non-agricultural population of more than two million. As China's urbanisation continued to expand and cities in the country continued to grow in size, the National Bureau of Statistics of China (2003) re-classified cities into the small, medium, large, extra-large, huge and mega city categories using the thresholds of 500,000, one million, two million, five million, ten million and more than ten million. In other words, only cities with an urban population of more than ten million are now considered 'mega cities'.

In fact, the Chinese government has put forward plans related to urbanisation and the associated implications on transport policy and planning. In its 12th

Table 4.1 Changing definitions of size of cities in China

	Source	City size and thresholds
1985	National Bureau of Statistics (1985)	Based on urban non-agricultural population: Small city: less than 200,000 Medium city: 200,000–500,000 Large city: 500,000–1 million Mega city: >1 million
1989	State Council of China (1989)	Based on urban and suburban non-agricultural population: Small city: less than 200,000 Medium city: 200,000–500,000 Large city: >500,000
1993	National Bureau of Statistics (1993)	Based on urban non-agricultural population: Small city: less than 200,000 Medium city: 200,000–500,000 Large city: 500,000–1 million Huge city: >1 million–2 million Mega city: >2 million
2003	National Bureau of Statistics (2003)	Based on urban population: Small city: less than 500,000 Medium city: 500,000–1 million Large city: 1 million–2 million Extra-large city: 2 million–5 million Huge city: 5 million–10 million Mega city: >10 million
2013	Zhou, Dai and Bu (2013)	Based on urban population: Small city: less than 500,000 Medium city: 500,000–1 million Large city: 1 million–5 million Megalopolis: 5 million–10 million Metropolis: >10 million

Source: Compiled by the author.

Five-Year Plan, the Chinese government explicitly stated that one of the focuses would be to stimulate and improve the urbanisation process in the Eastern, Central and Western regions (National People's Congress, 2011). In its 13th Five-Year Plan, explicit emphasis was placed on redressing the rural–urban disparity and supporting small towns as well (National People's Congress, 2016). A map of the geographical locations of the three regions is shown in Figure 4.6. Despite the fact that the Western region constitutes the largest share of land area, its population size and economic level are not as high as the other two regions. Table 4.2 shows the shares of the land area, population size and GDP of the three regions in 2010 and 2014. Although there is not a significant percentage change in both population and GDP in the three regions, a slight increase can be observed in the Western region. The proposed strategies and policies touched upon both quantity and quality of further developing cities in China. Understanding that solely boosting the urban population in all cities indiscriminately would

Figure 4.6 The three regions in China.
Source: The author.

Table 4.2 Land area, population and GDP by region in China, 2010 and 2014

Region	Land area (%)	2010		2014	
		Population (%)	*GDP (%)*	*Population (%)*	*GDP (%)*
Eastern	10.28	41.11	57.31	41.51	55.34
Central	18.63	31.96	24.06	31.45	24.48
Western	71.09	26.94	18.63	27.04	20.18

Sources: Based on National Bureau of Statistics (2011, 2015).

not be effective in enhancing overall economic development and people's living standards, the Chinese government planned to adopt differentiated and flexible urbanisation policies in cities with different levels of development.

Overall, the focus of mega cities with high population density like Beijing and Shanghai will be on improving "quality" rather than increasing "quantity" of urbanisation. For instance, the government advocates a better population size management tactic so as to avoid an over-expansion of cities which may lead to problems like pollution, traffic congestion, shortage of residential area and pressure on public services (National People's Congress, 2011). Zhou, Dai and Bu (2013) have analysed the city size distribution in China with reference to the impact of government policies. They suggested further distinguishing 'mega cities' into 'megalopolises' and 'metropolises' for guiding cities with five to ten million urban population, and more than ten million urban population respectively. These mega cities are also expected to be economic powerhouses of the country and the global economy (McKinsey & Company, 2012).

Unlike the mega cities, the major task for big and medium cities will be to further expand their population size mainly by absorbing the rural population, thus a better population management mechanism was emphasised (National People's Congress, 2011). Nonetheless, it is noteworthy that many of these cities already have an urban population size of one to two million (National Bureau of Statistics of China, 2003). Considering urbanisation in China, Zhou, Dai and Bu (2013) considered the urban population size of 0.5 to one million, and more than one million to five million, to be more appropriate for defining medium and large cities.

Regarding small cities, which possess plenty of room for expansion in urban population, the restrictions of *hukou* for migrant workers will be relaxed; welfare and public services like the right to compulsory education and medical insurance will be improved and provided to absorb the migrants into the urban population (National People's Congress, 2011). In particular, the *hukou* system, which is a household registration system in China, has for a long time kept track of population and served as a basis for the provision of government support (for example, education and social welfare). Recently, the system has been relaxed but residents of a place without a local *hukou* typically are generally still unable to receive all government benefits that local residents with *hukou* enjoy. These small cities generally refer to those with less than 500,000 urban population (Zhou, Dai & Bu, 2013; National Bureau of Statistics of China, 2003).

Apart from encouraging the rural population to move to cities, another plan of the Chinese government for stimulating urbanisation is to gradually form urban agglomerations with international competitiveness in the Eastern region and seek possible ways to group cities with relatively mature economies in the Central and Western regions (National People's Congress, 2011). The plan for a better coordination among cities by grouping them will have a great impact on the future development of China's transport system because it certainly requires a more efficient inter-city transport network. Due to China's large territory, railway is considered a critical transport means in linking cities. The government has planned to construct more inter-regional railways including the Zhengzhou-Chongqing Railway, the Lhasa-Shigates Railway and the second double line of the Lan-Xin Railway (National People's Congress, 2011). In terms of highways, the government has proposed to complete a national expressway network of 83,000 kilometres and increase the proportion of Class 2 or above national highways to over 70 per cent (National People's Congress, 2011). In the 13th Five-Year Plan, the huge expansion of the railway (especially high-speed railway) and expressway networks has been continued (National People's Congress, 2016). Nonetheless, their implications on transport sustainability have not been fully discussed in the Five-Year Plans.

Income disparity

While it is impressive that China has undergone rapid economic growth over the past few decades, it should be noted that the country's income inequality is growing at the same time. Figure 4.7 shows changes in the Gini index for China since 1981. The Gini index reflects the severity of income inequality. According to the World Bank (2017), a Gini index above 0.4 is already considered problematic in terms of income inequality. While China's national Gini index surpassed 0.4 in 2002, the level has not changed much over the entire decade since

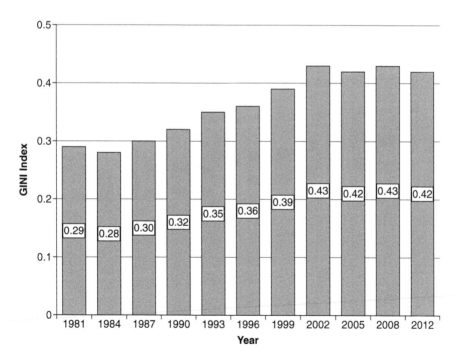

Figure 4.7 Gini index in China, 1981–2012.
Source: World Bank (2017).

then as the country went through rapid economic growth. The Gini index basically stabilised at about 0.42–0.43 in the early 2010s.

Figure 4.8 shows the share of income earned by the top 20 per cent compared to the lowest 20 per cent of income earners in China. In 1981, the 20 per cent of the population earning the highest income had around 40 per cent of the total income. This figure has been growing ever since. Meanwhile, the income share of the bottom 20 per cent of the population shows a continuous decrease from 8.7 per cent in 1981 to merely 5 per cent in 2005. By 2014, the top 20 per cent already had over half (51 per cent) of the total income and the bottom 20 per cent had only 7 per cent. Furthermore, the decline in the share of total income of the second and third highest 20 per cent over the last four decades has also been worrying. Overall, the gap between the richest and poorest has been more difficult to bridge with a weaker middle class as well. There are still huge disparities in the incomes of people living in China.

Implications on the sustainable transport transition

While the Chinese government has stated in its 12th and 13th Five-Year Plans that efforts will be devoted to reverse the trend of a widening income gap by carrying out measures like improving the minimum wage system and reducing the tax

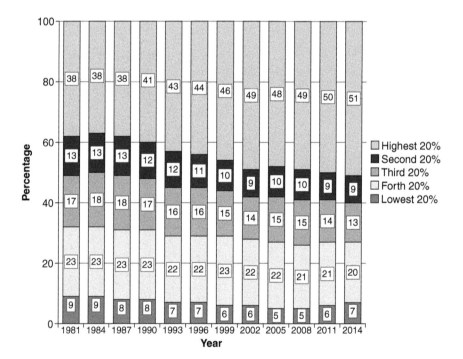

Figure 4.8 Income distribution in China, 1981–2014.

Source: National Bureau of Statistics (2015).

burden on low and middle income groups, it should be noted that the different financial strengths and living standards between the rural and urban areas, as well as among different cities, can be critical factors in deciding the possible patterns of the unsustainable transport transition up to 2030. For instance, in well-developed mega cities like Beijing, Shanghai, Nanjing and Wuhan, local governments with higher financial capabilities can afford to invest more on high-technology vehicles and systems like high-speed railway, electric cars and hybrid vehicles. These technologically products and systems would be of a high cost and would have to be backed up by people with higher purchasing more advanced power. However, for small cities, before they are economically developed enough to produce costly infrastructure and supporting facilities, the focus may be put on developing basic transport infrastructure like highways, bridges and conventional railways, as well as encouraging the use of environmentally friendly transport means that require less capital, such as bus rapid transit (BRT) and bicycles.

References

Ambler, J., Shaw, D.J.B. & Symons, L. (Eds.) (1985). *Soviet and East European Transport Problems*. London: Croom Helm.

Carnegie Endowment for International Peace. (2010). *The World Order in 2050*. Retrieved from www.carnegieendowment.org/files/World_Order_in_2050.pdf.

Cheng, C.Y. (1963). *Communist China's Economy 1949–1962: Structural Changes and Crisis*. Washington, D.C.: Seton Hall University Press.

Cheng, C.Y. (1982). *China's Economic Development: Growth and Structural Change*. Boulder, CO: Westview Press.

Chow, G.C. (1994). *Understanding China's Economy*. Singapore: World Scientific.

Dadush, U., & Stancil, B. (2010). *The World Order in 2050*. Retrieved from www.carnegieendowment.org/files/World_Order_in_2050.pdf.

Deutsche Bank Research. (2010). *China's Provinces: Digging One Layer Deeper*. Frankfurt: Deutsche Bank Research.

Economy Watch. (2013). *China (People's Republic of China) Economic Statistics and Indicators*. Retrieved from www.economywatch.com/economic-statistics/country/China/year-2013/.

Ehmer, P. (2011). *Structural Change in China: Economic Development Still Reliant on Industry for Now*. Frankfurt: Deutsche Bank Research.

Estrin, S., & Le Grand, J. (1989). Market socialism. *Market Socialism* (pp. 1–24). Oxford: Clarendon.

Haltmaier, J. (2013). *Challenges for the Future of Chinese Economic Growth*. Board of Governors of the Federal Reserve System (International Finance Discussion Papers Number 1072). Washington D.C.: Federal Reserve System.

Hawksworth, J. (2006). Projected relative size of economies in 2005 and 2050. The World in 2050: How big will the major emerging market economies get and how can the OECD compete? Pricewaterhouse Coopers. Retrieved from www.tepav.org.tr/upload/files/haber/1256628344r1748.The_World_in_2050.pdfwww.pwc.com/gx/en/world-2050/pdf/world2050emergingeconomies.pdf.

Hirschman, J. (1958). *The Strategy of Economic Development*. New Haven, CT: Yale University Press.

Hsu, R.C. (1991). *Economic Theories in China, 1979–1988*. Cambridge: Cambridge University Press.

Hunter, H. (1965). Transport in Soviet and Chinese development. *Economic Development and Cultural Change, 14*, 71–84. doi:10.1086/450142.

Kernig, C.D. (1987). *Yardsticks for Modernisation: Chinese Modernisation under Global Perspective*. China's Economic Reforms (Paper 17). Hong Kong: University of Hong Kong Centre of Asian Studies.

Li, Z., & Tao, X.A. (2011, March 11). The four priorities highlighted in the transport planning of the 12th Five-Year-Plan. *Hunan Daily*. Retrieved from http://news.hexun.com/2011-3-1/127860474.html.

Lyons, T.P. (1987). *Economic Integration and Planning in Communist China*. New York, NY: Columbia University Press.

Ma, L.J.C., & Cui, G. (1987). Administrative changes and urban population in China. *Annals of the Association of American Geographers, 77*, 373–395. doi:10.1111/j.1467-8306.1987.tb00165.x.

McKinsey & Company. (2012). Global cities of the future: An interactive map. *Urban World: Mapping the Economic Power of Cities*. Retrieved from www.mckinsey.com/tools/Wrappers/Wrapper.aspx?sid={C84CB74F-A3B1-7B1-265-252F6D85B68}&pid={4F5BEDB1-C1F-4243-A052-3ADBABE82DF}.

Marx, K. (1887). *Capital: A Critical Analysis of Capitalist Production*, 3 volumes (Volume 2, pp. 379–380 and 450). London: Swan Sonnenschein, Lowrey.

Marx, K. (1972). Manifesto. *Essential Writings of Karl Marx* (pp. 245, 250). New York, NY: Harper & Row.

Mellor, R.E.H. (1975). Soviet concept of a unified transport system and the contemporary role of the railways. In L. Symons & C. White (Eds.), *Russian Transport: An Historical and Geographical Survey* (pp. 75–77). London: G. Bell & Sons.

National Bureau of Statistics of China. (various years). *Urban Statistical Yearbook of China*. Beijing: China Statistics Press.

National People's Congress. (2011). *China's Twelfth Five-Year Plan*. Beijing: National People's Congress.

National People's Congress. (2016). *China's Thirteenth Five-Year Plan*. Beijing: National People's Congress.

Peterson, C. (1995). *Socialism after Communism: The New Market Socialism*. Philadelphia, PA: Pennsylvania State University Press.

Pricewaterhouse Coopers. (2009). Which are the largest city economies in the world and how might this change by 2025? *UK Economic Outlook November 2009* (p. 24). Retrieved from http://pwc.blogs.com/files/global-city-gdp-rankings-2008-025.pdf.

Selden, M. (1988). Mao Zedong and the political economy of Chinese development. *China Report, 24*, 125–39. doi:10.1177/000944558802400202.

State Council of China. (1989). *City Planning Act of China*. Beijing: State Council of China.

United Nations, Department of Economic and Social Affairs, Population Division. (2011). Average annual rate of change of the percentage urban by major area, region and country, 1950–2050. *World Urbanisation Prospects: The 2011 Revision*. Retrieved from www.un.org/en/development/desa/population/publications/pdf/urbanisation/WUP2011_Report.pdf.

United Nations, Department of Economic and Social Affairs, Population Division. (2014). *World Urbanisation Prospects: The 2014 Revision*. Retrieved from https://esa.un.org/unpd/wup/publications/files/wup2014-report.pdf.

Valli, V., & Saccone, D. (2009). Structural change and economic development in China and India. *The European Journal of Comparative Economics*, *6*, 101–129. doi:10.2139/ssrn.1486093.

Vetterling, P.W., & Wagy, J.J. (1972). China: The transportation sector, 1950–1971. In *People's Republic of China: An Economic Assessment* (pp. 147–184). Washington, D.C.: Joint Economic Committee of the United States Congress.

Wang, B., & Loo, B.P.Y. (2017). Hubs of internet entrepreneurs: The emergence of coworking offices in Shanghai, China. *Journal of Urban Technology*. Advance online publication. doi:10.1080/10630732.2017.1285124.

World Bank. (2017). *GINI Index (World Bank Estimate)*. Retrieved from http://data.worldbank.org/indicator/SI.POV.GINI?end=2012&locations=CN&start=2008&view=chart.

Zhou, S., Dai, J., & Bu, J. (2013). City size distributions in China 1949 to 2010 and the impacts of government policies. *Cities*, *32*, S51–S57. doi:10.1016/j.cities.2013.04.011.

5 Cities and the formation of city clusters

The top 100 Chinese cities by 2025

Given China's huge territorial extent, only the group of cities with the highest projected population in 2030 are included in the analysis. The Chinese government does not release population forecasts by city in the ten or 15 year time horizon. Hence, this study turns to the population forecast data for all major world cities of the United Nations (United Nations, 2011, 2014). Based on the United Nations' dataset, the 100 largest Chinese cities (in terms of population size) in 2025 (2030 data are not available) were selected for further analysis. The use of the United Nations population forecasts for the analysis has another key advantage in that it allows the current analytical framework to be adopted in other large developing economies, such as the top 100 cities in India or Brazil (see Chapter 9).

Table 5.1 shows the locations and population characteristics of these 100 Chinese cities with the largest expected population size in 2025. Their geographical locations, together with the three regions of Eastern, Central and Western China, are shown in Figure 5.1. Unless otherwise specified, all data refer to areas directly under each municipal government's jurisdiction instead of the whole city (National Bureau of Statistics of China, 2011). As discussed in Chapter 1, China's geographical diversity is huge. Before a more detailed statistical analysis of the city clusters (see next chapter), the three major regions – Eastern, Central and Western – provide us with some ideas about the characteristics of the cities included in this analysis. Readers may refer to Figure 4.6 for the regionalisation used. Among the 100 largest Chinese cities in the United Nations' population forecast, 54 are in the Eastern, 30 are in the Central and 16 are in the Western region. All provinces and provincial-level municipalities are included, except Tibet. In addition, although it is conventional to exclude the Special Administrative Regions of Hong Kong and Macau in detailed analysis, due to the different statistical, institutional and planning systems (among others), this study has chosen not to exclude Hong Kong in the United Nations' largest 100 Chinese city list because of the overriding belief that the unsustainable transport challenges among Chinese cities share both similarities and differences for lessons to be learnt.

Table 5.1 Top 100 Chinese cities by estimated population in 2025

	City	Population 2025 (thousands)	Population 2010 (thousands)	% change	Rank of population at 2025
Eastern region					
Fujian	Xiamen	4,869	2,702	80.2	28
	Fuzhou	4,236	2,799	51.3	33
	Putian	1,753	1,030	70.2	74
	Quanzhou	1,616	1,062	52.2	81
Guangdong	Shenzhen	15,545	10,222	52.1	3
	Guangzhou	15,474	10,486	47.6	4
	Foshan	9,790	6,208	57.7	9
	Dongguan	9,612	7,160	34.2	10
	Shantou	5,860	4,062	44.3	18
	Zhongshang	4,742	2,695	76.0	30
	Huizhou	2,991	1,760	69.9	42
	Maoming	1,656	1,004	64.9	80
	Jiangmen	1,600	1,103	45.1	82
	Zhanjiang	1,487	1,014	46.6	91
	Zhuhai	1,984	1,353	46.6	64
Hainan	Haikou	2,276	1,587	43.4	51
Hebei	Shijiazhuang	4,189	2,741	52.8	34
	Tangshan	2,774	1,871	48.3	44
	Handan	2,023	1,262	60.3	61
	Baoding	1,670	1,148	45.5	77
	Zhangjiakou	1,536	1,043	47.3	86
HKSAR	Hong Kong	8,160	7,053	15.7	14

continued

Table 5.1 Continued

	City	Population 2025 (thousands)	Population 2010 (thousands)	% change	Rank of population at 2025
Jiangsu	Nanjing	8,495	5,665	50.0	11
	Suzhou	5,833	3,248	79.6	19
	Wuxi	5,141	3,222	59.6	23
	Changzhou	3,535	2,323	52.2	38
	Xuzhou	3,462	2,144	61.5	41
	Nantong	2,479	1,550	59.9	48
	Yangzhou	2,245	1,566	43.4	52
	Huai'an	2,023	1,250	61.8	60
	Yancheng	1,936	1,290	50.1	67
	Lianyungang	1,662	965	72.2	79
	Zhenjiang	1,589	1,008	57.6	83
Liaoning	Dalian	4,483	3,305	35.6	31
	Shenyang	7,430	5,469	35.9	15
	Anshan	2,314	1,662	39.2	50
	Fushun	1,739	1,377	26.3	75
Shanghai	Shanghai	28,404	19,554	45.3	1
	Beijing	22,633	15,000	50.9	2
	Tianjin	11,934	8,535	39.8	7
Shandong	Qingdao	5,442	3,680	47.9	20
	Jinan	5,318	3,581	48.5	21
	Zibo	3,526	2,456	43.6	40
	Weifang	2,539	1,699	49.4	47
	Yantai	2,143	1,526	40.4	57
	Linyi	1,997	1,426	40.0	62
	Taian	1,843	1,240	48.6	69
	Jining	1,832	1,207	51.8	70
	Zaozhuang	1,757	1,175	49.5	73
	Dongying	1,523	949	60.5	88

Zhejiang	Hangzhou	8,450	5,189	62.8	12
	Ningbo	4,256	2,632	61.7	32
	Wenzhou	4,041	2,635	53.4	35
	Taizhou	1,802	1,338	34.7	72
Central region					
Anhui	Hefei	5,044	2,830	78.2	25
	Wuhu	2,122	1,172	81.1	58
	Huainan	2,064	1,396	47.9	59
	Huaibei	1,565	963	62.5	84
Heilongjiang	Haerbin	8,210	5,496	49.4	13
	Daqing	2,386	1,547	54.2	49
	Qiqihaer	2,200	1,588	38.5	55
	Jixi	1,507	1,043	44.5	90
Henan	Zhengzhou	6,019	3,796	58.6	17
	Luoyang	2,201	1,539	43.0	54
	Nanyang	1,997	1,164	71.6	63
	Anyang	1,530	1,129	35.5	87
	Xinxiang	1,507	1,016	48.3	89
	Pingdingshan	1,422	1,024	38.9	96
Hubei	Wuhan	12,727	8,904	42.9	6
	Xiangyan	2,182	1,531	42.5	56
	Jingzhou	1,553	1,040	49.3	85
	Yichang	1,380	980	40.8	99
Hunan	Changsha	4,942	3,212	53.9	27
	Yueyang	1,675	1,155	45.0	76
	Hengyang	1,670	1,099	52.0	78
	Zhuzhou	1,460	1,025	42.4	94
	Xiangtan	1,431	950	50.6	95

continued

Table 5.1 Continued

City		Population 2025 (thousands)	Population 2010 (thousands)	% change	Rank of population at 2025
Inner Mongolia	Baotou	2,568	1,931	33.0	46
	Hohhot	2,237	1,446	54.7	53
Jiangxi	Nanchang	3,529	2,331	51.4	39
Jilin	Changchun	5,173	3,598	43.8	22
	Jilin	2,765	1,889	46.4	45
Shanxi	Taiyuan	4,987	3,392	47.0	26
	Datong	1,977	1,355	45.9	66
Western region					
Gansu	Lanzhou	3,615	2,487	45.4	36
Guangxi	Liuzhou	1,984	1,359	46.0	65
	Nanning	2,915	2,096	39.1	43
	Guilin	1,407	968	45.4	97
Guizhou	Guiyang	3,569	2,458	45.2	37
	Zunyi	1,374	844	62.8	100
Chongqing	Chongqing	13,627	9,732	40.0	5
Ningxia	Yinchuan	1,903	1,052	80.9	68
Qinghai	Xining	1,815	1,185	53.2	71
Shaanxi	Xi'an	6,929	4,846	43.0	16
	Xianyang	1,471	1,019	44.4	93
	Baoji	1,393	901	54.6	98
Sichuan	Chengdu	9,965	6,397	55.8	8
	Mianyang	1,476	1,006	46.7	92
Xinjiang	Wulumqi	5,056	2,954	71.2	24
Yunnan	Kunming	4,821	3,388	42.3	29

Source: National Bureau of Statistics (2011).

Figure 5.1 Spatial distribution of the top 100 Chinese cities by estimated population in 2025.

Source: National Bureau of Statistics (2011).

Using 2010 as the baseline, the population increase projection was the lowest in Hong Kong (15.7 per cent) and the highest in Wuhan (81.1 per cent) in Central China, Yinchuan (80.9 per cent) in Western China and Xiamen (80.2 per cent) and Suzhou (79.6 per cent) in Eastern China. While these 100 major cities only accounted for 21.29 per cent of the total population in China in 2010, they constituted 50.22 per cent of the national GDP in the same year, indicating their important position in China's economy even nowadays. Overall, there are seven cities with over ten million population by 2025. They are Shenzhen (15.5 million), Guangzhou (15.5 million), Shanghai (28.4 million), Beijing (22.6 million) and Tianjin (11.9 million) in the Eastern region. It is also noteworthy that all of these cities, except Tianjin (8.5 million in 2010), already had a population of more than ten million even in 2010. The other two cities are Wuhan (12.7 million) in Central China and Chongqing (13.6 million) in Western China. Both of them were having less than but close to ten million population in 2010 (8.9 million in Wuhan and 9.7 million in Chongqing).

At the lower end of the spectrum, there are nine cities with up to 1.5 million population projected in 2025. In contrast to the opposite end of the spectrum, most of them are located in Western China. They include five cities of Guilin (1.4 million) in Guangxi, Xianyang (1.5 million) and Baoji (1.4 million) in Shaanxi, and Mianyang (1.5 million) in Sichuan. Four are in Central China, they are Pingdingshan (1.4 million) in Henan, Yichang (1.4 million) in Hubei, and Xiangtan (1.4 million) and Zhuzhou (1.5 million) in Hunan. One is in Eastern China: Zhanjiang (1.5 million) in Guangdong. Though partly due to their small population base in 2010, all these cities are expected to experience about a 40–50 per cent increase (ranging from 38.9 per cent in Pingdingshan to 54.6 per cent in Baoji) in population size in the coming two decades.

Nonetheless, the fastest-growing cities are more in the medium-size range of about two to five million population in 2025. Among the 100 largest Chinese cities, six of them are expected to experience more than 75 per cent growth in population from 2010 to 2025. In the Eastern region, they include Xiamen (80.2 per cent from 2.7 to 4.9 million) in Fujian, Zhongshan (76.0 per cent from 2.7 to 4.7 million) in Guangdong and Suzhou (79.6 per cent from 3.2 to 5.8 million) in Jiangsu. In Central China, they include Hefei (78.2 per cent from 2.8 to 5.0 million) and Wuhu (81.1 per cent from 1.1 to 2.1 million) in Anhui. The last city in this category is Yinchuan (80.9 per cent from 1.1 to 1.9 million) in Ningxia. Faced with the pressure of rapid population growth, these cities are expected to face new and rapidly emerging unsustainable transport challenges different in nature from the nine mega cities on the one hand, and the current problems they are facing now.

Ten key drivers of mobility

In pursuance of the ultimate goal of sustainable transport, ten key drivers are identified. They relate closely to a place's economic power, population, existing infrastructure and the society. These ten key drivers of mobility, together with the specific variables under each of these ten key drivers, are discussed below.

Population

Population and population density are two of the most important factors influencing a city's future development of the transport system. A densely populated city represents both unsustainable transport challenges and opportunities for a transition to sustainable transport. The latter is especially true for public transport, which needs to be supported by high and stable passenger demand to make it financially viable and economically feasible. Different public transport systems vary greatly in terms of capital investment and will have different applicability for cities of different population size (Loo & Cheng, 2010).

GDP

GDP and GDP per capita are two of the major measurements of a city's economic power and people's living standard. New sustainable transport strategies need to be supported by new infrastructure, ranging from energy, terminals and ways to vehicles (see Chapter 2). Different new sustainable transport strategies have different requirements of each of these four elements of the transport system. For instance, the introduction of electric cars will need new electric-charging points (energy) and affordable vehicles that people prefer (vehicles). Retrofitting the existing transport infrastructure with electric-charging points is highly challenging. The promotion of cycling will need additional parking bays for bicycles, including rental bicycles (terminals) and modifications in the road infrastructure to make cycling safer, more enjoyable and more convenient (ways) (Loo & Tsui, 2010; Yao and Loo, 2016). The introduction of railway lines typically requires exclusive railway tracks (ways), locomotives (vehicles) and train stations easily accessible to users (terminals) (Loo & Comtois, 2015). Some of the technologies, such as metro systems, can only be economically feasible for a city with sufficient economic power, which is important not only for the initial capital investment by the government or both the government and the private sector (through public-private partnership) but also for long-term maintenance by the operator and the ability of users to afford the metro services for daily travel (Loo & Cheng, 2010; Loo & Li, 2006).

Motorisation

The number of motor vehicles is certainly one of the key elements to be considered in sustainable transport because they are closely related to CO_2 emissions and road fatalities. In 2013, there were over 17.5 million private vehicles and 2.7 million trucks in China (National Bureau of Statistics of China, 2014). In cities, the number of motor vehicles per 1,000 population and per km^2 of road will need to be considered, especially for evaluating the city's need in adopting sustainable technologies related to the enhancement of vehicle performance such as using hybrid fuels and advanced combustion engines. The presence of a large vehicle fleet represents some constraints for a sustainable transport transition in the following manner. First, vehicles are capital assets and are likely to be used for a period of time, sometimes up to 10–15 years. Therefore, the mix of the vehicle fleet nowadays, especially in terms of fuel type and fuel efficiency, is unlikely to change drastically in the short term. In China, for example, over 90 per cent of the vehicle fleet comprises diesel and petroleum cars. In addition, when the replacement of the vehicle fleet does take place, existing habits and entrenched preferences can become major barriers to the adoption of alternative fuel vehicles. Second, lessons from existing studies show that the motorisation trend is almost irreversible. It will be much easier for people to use public transit or active modes of transport, that is, walking and cycling, when they have never owned a car. Once individuals in a society become automobile-dependent, it will be extremely difficult to change or to convince people 'out of the car' (James, Burke & Yen, 2017). Hence, if the city has a large vehicle fleet, efforts to promote public transit and other active transport modes must be supplemented by efforts to make the vehicle fleet cleaner. For cities not yet having a very large vehicle fleet, the opportunity and challenges of keeping a low car ownership (and usage) will stand out.

Road network

In cities, road transport still plays the most significant role in passenger and freight transport. Cities with well-developed road networks, however, can also encourage more people to use private cars more often if no traffic management and other transport policies are introduced. In areas where road pricing is introduced, the efficient use of scarce road space is encouraged (Hau, 1988, 1992; Hau *et al.*, 2011). Although many road pricing schemes have been studied in many Chinese cities (notably Beijing), no city in China has yet implemented a systematic road congestion charging scheme up to the end of 2016. Only toll roads of various kinds, such as tunnel and bridge tolls, or recovery tolls for expressways built through public-private partnership have been collected. Moreover, there is a concern whether the introduction of road pricing leading to a shorter travel time will make the remaining road users even harder to shift to other more sustainable transport modes. The social implications of road pricing, in discriminating low-income drivers, also pose challenges of inequity within the city.

In this study, road area and road area per capita are used to assess a city's current sufficiency of road network and its potential of adopting relevant sustainable technologies like bus rapid transit (BRT). As much on-road public transport, such as buses and minibuses, consumes road space and competes with other road users like motorcycles, cyclists and pedestrians, the existence of an extensive road network is an advantage for the rolling out of the comprehensive bus route schemes, for example. According to the National Bureau of Statistics of China, the data on road area does not include cycle tracks. Systematic data about the length and area of cycle tracks in Chinese cities are unavailable.

Current transport performance

As many sustainable transport technologies are related to road and rail transport, such as BRT and metro systems, the current transport performance of cities as a whole and the relative performance of the road and railway sectors can be critical factors reflecting on the readiness of these cities to adopt those technologies. The main variables included are passenger and freight volumes of the entire transport sector. Furthermore, in order to understand the significance and potential of selected cities in developing relevant sustainable technologies, additional indicators of percentages shared by the road sector and railway sector in total passenger and freight volumes are examined. The development of an attractive metro system that is able to cater for the needs of different people in a city, for example, will not be a matter of a few years for cities with no metro line at all. Most cities, including Hong Kong and Shanghai, started with short lines linking with the key activity centres of the city and then underwent continuous extension to the rest of the city over decades. In Hong Kong, the metro system started with the Initial Modified Line in 1979 and has undergone over three decades of almost non-stop extension to the Tuen Wan Line, Kwan Tong Line in the 1980s, the Tseng Kwan O Line in the 1990s, West Rail Line and Tung Chung Line in the 2000s and the Southern Lines in the 2010s (Loo, Cheng & Nichols, 2017). Similar extension history was observed in Shanghai. At present, the city has 14 lines and 364 stations totalling 588 km in operation. Line 1 was opened in 1993 and has been extending both northwards and southwards in the past two decades. From 2000 to 2005, 2 lines with 59 new stations were added to the system. By 2010, 11 lines and 280 stations with a total length of 410 km were in operation (Shen *et al.*, 2014). In recent years, Lines 12, 13 and 16 have been added to the system. It is expected that Shanghai's metro system will continue to extend in the future and there will be about 808 km of metro lines with over 500 stations by the end of 2020 (Shanghai Academy of Environmental Sciences, 2009).

Current bus services

Buses are high-capacity public transport that have a high potential for various emerging sustainable transport technologies to be introduced. It is believed that cities with better current bus services have a higher potential for further exploring related technologies like electric and hybrid buses, and for the introduction of traffic management measures like BRT. Moreover, the existence of a large bus network also suggests a population who are more used to using buses as their daily transport modes. Issues like bus route consolidation (especially in relation to reducing empty or low-capacity runs), bus branching, bus fleet modernisation, and other measures to further enhance the attractiveness of bus services should be actively explored. In this study, three indicators, including the number of buses in service, number of buses per 10,000 population and the number of passengers carried by buses, are collected and analysed.

Energy

Electricity as a source of energy for transport has been very much under-utilised in China to date. This has partly contributed to the heavy reliance of the urban transport sector on diesel and gasoline. The potential for using more electricity in transport is huge. In addition, the electricity grid can be more flexible to different clean energy sources, such as hydro-electricity and wind power. Yet, the total electricity generation capacity of the city needs to be considered before the electricity as a more sustainable source of transport energy can have any promise to be a key component in the sustainable transport strategy in a city. The total consumption of electricity, total consumption of electricity per 1,000 population, and the composition of the industrial and residential sectors are considered to gain a better understanding of the cities' electricity generation capacity.

Other energy factors include the potential of utilising alternative energy sources like natural gas as a source of energy for transport. The use of natural gases (including liquefied gas (LPG) and compressed natural gas) as a source of transport energy is quite mature in some countries. However, the use of these alternative fuel vehicles (AFVs) is still very limited in China and data on the number of AFVs at the city level are not available. Hence, they will be considered qualitatively whenever relevant rather than included in the main statistical analysis.

Availability of government support

Municipal governments' financial strength and willingness to support transport sector development are critical. Municipal governments' total income and expenditure will be examined in order to reveal their financial strength to undertake strategic policies and actions to overcome some of the key unsustainable transport challenges. As mentioned above, many of the transport policies and investments have to be made at the local level. A municipal government with poor financial capability will find the range of sustainable transport strategies affordable much more limited. For instance, while the Chinese central government has been eager to introduce electric vehicles, including bus fleets and taxis, in the country, these initiatives need to be supported by financial subsidies not always directly available from the central government. Even if subsidies to the public transport operators are provided by the central government, the modifications required of existing transport infrastructures to allow efficient and convenient electric charging are very expensive. In addition, key transport infrastructures, notably metro systems, require huge capital investment in foreign currency to be borne mainly by the local governments (Loo & Li, 2006). With so many cities in China, the sustainable transport strategy at the city level simply cannot rely solely on the central government (Loo & Chow, 2006). More importantly, the municipality governments' expenditure on research and innovation, which is critical to the development of some sustainable transport technologies like hybrid vehicles and advanced combustion engines, will be collected.

Citizens' expenditure on transportation

Citizens' expenditure on transportation can be an important factor restricting the choices of sustainable transport technologies that would be acceptable and affordable to local people. For cities with low per capita annual consumption expenditure on transport and communication, care is required to ensure that the recommendations of sustainable transport measures are not out of line with the local citizens' ability and willingness to pay. Currently, overseas countries suggest that about 15 per cent of people's expenditure is spent on transport.

Generally, the share in China is low. Part of the reason has been the state policy of making public transport affordable to the general public. For a long time, since 1990, the bus fare for services within cities in China has been kept at a uniform level of RMB1 yuan regardless of the distance travelled (Loo & Li, 2006). Moreover, this policy does not change regardless of a city's wealth or its location. Cities as rich as Shanghai have been charging the same bus fare as many inland cities. This is a rather special feature of China's urban transport system that reflects a legacy of the socialist doctrine of egalitarianism. Hence, looking into the future, public acceptability needs to be taken into consideration before any sustainable transport strategy is actively considered.

Road fatalities

Road fatality is certainly one of the most important concerns for cities in their process of transition to sustainable transport, especially under the rapid trend of motorisation in China. The number of road fatalities, road fatalities per million population, per million passengers carried and per 10,000 vehicles will be examined in this study to better understand selected cities' efficiency in ensuring road safety. Thus the urgency of adopting sustainable transport strategies to protect the life and well-being of local citizens can be better appreciated. While the road safety in China has improved substantially over time (see Chapter 3), there exists enormous variations within the country. The provincial disparity, together with the huge rural–urban divide, has been explained in Loo, Cheung and Yao (2011). In this study, we shall further examine the differences that exist among the largest 100 cities in China.

The overall picture

Data on the above 36 variables of the 100 Chinese cities in 2010 have been collected from the National Bureau of Statistics of China and individual provinces' statistical departments. In addition to the historical data, projection data about population and GDP up to 2030 have been gathered from the World Bank, United Nations and other international organisations. Table 5.2 gives an overall picture of the ten key drivers of the 100 cities and the variability among them.

As a group, these 100 Chinese cities had, in 2010, an average population density of 1,627.72 people per km^2 and GDP per capita of RMB60,372. The number of vehicles per million population was 78.38. The transport system carried 173.95 million tonnes of freight and 250.28 million passengers. The total electricity consumption per 1,000 population was 591. Municipal government income was about 2.3 million yuan (in 2010 dollars) but only about 2.41 per cent was spent on scientific research. Local citizens spent about 13.8 per cent of their consumption expenditure on transport. The road fatalities per 10,000 vehicles was 7.48.

Table 5.2 Characteristics of the ten mobility drivers in the top 100 cities

Indicator		Mean	Standard deviation
Population and population density			
Population 2010 ('000)		2,855	3,026
Population 2025 ('000)		4,250	4,410
Population density 2010 (people/km²)		1,627.72	1,612
GDP and GDP per capita			
GDP 2010 (billion RMB)		201.49	288
GDP per capita 2010 (RMB)		60,372	30,413
GDP 2025 (billion RMB)		671.32	1,127
GDP per capita 2025 (RMB)		110,618	72,720
Motorisation (2010)			
Total motor vehicles ('000)		54.27	56.61
Vehicles per million population		78.38	37.78
Vehicles per km of road		59.86	88.22
Current transport performance and patterns (2010)			
Freight transport	Total freight (10,000 tonnes)	17,395	13,372
	Freight by railway (10,000 tonnes)	1,968	2,790
	Freight by highway (10,000 tonnes)	12,461	9,372
	% of railway	11.96	12.74
	% of highway	74.25	18.60
Passenger transport	Total passengers (10,000)	25,028	48,565
	Passengers by railway (10,000)	3,055	16,545
	Passengers by highway (10,000)	21,326	34,043
	% of railway	9.01	9.19
	% of highway	88.13	12.57
Road network (2010)			
Road area (10,000 m²)		2,844	2,342
Road area per capita (m²)		11.56	4.96
Current bus services (2010)			
Total bus passengers (10,000)		51,444	72,212
Number of buses		3,053	4,247
Number of buses per 10,000 population		9.70	4.40
Electricity generation capacity (2010)			
Total electricity consumption (10,000 kwh)		1,663,315	1,915,699
Electricity consumption per 1,000 population		591	317
% of industry		66.16	17.67
% of residents		13.97	7.11
Availability of government support (2010)			
Total income (RMB10,000)		2,333,413	4,844,585
Total expenditure (RMB10,000)		2,694,869	4,934,917
Expenditure on scientific research (RMB10,000)		105,766	300,406
%		2.41	1.69

Table 5.2 Continued

Indicator	Mean	Standard deviation
Citizen's expenditure on transportation (2010)		
Per capita annual consumption expenditure (RMB)	15,348	11,535
Expenditure on transport (RMB)	2,144	1,320
%	13.80	3.44
Road fatalities (2010)		
Absolute number	322	233
Fatalities per million population	50.73	21.09
Fatalities per 10,000 vehicles	7.48	3.71

Source: Compiled by the author.

Formation of city clusters

While the above gives an average picture, the variability of most variables is also very high, with many standard deviations as large as the average. Hence, it is important to further divide the cities into clear clusters that share similar unsustainable transport challenges and potential future opportunities. Nonetheless, it is also recognised that there is no single solution which can be universally applied to all cities. To fulfil this objective, a hierarchical cluster analysis is conducted to group cities based on statistical similarities in the above 36 key indicators related to transport sustainability. The statistical method starts with each city in a separate cluster and then combines the clusters sequentially, reducing the number of clusters at each step until only one cluster is left. At each stage, the two clusters with the smallest distance (dissimilarity) will be merged. By looking at the value of distances at each stage, an optimal number of clusters will be determined.

Table 5.3 shows the distances at each stage of the hierarchical cluster analysis with the data collected for the 36 variables about the top 100 Chinese cities (see

Table 5.3 Results of the hierarchical cluster analysis of the top 100 Chinese cities

Number of clusters	Distance	Change of distance
12	43.938	
11	46.848	2.910
10	50.034	3.186
9	53.232	3.198
8	56.498	3.266
7	61.070	4.572
6	65.964	4.894
5	72.046	6.082
4	79.888	7.842
3	89.411	9.523
2	119.562	30.151

Source: Compiled by the author.

Table 5.1). By looking at the values of statistical distances at each stage, three should be the optimal number of city clusters in China as the statistical distance increases greatly when it is reduced to two clusters but it reduces insignificantly when there are four clusters. The three city clusters are labelled Clusters A, B and C.

Table 5.4 displays the results of the cluster analysis by showing the membership of each cluster. Figure 5.2 shows the geographical distribution of cities in each cluster. In terms of geographical distribution, there are cities in different clusters within each of the three regions – Eastern, Central and Western China. The results suggest that cities share more similarities in their sustainable transport challenges according to the cluster classifications than the three geographical regions alone. In each of the Eastern, Central and Western regions, there are cities belonging to Clusters A, B and C.

Summary

In this chapter, we provided the background for the analysis of the unsustainable transport challenges in China. More empirical data are presented to allow the

Table 5.4 Members of city clusters

Group A		Group B		Group C
Anshan	Qiqihaer	Baotou	Ningbo	Beijing
Anyang	Taian	Changchun	Qingdao	Chengdu
Baoding	Taizhou	Changsha	Quanzhou	Chongqing
Baoji	Xiangtan	Changzhou	Shantou	Guangzhou
Datong	Xiangyang	Dalian	Shenyang	Hong Kong
Fushun	Xianyang	Daqing	Shijiazhuang	Shanghai
Guilin	Xining	Dongguan	Suzhou	Shenzhen
Handan	Xinxiang	Dongying	Taiyuan	Tianjin
Hengyang	Yancheng	Foshan	Tangshan	Wuhan
Huai'an	Yichang	Fuzhou	Weifang	
Huaibei	Yinchuan	Fuzhou	Wenzhou	
Huainan	Yueyang	Guiyang	Wuhu	
Jiangmen	Zaozhuang	Haerbin	Wulumqi	
Jilin	Zhangjiakou	Haikou	Wuxi	
Jingzhou	Zhanjiang	Hangzhou	Xi'an	
Jining	Zhenjiang	Hefei	Xiamen	
Jixi	Zhuzhou	Hohhot	Xuzhou	
Lianyungang	Zunyi	Huizhou	Yangzhou	
Liuzhou		Jinan	Yantai	
Luoyang		Kunming	Zhengzhou	
Maoming		Lanzhou	Zhongshan	
Mianyang		Linyi	Zhuhai	
Nanyang		Nanchang	Zibo	
Pingdingshan		Nanjing		
		Nanning		
Putian	43	Nantong	48	9

Source: Compiled by the author.

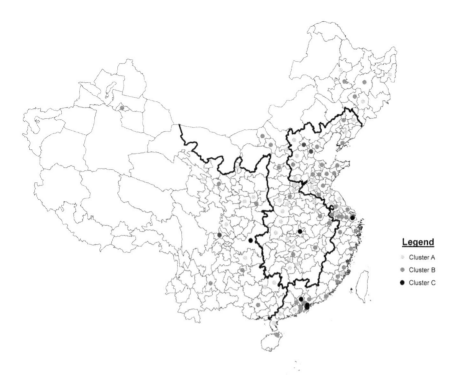

Figure 5.2 Geographical distribution of the three city clusters.
Source: Compiled by the author.

readers to get a better idea about various aspects of China's economy and society beyond its transport sector. It is important to recognise that whether a sustainable transport strategy will work or not depends critically not just on factors related to the transport system but beyond. Most importantly, ten key mobility drivers were identified, balancing data availability and the underlying transport sustainability challenges and opportunities. Justifications for narrowing down the focus from the country to the city level were then given. And the largest 100 Chinese cities (in terms of population size) were chosen for further analysis. Substantial efforts were spent to collect data about a relatively comprehensive list of 36 variables of the 100 cities based on the ten key mobility drivers. With a clear focus on sustainable transport, the cities are re-grouped statistically based on the statistical distances among the 36 variables. After the hierarchical cluster analysis, three city clusters were formed. The results are satisfactory both statistically (based on the statistical indicators) and analytically (with groupings not merely reflecting the population size or geographical location by region). The outputs of this chapter steer the endeavours of identifying potential sustainable transport strategies for different city clusters in the following chapters.

References

Hau, T.D. (1988). *A Refutation of the Second Law of Demand? The Case of the Hong Kong Cross Harbour Tunnel*. Unpublished manuscript, School of Economics, The University of Hong Kong, Hong Kong.

Hau, T.D. (1992). *Congestion Charging Mechanisms for Roads: An Evaluation of Current Practice* (Working Paper WPS1071). Washington, D.C.: World Bank.

Hau, T.D., Loo, B.P.Y., Wong, K.I. & Wong, S.C. (2011). An estimation of efficient time-varying tolls for cross-harbor tunnels in Hong Kong. *Singapore Economic Review*, *56*, 467–488. doi:10.1142/S0217590811004432.

James, B., Burke, M. & Yen, B.T.H. (2017). A critical appraisal of individualised marketing and travel blending interventions in Queensland and Western Australia from 1986–2011. *Travel Behaviour and Society*, *8*, 1–13. doi:10.1016/j.tbs.2017.03.002.

Loo, B.P.Y., & Cheng, A.C.H. (2010). Are there useful yardsticks of population size and income level for building metro systems? Some worldwide evidence. *Cities*, *27*, 299–306. doi:10.1016/j.cities.2010.02.003.

Loo, B.P.Y., & Chow, S.Y. (2006). China's 1994 tax-sharing reforms: One system, differential impact. *Asian Survey*, *46*, 215–237. doi:10.1525/as.2006.46.2.215.

Loo, B.P.Y., & Comtois, C. (2015). *Sustainable Railway Futures: Issues and Challenges*. Surrey: Ashgate.

Loo, B.P.Y., & Li, D.Y.N. (2006). Developing metro systems in the People's Republic of China: Policy and gaps. *Transportation*, *33*, 115–132. doi:10.1007/s11116-005-3046-2.

Loo, B.P.Y., & Tsui, K.L. (2010). Bicycle crash casualties in a highly motorised city. *Accident Analysis and Prevention*, *42*, 1902–1907. doi:10.1016/j.aap. 2010.05.011.

Loo, B.P.Y., Cheng, A.H.T. & Nichols, S.L. (2017). Transit-oriented development on greenfield versus infill sites: Some lessons from Hong Kong. *Landscape and Urban Planning*, *167*, 37–48. doi:10.1016/j.landurbplan.2017.05.013.

Loo, B.P.Y., Cheung, W.S. & Yao, S. (2011). The rural-urban divide in road safety: The case of China. *The Open Transportation Journal*, *5*, 9–20. doi:10.2174/1874447801105010009.

National Bureau of Statistics of China. (2011). *Urban Statistical Yearbook of China*. Beijing: China Statistics Press.

National Bureau of Statistics of China. (2014). *China Statistical Yearbook 2014*. Beijing: China Statistics Press.

Shanghai Academy of Environmental Sciences. (2009). *Shanghai Metro Planning (2010–2020)* (in Chinese). Retrieved 17 July 2017 from www.wendangku.net/doc/0dce 7ef69e314332396893c5.html.

Shen, S.-L., Wu, H.-N., Cui, Y.-J. & Yin, Z.-Y. (2014). Long-term settlement behaviour of metro tunnels in the soft deposits of Shanghai. *Tunnelling and Underground Space Technology*, *40*, 309–323. doi:10.1016/j.tust.2013.10.013.

United Nations, Department of Economic and Social Affairs, Population Division. (2011). Population of urban agglomerations with 750,000 inhabitants or more, 1950–2025. *World Urbanisation Prospects: The 2011 Revision*. Retrieved from www.un.org/en/development/desa/population/publications/pdf/urbanisation/WUP2011_Report.pdf.

United Nations, Department of Economic and Social Affairs, Population Division. (2014). *World Urbanisation Prospects: The 2014 Revision*. Retrieved from https://esa.un.org/unpd/wup/publications/files/wup2014-report.pdf.

Yao, S., & Loo, B.P.Y. (2016). Safety in numbers for cyclists beyond national-level and city-level data: A study on the non-linearity of risk within the city of Hong Kong. *Injury Prevention*, *22*, 379–385. doi:10.1136/injuryprev-2016-041964.

6 Overview of unsustainable transport challenges by city cluster

Characteristics of unsustainable transport challenges of the three city clusters

Tables 6.1 to 6.3 reveal the summary statistics of the three city clusters, including the means and standard deviations, in order to provide the background for further analysis. An overview shows that the city clusters do vary clearly by different dimensions. Though the differences in population size may be taken readily to represent the three city clusters, it is clear that population size is neither the only nor the dominant factor that distinguishes each city cluster. A note of caution is needed not to over-simplify the city-clustering exercise as one that is based on population only. It is a multi-dimensional statistical clustering that groups cities according to their various performances in areas relevant to the pathways to sustainable transport in 2030 and beyond.

Cluster A

Cities in cluster A generally consist of the least developed cities among the 100 cities with a relatively small population size and weak economic power. Table 6.1 summarises the main descriptive statistics of the ten key mobility drivers of cities in Cluster A. The average population size was 1.17 million in 2010 and is projected to be 1.75 million in 2025. These cities' local economies are not strong, with a GDP per capita of 42,691 yuan in 2010. As the population is projected to increase by around 50 per cent (49.57 per cent) in 2025 compared to 2010, it may create huge challenges to the cities that their currently small passenger and freight volumes, limited lengths of road networks and low degree of motorisation cannot catch up with the rapid population growth. The mean passenger and freight volumes in 2010 were 100.14 million and 114.47 million tonnes respectively. The road network only averaged 13 million m². The number of automobiles in these cities was still at a relatively low level of 23,760. The electricity generation capacity is also low for this city cluster. When compared to the 100-city average of 16.63 billion kwh, the electricity generation capacity of this city cluster was at 6.43 billion kwh.

There are altogether 43 cities in this city cluster. In the Eastern region they include Putian in Fujian, Maoming, Jiangmen and Zhanjiang in Guangdong,

Table 6.1 Summary statistics of the ten key mobility drivers for cities in Cluster A

Indicator	Mean	Standard deviation
Population and population density		
Population 2010 ('000)	1,170	224
Population 2025 ('000)	1,747	303
Population density 2010 (people/km^2)	1,292.17	953.05
GDP and GDP per capita		
GDP 2010 (billion RMB)	50.45	21.38
GDP per capita 2010 (RMB)	42,691	13,491
GDP 2025 (billion RMB)	95.98	50.58
GDP per capita 2025 (RMB)	54,199	24,172
Motorisation (2010)		
Total motor vehicles ('000)	23.76	14.24
Vehicles per million population	49.68	19.20
Vehicles per km of road	20.56	12.20
Current transport performance and patterns (2010)		
Freight transport Total freight (10,000 tonnes)	11,447	5,718
Freight by railway (10,000 tonnes)	1,553	1,884
Freight by highway (10,000 tonnes)	8,914	5,274
% of railway	14.29	14.62
% of highway	77.26	17.09
Passenger transport Total passengers (10,000)	10,014	5,315
Passengers by railway (10,000)	534	374
Passengers by highway (10,000)	9,360	5,281
% of railway	6.56	5.51
% of highway	91.98	7.28
Road network (2010)		
Road area (10,000 m^2)	1,312	514
Road area per capita (m^2)	11.41	4.74
Current bus services (2010)		
Total bus passengers (10,000)	14,224	8,499
Number of buses	943	472
Number of buses per 10,000 population	8.16	3.99
Electricity generation capacity (2010)		
Total electricity consumption (10,000 kwh)	643,406	437,843
Electricity consumption per 1,000 population	537	288
% of industry	69.15	17.67
% of residents	12.97	6.88
Availability of government support (2010)		
Total income (RMB10,000)	482,787	296,233
Total expenditure (RMB10,000)	777,770	288,015
Expenditure on scientific research (RMB10,000)	12,082	7,570
%	1.53	0.83

Table 6.1 Continued

Indicator	Mean	Standard deviation
Citizen's expenditure on transportation (2010)		
Per capita annual consumption expenditure (RMB)	11,854	1,898
Expenditure on transport (RMB)	1,434	455
%	11.92	2.48
Road fatalities (2010)		
Absolute number	182	98
Fatalities per million population	39.52	18.62
Fatalities per 10,000 vehicles	8.77	4.20

Source: The author.

Handan, Baoding and Zhangjiakou in Hebei, Huaian, Yancheng, Lianyuangang and Zhenjiang in Jiansu, Anshan, Fushan, Liaoning, Taian, Jining and Zaozhuang in Shandong, and Taizhou in Zhejiang (18). In the Central region they include Huainan and Huaibei in Anhui, Qiqihaer and Jixi in Heilongjiang, Luoyang, Nanyang, Anyang, Xinxiang and Pingdingshen in Henan, Xiangyan, Jingzhou and Yichang in Hubei, Yueyang, Hengyang, Zhuzhou and Xiangtan in Hunan, Baotou in Inner Mongolia, and Datong in Shanxi (18). In the Western region they include Liuzhou and Guilin in Guangxi, Zunyi in Guizhou, Yinchuan in Ningxia, Xining in Qinghai, Baoji in Shaanxi, and Mianyang in Sichuan (7). In other words, it seems that Cluster A cities are rather evenly spread. The share of cities in Cluster A for the regions of the Eastern, Central and Western regions is 30.51 per cent (18/59), 60 per cent (18/30) and 43.75 per cent (7/16) respectively. Based on the fact that these cities are generally smaller but extremely vibrant and expected to be large in terms of number, they may be called the 'ant cities'. This analogy is intended for the more imaginative readers who (like me) tend to associate sets of characteristics with familiar insects, animals and/or objects in daily life. There is no intention to suggest that these cities will not transform themselves into much bigger cities in the future, like those currently in Clusters B or C.

Cluster B

Table 6.2 shows the summary statistics of the ten key mobility drivers for cities in Cluster B. This cluster is mainly comprised of medium and large cities which are close to the mean of the 100 cities in terms of population size, GDP, GDP per capita, motorisation rate, transport performance and other variables. We can see that these cities had an average population of 2.9 million, 70,014 yuan GDP per capita, a motorisation rate of 96.98 vehicles per million population, 206.33 million passengers and 171.96 million tonnes. These figures were close to the averages of 2.85 million people, 60,372 yuan GDP per capita, a motorisation rate of 78.38 vehicles per million population, 250.28 million passengers and

Table 6.2 Summary statistics of the ten key mobility drivers for cities in Cluster B

Indicator		Mean	Standard deviation
Population and population density			
Population 2010 ('000)		2,901	1,437
Population 2025 ('000)		4,404	2,110
Population density 2010 (people/km^2)		1,669	1,883.10
GDP and GDP per capita			
GDP 2010 (billion RMB)		197.28	112.70
GDP per capita 2010 (RMB)		70,014	27,161
GDP 2025 (billion RMB)		643.78	505.53
GDP per capita 2025 (RMB)		138,051	56,117
Motorisation (2010)			
Total motor vehicles		59.63	29.23
Vehicles per million population		96.98	27.65
Vehicles per km of road		68.49	45.87
Current transport performance and patterns (2010)			
Freight transport	Total freight (10,000 tonnes)	17,196	8,149
	Freight by railway (10,000 tonnes)	1,771	2,542
	Freight by highway (10,000 tonnes)	12,899	7,005
	% of railway	9.96	10.76
	% of highway	74.47	16.98
Passenger transport	Total passengers (10,000)	20,633	14,691
	Passengers by railway (10,000)	1,332	1,046
	Passengers by highway (10,000)	18,807	14,238
	% of railway	9.68	9.87
	% of highway	87.14	11.75
Road network (2010)			
Road area (10,000 m^2)		3,233	1,626
Road area per capita (m^2)		12.37	5.23
Current bus services (2010)			
Total bus passengers (10,000)		51,888	35,675
Number of buses		2,957	1,709
Number of buses per 10,000 population		10.42	3.57
Electricity generation capacity (2010)			
Total electricity consumption (10,000 kwh)		1,763,329	1,123,967
Electricity consumption per 1,000 population		647	358
% of industry		66.08	16.32
% of residents		14.35	7.61
Availability of government support (2010)			
Total income (RMB10,000)		1,863,082	1,272,275
Total expenditure (RMB10,000)		2,122,879	1,226,338
Expenditure on scientific research (RMB10,000)		66,395	60,741
%		2.88	1.71

Table 6.2 Continued

Indicator	Mean	Standard deviation
Citizen's expenditure on transportation (2010)		
Per capita annual consumption expenditure (RMB)	15,577	3,236
Expenditure on transport (RMB)	2,443	982
%	15.30	3.37
Road fatalities (2010)		
Absolute number	365	177
Fatalities per million population	60.70	18.69
Fatalities per 10,000 vehicles	6.79	3.03

Source: The author.

173.95 million tonnes respectively. A notable point is that these cities face the problem of high road fatalities already. Their road fatality rate averaged 365, while the 100-city average and standard deviation was only 322. However, the government financial capacity is not high. The financial capacity, as shown by the governments' budget, was 18.63 billion yuan in 2010. Nonetheless, the expansion of the road network has already taken off in this city cluster; probably an expressway network was already in place for motorisation to further grow as the income of citizens further grew in the next decade or so. The road area per capita is the highest amongst the three clusters. The figure stayed at 12.37 m²/person in 2010, in contrast to 11.41 m²/person for Cluster A and 7.96 for Cluster C. Overall, we see that these cities are bustling but they are not the 'stars'. Hence, they may be nicknamed the 'bee cities', because these medium-size cities are extremely dynamic with 'hustle and bustle' day and night. The 'honey' that they generate greatly boosts the overall economic growth of the nation, and they often also form the 'hubs' of emerging city-networks in their respective districts.

There are 48 cities altogether in this cluster, by far, the most numerous. In the Eastern region, they include Xiamen, Fuzhou and Quanzhou in Fujian, Foshan, Donggen, Shantou, Zhongshan, Huizhou and Zhuhai in Guangdong, Haikou in Hainan, Shijiazhuang and Tangshan in Hebei, Naning, Suzhou, Wuxi, Changzhou, Xuzhou, Nantong and Yangzhou in Jiansu, Dalian and Shenyang in Liaoning, Qingdao, Jinan, Zibo, Weifang, Yantai, Linyi and Dongying in Shandong, and Hangzhou, Ningbo and Wenzhou in Zhejiang (31). In the Central region, they include Hefei and Wuhu in Anhui, Haerbin and Daqing in Heilongjiang, Zhengzhou in Henan, Changsha and Hohhot in Hunan, Nanchang in Jiangxi, Changchun and Jilin in Jilin, and Taiyuan in Shanxi (11). In the Western region, they include Lanzhou in Gansu, Naning in Guangxi, Guiyang in Guizhou, Xian and Xianyang in Shaanxi, Wulumqi in Xinjiang, and Kunming in Yunnan (7). In other words, Cluster B cities are more abundant in the Eastern region. The share of cities in Cluster B for the Eastern, Central and Western regions is 52.54 per cent (31/59), 36.67 per cent (11/30) and 43.75 per cent (7/16) respectively.

Cluster C

This cluster mainly consists of large cities but still has impressive growth potentials in terms of population size, GDP and GDP per capita between 2010 and 2025. Their summary statistics are shown in Table 6.3. Despite the high average population size at 10.65 million in 2010, the figure was still expected to grow by

Table 6.3 Summary statistics of the ten key mobility drivers for cities in Cluster C

Indicator		Mean	Standard deviation
Population and population density			
Population 2010 ('000)		10,654	4,150
Population 2025 ('000)		15,385	6,381
Population density 2010 (people/km²)		3,008.96	1,944.25
GDP and GDP per capita			
GDP 2010 (billion RMB)		945.59	449.49
GDP per capita 2010 (RMB)		93,424	51,858
GDP 2025 (billion RMB)		3,567	1,726.67
GDP per capita 2025 (RMB)		233,864	71,833
Motorisation (2010)			
Total motor vehicles ('000)		171.45	113.80
Vehicles per million population		116.25	55.89
Vehicles per km of road		201.57	227.66
Current transport performance and patterns (2010)			
Freight transport	Total freight (10,000 tonnes)	46,870	21,981
	Freight by railway (10,000 tonnes)	5,003	5,311
	Freight by highway (10,000 tonnes)	27,075	18,540
	% of railway	11.49	12.36
	% of highway	58.69	27.05
Passenger transport	Total passengers (10,000)	120,203	127,489
	Passengers by railway (10,000)	24,282	53,117
	Passengers by highway (10,000)	91,929	81,173
	% of railway	17.16	14.32
	% of highway	75.06	24.23
Road network (2010)			
Road area (10,000 m²)		8,094	2,531
Road area per capita (m²)		7.96	2.65
Current bus services (2010)			
Total bus passengers (10,000)		226,910	120,792
Number of buses		13,649	7,390
Number of buses per 10,000 population		13.25	7.10
Electricity generation capacity (2010)			
Total electricity consumption (10,000 kwh)		6,002,805	3,185,976
Electricity consumption per 1,000 population		548	146
% of industry		52.27	19.86
% of residents		16.71	4.88

Table 6.3 Continued

Indicator	Mean	Standard deviation
Availability of government support (2010)		
Total income (RMB10,000)	13,683,724	10,761,132
Total expenditure (RMB10,000)	14,904,952	10,132,273
Expenditure on scientific research (10,000)	763,351	742,864
%	4.13	2.38
Citizen's expenditure on transportation (2010)		
Per capita annual consumption expenditure (RMB)	30,820	35,084
Expenditure on transport (RMB)	3,940	2,817
%	14.81	3.72
Road fatalities (2010)		
Absolute number	767	310
Fatalities per million population	51.05	18.87
Fatalities per 10,000 vehicles	5.02	2.28

Source: The author.

44.41 per cent to 15.39 million in 2025. The GDP and GDP per capita were 945.59 yuan and 93,424 yuan/person respectively, which were 369.30 per cent and 54.75 per cent higher than the 100-city average. Cities in Cluster C currently top the lists of the number of motor vehicles (with 171,450 vehicles), electricity generation capacities (averaging 60.13 billion kwh), governments' financial strengths (at 136.84 billion yuan per year), proportion of government expenditure on scientific research (averaging 4.13 per cent) and total transport volume (at 1.20 billion passengers and 468.70 million tonnes). Due to their huge population size and high degree of motorisation, the cities in this cluster have the lowest road area per capita coupled with the highest number of vehicles per km of road, leading to serious traffic congestion. The road area per capita was at $7.96\,m^2$/person, and the number of vehicles per km of road was at 201.57. In comparison, the 100-city averages were $11.56\,m^2$/person and 59.86, respectively. These cities are nicknamed the 'cat cities', because they often form extended metropolitan regions with strong economic and social ties with their surrounding areas. To a large extent, they already form relatively independent urban and economic systems. The economic leadership of 'cat cities' within their respective extended metropolitan regions is well-established. They tend to be not only economic powerhouses but also centres of innovation and creativity (Wang and Loo, 2017). Therefore, the success of the 'cat cities' is crucial for the sustained economic growth of the country and the eventual economic transformation of the nation beyond export-oriented industrialisation.

There are only nine cities in this cluster and they are mostly in the Eastern region. In the Eastern region, they include Shenzhen and Guangzhou in Guangdong, Hong Kong, Shanghai, Beijing and Tianjin. In the Central region, there is Wuhan in Hubei. In the Western region, they include Chongqing, and Chengdu in Sichuan. The shares of cities in Cluster C for Eastern, Central and Western China are 10.17 per cent (6/59), 3.33 per cent (1/30) and 12.5 per cent (2/16) respectively.

Comparison of the three city clusters

In order to provide a comparative framework, the relative characteristics of the city clusters are shown in Table 6.4. The statistical distance among the three city clusters is the greatest for variables Population 2010, Population 2025, GDP 2010 and GDP 2025. With the 100 cities taken as a group, the mean population in 2010 was 2,855 million and it is expected to increase to 4,250 million. The range of the statistical distances is above 3.0. For both 2010 and 2025, Cluster C has the maximum average distance from the respective means, while Cluster B has the minimum average distance from the respective means.

Furthermore, the differences in terms of statistical distance are also huge (with the range of statistical distances between 2.51 and 3.1) for the variables of total motor vehicles, total freight volume, road areas, total bus fleet, total government income, total government expenditure and the absolute number of road fatalities. For the number of buses, the maximum average distance from the mean is 2.49 for Cluster C while the minimum is –0.50 for Cluster A. The range is 2.99. Cities in the three clusters are the most similar (with the range of statistical distances between 0.51 and 1.0) in terms of road area per capita, electricity consumption per 1,000 population, the share of electricity used for residential purpose, share of transport expenditure in people's income, and road traffic fatalities per million population. To illustrate, the maximum average distance from the mean of road area per capita of Cluster C is –0.73, while the minimum is –0.03 from Cluster A. The difference is only 0.70.

Growth potentials of the city clusters

By comparing the statistics in 2010 and 2025 (projected by the UN and McKinsey & Company) in terms of population, GDP and GDP per capita, the growth potentials of the three city clusters can be shown (McKinsey & Company, 2012). Figure 6.1 shows the projected percentage increases of these three mobility driver variables between 2010 and 2025.

For all three clusters, the increase in population is projected not to be as large as that of GDP and GDP per capita, reflecting a higher accumulation of wealth in these cities. The projected percentage increases of population in the three clusters are around 50 per cent and they are very close. The greatest population growth (in terms of percentage increase) was expected to take place in Cluster B cities (increase of 52 per cent), followed by Cluster A cities (increase of 49 per cent) and Cluster C cities (increase of 44 per cent). As the population size of Cluster C cities (averaging 10.54 million) was nearly four times higher than that in Cluster B cities (2.90 million) and nearly ten times higher than those in Cluster A (1.17 million) in 2010, Cluster C will still consist of the largest cities

Table 6.4 Statistical distances among the three city clusters

Indicator		Mean of 100 cities	Average distance from the mean		
			Group		
			A	B	C
Population and population density					
Population 2010		2,855	−0.56	0.02	2.58
Population 2025		4,250	−0.57	0.03	2.53
Population density 2010 (people/km²)		1,627.72	−0.21	0.03	0.86
GDP and GDP per Capita					
GDP 2010 (billion RMB)		201.49	−0.52	−0.01	2.58
GDP per capita 2010 (RMB)		60,372	−0.58	0.32	1.09
GDP 2025 (billion RMB)		671.32	−0.51	−0.02	2.57
GDP per capita 2025 (RMB)		110,618	−0.78	0.38	1.69
Motorisation (2010)					
Total motor vehicles (`000)		54.27	−0.54	0.09	2.07
Vehicles per million population		78.38	−0.76	0.49	1.00
Vehicles per km of road		59.86	−0.45	0.10	1.61
Current transport performance and patterns (2010)					
Freight transport	Total freight (10,000 tonnes)	17,395	−0.44	−0.01	2.20
	Freight by railway (10,000 tonnes)	1,968	−0.15	−0.07	1.09
	Freight by highway (10,000 tonnes)	12,461	−0.38	0.05	1.56
	% of railway	11.96	0.18	−0.16	−0.04
	% of highway	74.25	0.16	0.01	−0.84

continued

Table 6.4 Continued

Indicator		Mean of 100 cities	Average distance from the mean		
			Group		
			A	B	C
Passenger transport	Total passengers (10,000)	25,028	-0.31	-0.09	1.96
	Passengers by railway (10,000)	3,055	-0.15	-0.10	1.28
	Passengers by highway (10,000)	21,326	-0.35	-0.07	2.07
	% of railway	9.01	-0.27	0.07	0.89
	% of highway	88.13	0.31	-0.08	-1.04
Road network (2010)					
Road area (10,000 m²)		2,844	-0.65	0.17	2.24
Road area per capita (m²)		11.56	-0.03	0.16	-0.73
Current bus services (2010)					
Total bus passengers (10,000)		51,444	-0.52	0.01	2.43
Number of buses		3,053	-0.50	-0.02	2.49
Number of buses per 10,000 population		9.70	-0.35	0.16	0.81
Electricity generation capacity (2010)					
Total electricity consumption (10,000 kwh)		1,663,315	-0.53	0.05	2.27
Electricity consumption per 1,000 population		591	-0.17	0.18	-0.14
% of industry		66.16	0.17	0.00	-0.79
% of residents		13.97	-0.14	0.05	0.39

Availability of government support (2010)				
Total income (RMB10,000)	2,333,413	−0.38	−0.10	2.34
Total expenditure (RMB10,000)	2,694,869	−0.39	−0.12	2.47
Expenditure on scientific research (RMB10,000)	105,766	−0.31	−0.13	2.19
%	2.41	−0.52	0.28	1.02
Citizen's expenditure on transportation (2010)				
Per capita annual consumption expenditure (RMB)	15,348	−0.30	0.02	1.34
Expenditure on transport (RMB)	2,144	−0.54	0.23	1.36
%	13.80	−0.55	0.44	0.29
Road fatalities (2010)				
Absolute number	322	−0.60	0.18	1.91
Fatalities per million population	50.73	−0.53	0.47	0.02
Fatalities per 10,000 vehicles	7.48	0.35	−0.19	−0.66

Source: The author.

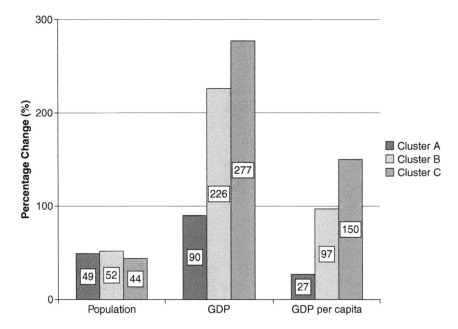

Figure 6.1 Projected increases in population, GDP and GDP per capita of the three city clusters, 2010 vs. 2025.

Source: Compiled by the author.

in the country. Nonetheless, cities in Cluster B are likely to become much bigger than those in Cluster A with their higher population base in 2010 and the more rapid growth rate up to 2025. Overall, the current distinction among the three clusters in terms of population size will remain significant.

While the average GDP and GDP per capita of the cities in Clusters B (RMB197.28 billion and RMB70,014 per capita) and C (RMB945.59 billion and RMB93,424 per capita) are already much higher than in the cities in Cluster A (RMB5.45 billion and RMB42,691 per capita) in 2010, the gap is projected to grow larger and larger as shown in Figure 6.1. Overall, the percentage increase of GDP for cities in Clusters A, B and C will be 90 per cent, 226 per cent and 277 per cent respectively. When the GDP per capita is considered, the percentage increase for Clusters A, B and C will vary even more substantially at 27 per cent, 97 per cent and 150 per cent. In other words, both the economic power and the overall living standard of cities in Cluster C are expected to increase much more noticeably than cities in the other clusters. The rapid economic growth of the mega and medium-sized cities including Beijing (Cluster C), Shanghai (Cluster C), Guangzhou (Cluster C), Suzhou (Cluster B), Hangzhou (Cluster B) and Nanjing (Cluster B) will further favour their process of transition to sustainable transport by making local governments and people more able to afford sustainable transport technologies which require strong financial capacity and technological advancement. According to a study by Pricewaterhouse Coopers in 2009, Shanghai, Beijing and Guangzhou will be among the world's top 30 cities with the highest GDP in 2025 and their rankings will be 9, 17 and 21 respectively (25, 38 and 44 in 2008) (Pricewaterhouse Coopers, 2009). In contrast, the relatively slow economic growth of the cities in Cluster A will probably constrain their ability in adopting sustainable transport technologies that are more expensive in building, operating and maintaining. Therefore, a transition period where technologies like bicycles and BRT will be promoted before they are economically prepared for more advanced technologies for the period beyond 2030.

Emerging urban transport problems

Cluster A

Most notably, the 2025 population of cities in Cluster A is projected to increase by around 50 per cent compared to that of 2010. This may create serious problems in these cities because their currently small passenger and freight volumes, limited length of road network and low degree of motorisation may not be able to catch up with the rapid population growth. The further development and expansion of transport infrastructure may be constrained by their relatively small GDP, low GDP per capita, limited government financial capacity and weak electricity generation capacity. As a result, the physical movements of people and freight may be hindered due to the lack of competitive transport-related facilities and services. In other words, the transport capacity problem is obvious. A clear policy to ensure that the sustainable transport measures are affordable to local governments and people will be crucial in its sustainable transport transition.

Cluster B

Being the city cluster with the highest road fatality per million population, how to enhance road safety is a major urban transport issue and a core question that cities in Cluster B need to carefully consider. The serious road safety problem will further aggravate as the motorisation rate of these cities continues to climb, together with their strong growth in population size and economic power. The rapid increase in motorisation rate may also escalate the problem of air pollution in Cluster B cities. Smog, which has become a major transport problem in many large Chinese cities, is likely to be a serious emerging problem for cities in Cluster B in their transition to 2030. While cities in Cluster B have the highest road area per capita, which implies greater room for expansion in the number of motor vehicles, the cities may not be able to efficiently alleviate the associated problem with their weak financial position. A clear policy to manage vehicle growth and road space to tackle road safety challenges will be crucial in its sustainable transport transition.

Cluster C

Due to their huge population size and high degree of motorisation, the cities in Cluster C have the lowest road area per capita and the highest number of vehicles per km of road, leading to serious traffic congestion. Traffic congestion does not only cause time delays and the loss of productivity, but also makes the problems of traffic accidents and CO_2 emissions worse. A clear policy to support the extremely large passenger and freight movements without generating unbearable congestion challenges will be crucial in its sustainable transport transition.

References

McKinsey & Company. (2012). Global cities of the future: An interactive map. *Urban World: Mapping the Economic Power of Cities*. Retrieved from www.mckinsey.com/tools/Wrappers/Wrapper.aspx?sid={C84CB74F-A3B1-7B1-265-252F6D85B68}&pid={4F5BEDB1-C1F-4243-A052-3ADBABE82DF}.

Pricewaterhouse Coopers. (2009). Which are the largest city economies in the world and how might this change by 2025? *UK Economic Outlook November 2009* (p. 24). Retrieved from http://pwc.blogs.com/files/global-city-gdp-rankings-2008-025.pdf.

Wang, B., & Loo, B.P.Y. (2017). Hubs of internet entrepreneurs: The emergence of coworking offices in Shanghai, China. *Journal of Urban Technology*. Advance online publication. doi:10.1080/10630732.2017.1285124.

7 Initial strategies for sustainable transport

The sustainable transport 'toolbox'

Focusing on passenger transport, the urban transport hierarchy can be analysed from the perspectives of environmental impact and passenger carrying capacity (Loo, 2009). Figure 7.1 presents the major transport modes of walking, cycling, taxis, private cars, minibuses and other paratransit modes, buses, light rails and metro systems against these two dimensions. Paratransit modes include different formal and informal transport means like motorcycle taxis, tuk-tuk, tricycle taxis, jeepneys, residential coaches common in many developing countries. Generally, transport modes with a lower environmental impact per passenger (environmentally friendly) are more sustainable and, hence, more desirable. However, some sustainable transport modes may not have sufficiently large

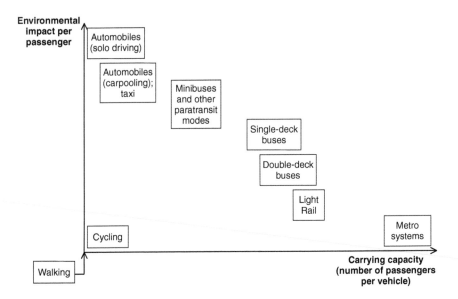

Figure 7.1 The urban transport hierarchy.

Source: Modified from Loo (2009). Copyright obtained from Elsevier.

carrying capacity to handle peak travel demand along busy corridors in cities, especially during the morning peak hours of commuting. Conversely, the lack of a stable large customer pool and various financial constraints may make certain sustainable transport modes with large passenger carrying capacity infeasible and 'out of reach' to local transport policy-makers and planners. Some capital-intensive transport infrastructure like metros may not be economically or financially viable in cities with a low population size and/or a weak economy. Loo and Cheng (2010), for example, have found that the first lines of metro systems were generally built only in cities with at least 5.0 million population and a GDP per capita higher than US$11,400 (2008 dollars). When all 60 metro lines in 21 countries were considered, the average city population size was 6.6 million and the average city income per capita was US$22,800 (2008 dollars) (Loo & Cheng, 2010).

Within a city, Figure 7.1 can be considered at the corridor level. Given a city's main urban form, there will be specific corridors/routes that require higher-capacity transport modes and others that warrant lower-capacity transport modes. There is a need for policy-makers and planners to consider the lag time in building and providing various transport infrastructure and services, especially for newly developed areas. Depending on the sequence of transport availability and population growth in a district/region, the transport-development strategies may be classified as transport-led, development-led and integrated (Loo & Chow, 2009). In other words, even for the same sustainable transport mode (such as metros), there exists enormous variability in the timing and scale of development within the same city.

The key variables in the initial sustainable transport strategies considered in this chapter are bus rapid transit (BRT), bike/e-bike, light rail, metro and electric cars. The range of initial sustainable transport strategies considered covers transport modes suitable for cities of different sizes and requires integration to ensure that the leading bundle of sustainable modes recommended can stand a chance of redressing unsustainable transport problems faced by cities around the world. In order to provide a better understanding of these major 'tools' or leading sustainable transport modes, the following section will provide a brief overview of them in terms of the definition, the hardware and software required, the key advantages and potential disadvantages.

Bus rapid transit (BRT)

BRT is a public transport mode that combines the quality of rail transit and the flexibility of buses. The huge variability of BRT systems around the world has made the definition of BRT one of the most challenging in the public transport literature. Systematic attempts to identify and generalise BRT characteristics range from the early attempts of Jarzab, Lightbody and Maeda (2002) and Levinson *et al.* (2002) to the more recent ones of Wirasinghe *et al.* (2013) and Nikitas and Karlsson (2015). One the one hand, BRT distinguishes itself as a transport mode that offers more than conventional bus services in terms of providing faster and more reliable services due to its rights-of-way (ranging from priority use to exclusive lanes on streets), exclusive bus platforms/stops, pre-board fare payment system, frequent services (at least 16 hours per day with headways within ten minutes during peak hours, according to Levinson *et al.*, 2003), and the use of advanced information and communication technologies (ICT) (ranging from real-time arrival time on platforms to various bus information delivered to smartphones). On the other hand, BRT distinguishes itself from light rail in terms of using rubber-tyred buses (including articulated buses) on a city's road network without rail tracks. As such, BRT often operates as a discrete brand with a distinct name and logo on its rolling stock (buses), infrastructure (like terminals) and marketing plans. Some notable examples are RIT in Curitiba (Brazil), TransMilenio in Bogota (Colombia), Metrobüs in Istanbul (Turkey), TansJakarta in Jakarta (Indonesia), HealthLine in Cleveland (USA) and Brisbane Busway in Brisbane (Australia) (Nikitas & Karlsoon, 2015).

With the high flexibility of BRT, the hardware required in terms of infrastructure is relatively simple with bus-only or bus-priority lanes, and typically stations with wider spacing (stops of one mile or more according to Jarzab, Lightbody & Maeda, 2002) than conventional bus services. Although buses running in BRT can be powered by diesel fuel, electricity or an alternative fuel is often used to fulfil its image of being more environmentally friendly and to justify the allocation of scarce road space for dedicated use by BRT. These features, in turn, mean that BRT can be implemented incrementally and is often much less capital-intensive than the light rail option.

In terms of software, there are challenges to manage the competition for road space among all road users, increase efficiency and ensure high service frequency. BRT is the most efficient when fully integrated with an intelligent transport system (ITS). The early applications only include in-vehicle displays of station names and arrival time at platforms. Nowadays, smartphone apps that provide real-time traffic and other relevant information, especially on interchange with other transport modes and nearby attractions, are essential in making BRTs successful.

The key advantages of BRT are its cost-effectiveness compared to light rail and metro systems, short implementation period (typically less than two years) and flexibility. While the costs of building BRT systems can vary significantly, many were achieved with a capital cost of less than US$5 million per km (Hidalgo & Carrigan, 2010). In comparison, Nikitas and Karlsson (2015) suggest that rail systems with similar capacities typically cost three to ten times more. Loo and Li (2006) indicate that the construction costs of different metro lines in Hong Kong varied from US$47 million per km back in the late 1970s to over US$0.3 billion per km in the early 2000s. In the case of BRT-Lite in Lago (Nigeria), the scheme only took 15 months from conception to operation (Brader, 2009). Similarly, BRT systems in China typically took less than two years from planning to opening for public use. Guangzhou currently has the highest-capacity BRT line in China (Salon, Wu & Shewmake, 2014). Last but not least, the high flexibility of BRT means that it is possible for a city to implement the system in stages as finances become available and the city's urban form evolves. Moreover, there is increasing evidence to show that BRT, when planned well and integrated with other transport modes in the city, can become a successful 'anchor' for TOD communities and realise substantial value uplifts of nearby properties (Salon, Wu & Shewmake, 2014; Xu, Zhang & Aditjandra, 2016).

The potential disadvantages are threefold. First, it may be difficult to assign dedicated lanes for BRT in cities with low road area per capita. The introduction of BRT lines in cities already exhibiting unsustainable transport problems like severe traffic congestion and high traffic fatalities is likely to face strong opposition from car users for aggravating congestion on the one hand and existing stakeholders (notably conventional buses and paratransit operators) as threats on the other. Second, buses are sometimes considered slow, inefficient and old-fashioned. This consideration looms large especially in cities where rail alternatives are presented in electoral debates and public consultation. The latter are still generally considered more favourably as clean, modern, more permanent and more comfortable (Nikitas & Karlsson, 2015). Third, BRT service is less predictable or reliable than light rail and the metro system because of the need to share road space and, hence, the increased chance of disruptions caused by major traffic incidence. In circumstances like the TranSantiago BRT system in Santiago (Chile), where we have conducted fieldwork, the high unreliability of services caused by the sharing of road space in many road sections, together with the relatively chaotic and hasty rolling-out of the system, has made it rather unattractive to the local population.

Bike/electric bike

A pro-cycling city is a city characterised by a transport system that gives priority to cycling over motor vehicles. Urban cycling is the norm for moving around, and is made easy through the entire urban fabric of buildings and infrastructure to people's attitudes and actual travel behaviour. A look around the world, however, shows that there are only a handful of pro-cycling cities, with Copenhagen, Amsterdam and some Dutch cities as exemplary. Through an ethnographic study of 'the making of' a pro-cycling city in Copenhagen, Larsen (2017) rightly points out 'Copenhagenising low-cycling cities' is hardly easy and it goes much beyond the building of cycle tracks. While world-class cycling facilities (from cycle tracks, racks, bike availability to bike repairs) can be replicated, the 'normalisation' of cycling is hardly government-driven or directly caused by 'world-class' cycle tracks. A striking analogy was that 'for many Copenhageners cycling is as routinised as "brushing one's teeth"' (Larsen, 2017, p. 883). While 'the development of a "cycling city" is a slow moving, complex, multifaceted process' (Larsen, 2017, p. 889), policies that encourage and support cycling as a sustainable transport mode have been rolled out in all major continents of the world in the last decade or so (Fishman, 2016a).

Promoting cycling as a sustainable transport mode in cities, however, does require substantial hardware support. First and foremost is perhaps the provision of segregated cycle tracks or paths, especially in cities where cycling is only a minor mode and vehicular traffic is both dense and mixed (Loo & Tsui, 2010). The safety-in-numbers phenomenon (that is, places with fewer cyclists tend to be more dangerous and vice versa) has recently been found to hold at the local scale within the same city (Yao & Loo, 2016). Hence, contrary to the conventional wisdom that cycle tracks should be built only when there is sufficient proven demand or cyclists using a particular route, the research suggests that cycling infrastructural investment is most needed when and where cycling is only a minor mode. Until and unless such infrastructure is provided, the huge cycling risk can stifle any attempt to make cycling a leading sustainable transport mode. Moreover, the easy availability of affordable and good-quality bikes, together with helmets, and the provision of parking facilities at convenient locations are necessary. These two related issues may be addressed simultaneously with bike-sharing schemes, largely inspired by the 'Paris Velib' system (launched in 2007) and now available in over 800 cities worldwide (Fishman, 2016b). Nonetheless, apart from ensuring the financial viability of the schemes, the designation of a sufficient number of conveniently located (including the downtown) bicycle collection/drop-off points (or docking stations) requires fundamental changes in the car-oriented mentality.

In terms of software, management measures range from the maintenance of cycle tracks (especially during seasons with adverse weather such as heavy rain or snow), the enforcement of laws against the illegal use of and the parking of private vehicles on cycle tracks (especially in developing countries), traffic demand management measures to minimise potential vehicle–bicycle conflicts, and the provision of training programmes on safe cycling. Where bicycle-sharing schemes have been rolled out, the maintenance, parking and deployment of shared bicycles can become substantial burdens and offset hard-gained environmental benefits. Moreover, the chaotic parking of shared bicycles (occupying pedestrian walkways, transit stops and open space) and the scrapping of poor-quality and badly maintained bicycles for many bicycle-sharing schemes in China are already creating new unsustainable transport challenges for city management (Anonymous, 2017). Moreover, there is a need to make cycling maps and set up information centres and specific regulations for cyclists so that they consider cycling easy, fun, fast and safe.

The key advantage is that cycling is cheaper than motor vehicles and thus more affordable to the users in developing countries. It can reduce travel time for journeys less than 8 km. When bicycles are powered by human energy, it eliminates transport carbon emissions altogether and can have health benefits by ensuring physical activity for people in cities who have a sedentary lifestyle. Even when e-bikes are used, the transport carbon emissions are estimated to be 40 times less than cars (Shao *et al.*, 2012). The disadvantages are that cycling is limited to relatively short journeys, it has limited capacity, and there are bicycle safety concerns, especially in mixed traffic situations. Once again, the e-bikes hold some promise here. The use of e-bikes – maximum motor output lower than 0.25 kilowatts – has been common in Japan. More recently, e-bikes of 0.2 to one kilowatt, with an electric range of 40–150 km are available (Fishman & Cherry, 2016). Weinert *et al.* (2008) estimated that China already had about 65 million electric bicycles and scooters by the mid-2000s. This figure had risen to 120 million by 2010 (Yao & Wu, 2012). The use of e-bikes can have the potential benefits of overcoming many barriers of bicycle use, especially for the elderly and in more difficult terrains and weather conditions. However, higher costs, safety concerns, limited knowledge and a range of anxieties can greatly limit their use (Fyhri *et al.*, 2017; Popovich *et al.*, 2014). In addition, the possible environmental impact associated with the use of old lead-acid batteries and improper disposal/recycling can be enormous (Fishman & Cherry, 2016). Where the conditions are right, bicycles can account for as high as 40 per cent of the trips made in cities (Pucher, Dill & Handy, 2010). Nonetheless, the efforts required and the risk of failure to promote cycling in car-dependent societies should not be underestimated. Despite the ambitious goal of doubling cycling in Australia from 2011 to 2016, the national cycling participation survey has, however, shown a decline (Austroads, 2015; fieldwork in Brisbane in 2015 and 2017). Hence, detailed studies are required before cycling can become a leading sustainable transport mode to overcome unsustainable transport problems in cities.

Light rail

This public transport mode uses lightweight passenger rail cars to operate singly on fixed steel rails in a row that is not separated from other traffic for much of the day. Compared to heavy rail systems with exclusive tracks, light rail tends to have a lower speed, averaging around 10–40 km/hr, and smaller transport capacity, typically ranging from 8,000 to 15,000 passengers per hour (Kolos & Taczanowski, 2016). Some examples are the Docklands Light Railway in London, Metrolink in Manchester and Supertram in Sheffield within the UK, Skytrain in Vancouver, Canada and mini-Metro in Copenhagen, Denmark (Ferbrache & Knowles, 2016).

Compared to BRT, light rail systems generally require relatively heavy investment in infrastructure and hardware with trackways, stations, storage yards and electrical substations for electricity supply. Other capital stock investment includes railcars ranging from 46 to 93 feet, carrying up to 300 persons each. A light rail carriage, with an average capacity about twice as high as, and an expected lifetime approximately three times longer than a bus, also tends to be more expensive than the latter (Kolos & Taczanowski, 2016). In terms of software, light rail requires proper management and communication via control centres and an automatic monitoring system. Measures to ensure good integration with other public transport are also important. As light rail does not typically have fully segregated right-of-way, potential conflicts with other vehicles, bicycles and pedestrians can pose traffic safety problems (Chira-Chavala *et al.*, 1996; Porter, Hansen & Gallardo, 1995; Walmsley, 1992). Continuous efforts have been made to improve traffic safety related to the shared use of road space by light rail with other road users (MacNeill *et al.*, 2015).

Light rail offers many advantages as a sustainable transport mode. In the first place, it is much cheaper than conventional heavy rail systems in terms of construction and operating costs. In Europe, Kolos and Taczanowski (2016) cited capital cost to be in the range of €10.5 to 27 million per km. It is environmentally friendly because the rail cars are powered by electricity, rather than diesel or gasoline. Compared to buses, its higher capacity can help reduce traffic congestion (Bhattacharjee & Goetz, 2012). Moreover, light rail stops, being at grade, have had some success in terms of better integration with cycling and walking in some French cities (Olesen, 2014). Nonetheless, concerns have also been expressed regarding low actual patronage on light rail, which would result in minimal, if any, impact vis-à-vis diverting highway traffic and reducing traffic congestion (Ransom & Kelemen, 2016).

Compared to BRT, light rail requires larger initial capital for the construction of trackways, stations and storage yards. Hence, the planning and implementation process also tends to be longer. In the two European cases discussed in Olesen and Lassen (2016), a lag time of ten to 15 years was reported. Mostly attributable to the higher capital costs and more expensive trains, light rail fare tends to be higher than that of conventional buses. Spatially, the more capital-intensive nature can make light rail less affordable to low-income neighbourhoods and may result in social inequity within the city. In Chicago (USA), for example, light rail typically runs through the middle-class white neighbourhoods rather than the working-class Latino, African-American and other minority neighbourhoods (Farmer, 2011). However, the contrary was found in Bordeaux, where social equity was enhanced (Sari, 2015). Safety can be problematic as railcars need to intersect with other on-road traffic transport. Once again, when the conditions are right, light rail stations hold great promise as the 'anchors' in TOD for supporting smart growth, and as 'a means to remodel the city' (Olesen & Lassen, 2016, p. 378). Yet, the associated financial commitments can also be overwhelming and limit the initial success of light rails, as the case of Denver, Colorado (USA) well illustrated (Goetz, 2013). Typically, light rail is more appropriate in mid-sized cities (as low as 100,000 inhabitants) with healthy economies and medium urban density (Kolos & Taczanowski, 2016). Moreover, Ferbrache and Knowles (2016) have underlined the failure to integrate light rail with existing and new urban policies as a key factor in 'under-achievement' of light rail as a sustainable transport mode so far.

Metro

Metro refers to a tracked, electrically driven local means of transport which has an integral, continuous track bed of its own, having huge carrying capacity and high service frequency (Fouracre, Dunkerley & Gardner, 2003). While the first track of the London Tube (UK) was built more than 100 years ago in 1863, most metro systems in cities were built only in the 1970s or after (Allport, 1990; Loo & Cheng, 2010). Some notable exceptions are the Tokyo Metro (Japan) built in 1927 and the Toronto Subway (Canada) built in 1954. Today, there are more than 200 metro systems operating in major world regions, with the African continent having the fewest (Cairo in Egypt and Algiers in Algeria) and Asia having the most rapid expansion. In mainland China (that is, excluding Taiwan, Hong Kong and Macau), Loo and Li (2006) reported that there were 'a few cities with metro systems' (p. 121) (that is, Beijing, Guangzhou, Shanghai, Shenzhen and Tianjin) and seven cities with metro systems under construction in the mid-2000s. There are now as many as 27 mainland Chinese cities having metro systems. Among these 27 metro systems, 24 (88.9 per cent) were newly built and operated only in 2000 or after. Moreover, more than half (17 or 63.0 per cent) were opened since 2010. With the operation years shown in brackets, they are Changsha in Hunan (2014), Chengdu in Sichuan (2010), Dongguan in Guangdong (2016), Fuzhou in Fujian (2016), Hangzhou in Zhejiang (2012), Harbin in Heilongjiang (2013), Hefei in Anhui (2016), Kunming in Yunnan (2012), Nanchang in Jiangxi (2015), Nanning in Guangxi (2016), Ningbo in Zhejiang (2014), Qingdao in Shandong (2015), Shenyang in Liaoning (2010), Suzhou in Jiangsu (2012), Wuxi in Jiangsu (2014), Xian in Shaanxi (2011) and Zhengzhou in Henan (2013) (Metrobits.org, 2017). The ready acceptance of metro systems among the Chinese is not unrelated to the historical importance and major role of railways in the country's passenger transport (see Chapter 3).

Infrastructure investment required for metro systems, however, is especially heavy, with tracks (underground tunnel, street-level railway or elevated railway), stations and depots. In addition, investment in the rolling stock of electricity-powered trains with up to ten cars operating at a high speed (e.g. 80 km/hr for Hong Kong's urban metro lines) is high. The magnitude of the financial cost of metro systems has been escalating in recent decades. Flyvbjerg, Bruzelius and van Wee (2008) conducted a very useful analysis of the total capital costs per route-km of major metro systems worldwide. Their study suggested that the total capital costs (2002 prices) per route-km were US$26.7–329.9 million in Europe, US$43.8–147.5 in the Americas and US$54.5–65.8 in Asia. Excluding the outliers, the benchmark figures are between US$50 to 150 million per km. While many city governments have focused on the challenge of funding the initial capital investment, the needs to maintain, properly pay for capital stock depreciation and eventually upgrade the expensive infrastructure can even be more demanding.

Management and software support is also critical because of the huge financial commitments involved in building metro systems. For a metro system to avoid being considered a 'white elephant' (especially in view of other competing investments in a society for education and health care, for example), it needs to fulfil its unique advantages of being able to move a huge volume of passengers efficiently within the city. With a network length of 220.9 km, the Mass Transit Railway Corporation (MTRC) in Hong Kong moved over 5.5 million passengers on an average weekday in 2015 (MTRC, 2016). Referring to Figure 7.1, the low environmental impact of a metro system cannot be separated from its huge passenger carrying capacity, and the condition that the latter is well utilised. To do so, a metro system needs to be well integrated with other public transport to ensure a pleasant door-to-door passenger experience. As metro stations are generally farther apart, multi-modal transfers are often required for the first and last miles. Even in Hong Kong, where the transport policy is 'railways as the backbone', Loo, Cheng and Nichols (2017) found that metro-only trips were still less common than multimodal metro trips, even for residents living within 500 m of the metro station. Furthermore, enhancing safety standards such as putting up platform screen doors is essential, though extra costs are involved. There may also be a need to set up specific regulations for metro transport due to the high risk of any accident or terrorist attack in trains underground.

The key advantages of a metro system are its huge carrying capacity, frequent services and fast speed. A metro system requires less space for operation than road transport in transporting the same number of passengers off-road. Running on electricity, metro is also of higher energy efficiency than road transport. Nonetheless, the high cost in constructing, operating and maintaining the metro system can be prohibitive for many cities in developing countries. A metro system also requires a long planning and implementation period (Loo & Li, 2006). The ability to identify and implement a financially sustainable business model to build a metro system in the first place, and to maintain and upgrade it in the long term, is a determining factor for the metro to become the leading sustainable transport mode in transforming a city's unsustainable transport.

Another critical factor, which is also mentioned above for BRT and light rail, is the planning of nearby areas around rail transit stations (Loo, Chen & Chan, 2010). With density, diversity and design (the three Ds) as the guiding principles, Loo, Cheng and Nichols (2017) have highlighted the need to consider the pre-existing conditions around the rail stations. While the railway operator plays a role, the city's historical development and overall planning also affect the resulting patterns of population, employment, land use and change to travel behaviour. Greenfield sites have the greatest potential for realising a strong modal shift to metro, housing a rapidly expanding population and realising new planning concepts like 'comprehensive development areas'. Infill sites have huge potential for urban regeneration and generating new employment hubs.

Electric cars

Electric cars are those propelled by an electric motor that is powered either solely by a battery, or together with an internal combustion engine using hydrogen, gasoline or diesel or by a fuel cell. The promotion of electric cars as a sustainable transport mode has the main characteristic of not making a drastic change in people's mode choice or travel behaviour as a prerequisite for addressing the unsustainable transport problems. With the use of electricity as the energy for vehicles on roads, the main advantages are the reduction in the direct consumption of non-renewable fossil fuels for road transport, and the associated reduction in transport carbon emissions, other harmful greenhouse gases and particulate matters (PM). Unlike other the sustainable transport 'tools' described above, the use of electric cars, however, cannot address directly some notable unsustainable transport problems like traffic congestion, traffic injury and social inequity. The use of electric cars essentially focuses on the environmental dimension only of preserving environmental resources (notably fossil fuels) and minimising environmental impact (through reducing the emissions of CO_2, other greenhouse gases, harmful chemicals and particulate matters). The ability to drastically reduce transport carbon emissions in order to meet national, regional (in the European Union, for example) and world targets set in the Kyoto Protocol in 1997 and more recently COP21 in 2015 (21st Yearly Session of the Conference of the Parties, 2015) makes electric cars a potential candidate in the sustainable transport strategies towards 2030.

Infrastructural support in terms of public charging stations and home charging equipment is required. In particular, Neaimeh *et al.* (2017) find that the availability and distribution of fast charging facilities can affect people's intention to shift to electric vehicles significantly. These fast charging facilities, however, require considerable investment (Egbue, Long & Samaranayake, 2017). Other hardware support is also high with battery electric vehicles, hybrid electric vehicles, plug-in hybrid electric vehicles and fuel-cell electric vehicles. As only the battery electric vehicles operate in all-electric mode at all times and are powered solely by electricity, we refer mainly to them as 'electric vehicles' in this book. The other hybrid electric vehicles, including those which support plug-in, fall within the umbrella of 'electric cars' but are not our main focus. Apart from the charging system, electric cars are generally more expensive than conventional ones, largely due to the more expensive battery. The US Department of Energy, for example, has been targeting a reduction in the costs by about 75 per cent (to $125 per kWh in 2022) in its EV Everywhere Grand Challenge (DOE, 2014). There are not as many vehicle manufacturers and models to choose from either. While the potential for using electric cars goes beyond private cars, research and development is badly needed for the electric car technology to be widely used in buses, goods vehicles and other heavy vehicles.

In terms of software, evidence of the limited success of many voluntary travel behavioural policy bundles in 'getting drivers out of their cars' (James, Burke & Yen, 2017) has urged us to actively explore making electric vehicles acceptable to drivers. Given the huge diversity of people's needs and preferences in cities, private cars do have a niche in the sustainable urban transport hierarchy. Nonetheless, policies to encourage and support people to shift to electric cars are still essentially limited to the provision of infrastructure and purchase/tax subsidies (Massiani, 2015; Melton, Axsen & Goldberg, 2017; Zhang *et al.*, 2014). More research into the actual travel patterns and preferences of the driving population will be needed to increase the electric car option uptake worldwide (Egbue, Long & Samaranayake, 2017; Li, Long & Chen, 2016; Yang *et al.*, 2017). The more drastic policies being the French and British governments' proclamation to ban the sales of diesel and petrol cars and vans by 2040.

The greatest advantages of the electric car option are the higher energy efficiency and lower pollution. When the technology develops further, electric cars can be widely used not only for private cars but also for public transport (such as buses) and goods vehicles. They are quiet, reliable and offer smooth rides. Electric cars emit no tailpipe pollutants. In China, enormous efforts have been made to reduce the high emissions of its vehicular fleet, especially through the promulgation of fuel economy standards (based on the vehicle weight classification system) effective since July 2005 (Anonymous, 2015; An & Sauer, 2004). It was estimated that the national average emission levels of China's vehicle fleet have already reduced from 210 g CO_2 per km in 2002 to 180 g CO_2 per km in 2009 (Anonymous, 2015). Moreover, the national government has supported local automobile companies, notably BYD, not only to do research and development but also to manufacture electric vehicles domestically.

However, electric cars still have limited driving distance before needing a recharge (the range). The more basic models (such as Nissan Leaf) using a 24 kWh lithium-ion battery pack have a US Environmental Protection Agency (EPA) estimated range of only 84 miles (Egbue, Long & Samaranayake, 2017). At the higher end of the spectrum, the 2016 Tesla Model S uses a 70–80 kWh lithium-ion battery pack and has an estimated range of 240 to 270 miles (Egbue, Long & Samaranayake, 2017). Without fast charging technology and facilities, they can take four to eight hours to re-charge. Furthermore, electric cars are also more expensive than conventional vehicles, making them unaffordable to many drivers in developing countries. Therefore, some government incentives and policies are necessary for this option to work. In China, the 'ten cities, 1,000 EVs' plan was introduced in 2009, though the targets seem not to have been achieved (Zhang *et al.*, 2014). In essence, the aim of the plan is to have 1,000 electric vehicles in operation within three years for each of the ten cities selected every year. Since 2010, incentive schemes to subsidise the purchase of electric cars were also piloted in Shanghai, Hefei, Hangzhou, Shenzhen and Changchun (Zhang *et al.*, 2014). From 2012 to 2015, the Chinese government further introduced policies to support domestic electric car manufacturers, issued an electric vehicle charging infrastructure development guide, and announced a ten-year roadmap for new energy vehicles (An, 2016). The resulting increase the sale of battery electric and plug-in electric vehicles in 2015 by 343 per cent has been most impressive; and the latest target was to reach two million by 2020 (Wang *et al.*, 2017). In comparison, the US government's goal of having one million plug-in electric vehicles on US roads by 2015 was much more modest (Voelcker, 2011). While electric cars do not have tailpipe emissions, various types of pollution can happen at the source of electricity generation. Moreover, it is also argued that the better and better fuel economy standards of the internal combustion engine using fossil fuels may actually make the gains from the transition to electric cars minimal. In particular, China is still highly reliant on coal in its electricity generation. Figure 7.2 shows the current energy mix in China. It can be seen that China's reliance on coal as a source of energy has not actually reduced over time, despite the development of more environmentally friendly and renewable energy sources of hydro power, nuclear power and wind power. As a result, electric cars are not associated with much lower CO_2 emissions per passenger-km than countries whose electricity is largely generated from renewable and environmentally friendly sources, like Norway.

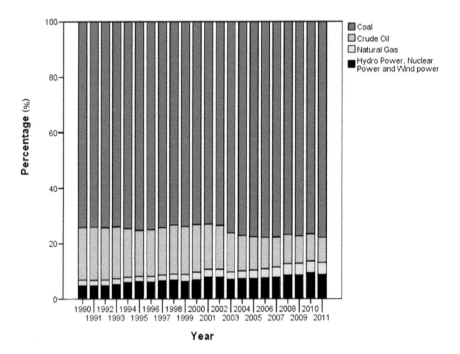

Figure 7.2 Energy mix in China, 1990–2011.

Source: Compiled by the author based on National Bureau of statistics of China (2015).

Nonetheless, the gains can still be substantial. Table 7.1 shows estimations of the CO_2 emissions of different passenger transport modes in China. Table 7.2 shows estimations of CO_2 emissions generated by private cars running on different fuel types in the context of China. (The estimations are made based on a number of assumptions, all of which are listed in the note to the table.) When compared to diesel and gasoline (120–133 g CO_2 per passenger-km), the potential reduction of shifting to electricity is comparable to LPG (115–116 g CO_2 per passenger-km). Hence, the natural gas option may also be further explored in China. Moreover, the reduction of 4–13 g CO_2 per passenger-km by shifting to electricity should not be underestimated as China has over 150 million vehicles (excluding motorcycles) and the passenger turnover is as high as 2,789.4 billion passenger-km in 2014 (see Chapter 3).

Furthermore, the other negative transport externalities associated with the unrestrained use of electric cars need to be carefully monitored and regulated. Along with this sustainable transport option, associated measures that should be actively incorporated include different forms of car-sharing and autonomous vehicles with not only low emissions standards but also high safety features. Car sharing, in particular, has been developing in Paris, France with the Autolib car sharing programme. Around 4,000 electric cars are accessible from 700 pick-up/drop-off

Table 7.1 CO_2 emissions per passenger in China, 2009

Mode	Fuel consumption per passenger-km (g)	CO_2 emissions per passenger-km (g)
Road	Gasoline: 31 Diesel: 6 (only used for highway buses)	71
Highway buses	Gasoline: 6 Diesel: 6	19
Taxis	60 (gasoline)	185
City buses	16 (gasoline)	49
Private car and institutional vehicles	51 (gasoline)	157
Motorcycles	17 (gasoline)	51
Rail	6 (coal) 3 (diesel)	10
Air	28 (jet kerosene)	87
Water	3 (diesel)	10

Sources: Ding *et al.* (2013); He *et al.* (2005); IPCC (2006); Loo and Li (2012); National Bureau of Statistics of China (2011); Ou, Zhang and Chang (2010). Copyright obtained from Elsevier.

Note
It is assumed that the average load for private cars in China is 1.3 (Loo & Li, 2012). The average fuel consumption for diesel, gasoline, LPG and electricity is about 0.4747 km/MJ, 0.4002 km/MJ, 0.4224 km/MJ and 21.1 kWh/100 km, respectively. The CO_2 emissions factor defaults for coal, diesel, gasoline, LPG and crude oil are 96,100, 74,100, 69,300, 63,100 and 73,300 kg/TJ respectively. Standard coal consumption per unit of electricity generation in China is about 340 g/kWh in 2009 and the generation source of electricity is coal (81.33%) and crude oil (1.46%). Coal is equal to 0.7143 tonnes standard coal per tonne and crude oil is 1.4286 tonnes standard coal per tonne.

Table 7.2 CO_2 emissions for private cars fuelled by different energy sources in China, 2009

Fuel type	CO_2 per passenger-km (g)
Diesel	120
Gasoline	133
LPG	115
Electricity	116

Sources: Ding *et al.* (2013); He *et al.* (2005); IPCC (2006); Loo and Li (2012); National Bureau of Statistics of China (2011); Ou, Zhang and Chang (2010).

Note
See Table 7.1.

points in Paris for public use (Spinak, Chiu & Casalegno, 2008). Similar schemes have been rolled out in in Shenzhen, Shanghai and other large cities in China. Other schemes like Uber and Didi can facilitate people using their own cars to provide transport services to other people in a 'car-like' manner without substantially expanding the taxi or public transport fleet. After all, a sustainable transport strategy will only have a chance to succeed if it has 'something for everyone' and is able to build consensus among the community. A similar process has been described by Larsen (2017) in the making of the pro-cycling city.

Walking

It must be emphasised that walking is not considered separately as a sustainable transport mode for selective inclusion in the sustainable transport strategy because it is seen to be fundamental in all cities. Walking, as the most primitive form of mobility for human beings, is also one of the most sustainable forms of transport in the contemporary world. In the last decade or so, issues and challenges related to the promotion of walking in cities have attracted much interest from academics and professionals across different sectors and researchers from different disciplines, including design, ergonomics, public health, transport and urban planning, among others.

While city-scale factors (such as urban form, population and income) may be more relevant in explaining car use, neighbourhood-scale factors (such as road connectivity and urban design) are more relevant in affecting walking behaviour (Naess, 2011; Loo *et al.*, 2017a). It is clear that promoting walking needs to take into account local neighbourhood-scale factors and people perceptions.

In global cities, such as New York City, London, Tokyo, Singapore and Hong Kong, the high density of population, employment and other key facilities offer rare opportunities for short-distance trips to be completed by walking only. These short trips are generally considered to be within a ten-minute walk or approximately 500 metres, though it is recognised that people's willingness to walk actually differs by individual ability, taste, trip purpose, time and various environmental settings (Loo, Chen & Chan, 2010; Quade, Douglas & Cervero, 1996).

Moreover, as public transport, especially the rail transit system, cannot provide point-to-point service, there is often a need to make short-distance connecting trips or transfer trips (that is, the first/last miles) even in a transit society. Transit-oriented development (TOD) refers to a combination of characteristics about the built environment which promotes walking and the use of public transport (Ewing & Cervero, 2010; Jacobson & Forsyth, 2008; Loo & du Verle, 2017; Reconnecting America, 2011; Victoria Transport Policy Institute, 2015).

At the neighbourhood scale, these TOD characteristics range from the road network, parking availability, public transport services, pedestrian and cycling facilities, general land-use patterns, housing types and density, public and private facilities and public space (Loo, 2009). Even with a good public transport system, walking is still crucial in facilitating seamless transport for transfers (whether intermodal or not) and the 'first/last mile' of most trips (Li & Loo, 2016). It is particularly important at the neighbourhood level in promoting people's physical and mental health, and developing a sense of community. According to the Organisation of Economic Co-operation and Development (OECD), social capital refers to the 'networks together with shared norms, values and understandings that facilitate co-operation within and among groups' (OECD, 2001). There is increasingly strong evidence to suggest that walking is beneficial to the formation of social capital in local communities and is good for people's physical and mental health (Loo *et al.*, 2017a, 2017b). Walkability, especially near critical facilities like hospitals (Loo & Lam, 2012) and schools, is particularly important and fundamental. The effects have been demonstrated in the recent work of Loo *et al.* (2017a) on the three Asian cities of Hong Kong, Singapore and Tokyo. To the elderly, encouraging 'walking buddies' is helpful for social capital.

Hence, walking can be considered a key component of mobility in a sustainable city, which balances the environmental, economic and social needs of the present and future generations. In cities, both single-mode walking and multimodal walking involving transfers to other transport modes need to be carefully considered. Walking is seen as the glue that links all the other transport modes together in a multimodal urban transport system. While we are not going to delve into the critical importance of improving walkability in cities, it is sufficient to emphasise walkability as a largely pleasant pedestrian experience. Enhancing 'walkability' is about building a safe, comfortable environment (with amenities) through which pedestrians can travel conveniently to other places and enjoy a pleasant experience. With this people-centred and place-based approach, and the three core principles of safety, comfort and convenience, street connectivity and all relevant design (and non-design) attributes can be identified and incorporated holistically for the ultimate purpose of allowing easy pedestrian access to relevant places and enhancing the pedestrian experience (Loo & Lam, 2012; Loo, 2017a).

Further remarks

The above list is not intended to preclude new sustainable transport modes or services, such as the Hyperloop envisioned to transport people through an electro-magnetic train/pod in a tube under light vacuum at supersonic speed (Decker *et al.*, 2017). Moreover, we see mobility-as-a-service (Mulley, 2017) as an innovative combination of different transport modes rather than a separate sustainable transport 'tool'/mode. Nonetheless, these options are not further examined as the main 'tools' for a large-scale transition of over 100 cities in a developing country to sustainable transport in the next 15 years.

Moreover, it must be emphasised that the relationship between transport and land use has long been recognised as inseparable and mutually reinforcing. In the context of sustainable transport, there is perhaps no better example than the concept of transit-oriented development (TOD), which not only includes a public transit station but also high-to-medium-density population and development, and mixed land use, including the availability of public open spaces. A walkable community centred upon a quality public transport stop. Table 7.3 compares and contrasts the major dimensions of a road network, parking availability, public transport services, pedestrians and cyclists, general land-use pattern, housing types and density, public and private facilities, and public space for a transit-oriented community and an automobile-dependent community (Loo, 2009).

Table 7.3 reveals that this broad definition of TOD includes elements of the smart growth strategy, the location efficient strategy and walkable communities. While these various initiatives have slightly different emphases, they all aim to reduce the automobile dependency of the community and to encourage the

Table 7.3 Characteristics of automobile and transit-oriented development

	Automobile-oriented development	Transit-oriented development
Road network	• Expressway-oriented road system with hierarchical street patterns designed to maximise traffic volume and speed.	• Few expressways. • Highly interconnected streets with traffic calming measures.
Parking availability	• Abundant, easily accessible parking lots at low or no cost.	• Parking management in force. • Limited and multi-storey parking charged at relatively high cost.
Public transport services	• Very poor and/or restricted to paratransit only.	• Very good, in terms of comfort, frequency, reliability and speed.
Pedestrians and cyclists	• Not friendly to pedestrians and cyclists, no pedestrian walkways on some streets.	• Friendly to pedestrians and cyclists with high accessibility to all major attractions. In some circumstances, the multi-exit railway station forms a well-connected and segregated pedestrian walking system.
General land-use pattern	• Segregated and dispersed land-use pattern at the urban fringe, with little in-fill development.	• Dense, compact and a balanced mixed land-use pattern around transit stops, particularly railway stations.
Housing types and density	• Single-lot, single-household detached houses in a spread out manner.	• A variety of affordable housing types with high-rise and mixed residential and commercial buildings near the transit stations acting as the centres of towns or suburban communities. Residential density declines progressively outward.
Public and private facilities	• Major city facilities, such as shopping malls, public services, schools, stadiums and other leisure venues are located at major expressway exits requiring automobile access. • Large-scale single-storey or low-rise retail malls away from the city centre, surrounded by free parking lots.	• The Central Business District remains the main transit hub and the centre of major business, entertainment, government/institutional and retail activities. • Medium-scale retail shops on the lower floors of the commercial and resident buildings near transit stations. • Schools, cafes and neighbourhood stores on the ground level of residential buildings to help create attractive street life.
Public space	• Limited. • Private club facilities, large private yards, and gated communities are common.	• Abundant and well-planned. • Provision of public parks, sports centres, libraries and other public facilities.

Source: Loo (2009).

development of a sustainable urban transport system in the long-run. In particular, the smart growth strategy was first proposed as an alternative to urban sprawl. Hence, the strategy puts emphasis on the smart use of the existing urban areas and the slowing down of the spatial expansion of cities. The location efficient strategy likewise emphasises the possibility of infill development in cities but it also puts much importance on housing affordability. Lastly, walkable communities advocate walking as the primary mode of passenger transport in cities. In addition, it is worth mentioning that there have also been renewed interests in developing paratransit modes in the United States, as they are more flexible and adaptable to the low-density and dispersed suburbanisation process.

In addition, selective policies can include restricting the use of old and low fuel efficiency vehicles to certain parts of the road system only, and to promulgating car-free or low-emissions developments. Based on Loo (2017b), the former typically refers to the banning or severe restriction of the use of private cars within specified boundaries. Depending on the physical size, these areas may be called car-free cities, car-free districts or car-free zones. Nonetheless, public cars, such as police cars, fire engines, ambulances and other service vehicles, and heavy goods vehicles for delivery are not banned (Nieuwenhuijsen & Khreis, 2016). Specific time delivery on designated roads may be allowed. Moreover, car-sharing clubs are a distinctive feature of many car free zones in Europe. These shared cars are not privately-owned; and a limited fleet is permitted and sometimes promoted within or at the periphery of the car-free development to facilitate mobility (Coates, 2013). When further relaxation allows all private cars that meet certain air quality standards to enter the zone, the area may be called a low-emission zone. In all of these cases, the importance of land-use zoning and careful planning to ensure that the needs of residents are satisfied is an essential step for the 'virtuous cycle' of like-minded individuals to choose to live in these car-free developments and making them sustainable. Similarly, ferry-oriented developments – with residents' needs most served by efficient and environmentally friendly ferry services – will need careful planning.

Last but not least, we recognise that transport is not being seen as a service industry or a form of consumption necessary for economic activities to take place. The transport sector is a major economic sector in its own right. Furthermore, innovations of the transport sector, including the applications of e-technologies like intelligent transport systems and the invention of new forms of transport modes, notably high-speed railways, and new forms of vehicles, such as electric vehicles, are becoming major sectors in generating new research and development that drives the national economy as well. The export of Chinese automobiles and railway systems, especially in Africa, has long been happening. More recently, the export of a series of technologies from the train scheduling to station design related to high-speed railways has become increasingly significant in the country (Ho, 2015). Once again, recognising that transport is an economic sector by itself may pose both opportunities and challenges to sustainable transport. The development of electric vehicles can take advantage of venture capital, for example, rather than rely on governments to overcome the barriers to its wider adoption. The success of Tesla in changing consumer preferences towards electric vehicles is notable. On the other hand, this can pose barriers. The existence of the extremely large and economically powerful automobile manufacturing industry in the USA, for example, makes governments think twice before any automobile restraint policy is adopted. The Chinese automobile manufacturing industry is no exception. The fact that it employs so many people, from factories to design and management means that the central government in China has not put reducing automobile ownership and usage as a policy in any of its Five-Year Plans. The fact that the automobile industry is an industry with strong forward and backward linkages means that when it is hard hit, many other related industries – for example rubber tyres, window glass – will be severely affected. The automobile industry in China has been particularly concentrated in northeast China. The decline in automobile sales can trigger major economic crisis in provinces like Liaoning and Jilin. A transformation of the automobile manufacturing industry to produce electric or other alternative fuel vehicles may be more realistic in the next 15 years.

Initial recommendations by the three city clusters

Based on the characteristics of the three city clusters and the sustainable mobility strategies identified, specific matching is suggested below. For each city cluster, one sustainable transport strategy consisting of two major or leading sustainable transport modes, selected from the sustainable transport 'toolbox' above, are introduced in order to spearhead changes and focus local discussion.

Cluster A

Given the relatively small population size, low GDP per capita and weak electricity generation capacity, it may not be viable for cities in Cluster A to choose a metro system as a method to deal with the increasing demand for mobility. Furthermore, it is not realistic to promote the ownership of electric cars due to the relatively low income of the citizens. Facing the increasing population size and the low cost in implementing and operating, BRT can be a sustainable choice that the cities in Cluster A may consider in order to meet the increasing demand for passenger transport. BRT may become the major means of road passenger transport in these cities as people may rely more on public transport due to the low motorisation rate. Its large carrying capacity, lower capital requirement in implementation and operation, compared with metro systems, and short period required for implementation (usually less than two years for Chinese cities) are also salient (Zhou, 2009).

Given that the roads are not yet too full of cars, promoting cycling in order to maintain mobility may be a good choice for the cities in Cluster A with a small population size and low population density. However, the governments must at the same time set up relevant regulations to ensure the safety of cyclists such as constructing more cycling tracks on busy roads with high vehicular flows.

Cluster B

In order to deal with the possible escalation of road fatality and air pollution due to the further increase in motorisation rate, one of the solutions is to promote BRT. Different from the case of cities in Cluster A, cities in Cluster B need, because of their larger population size, to operate more double-deck buses, which have a higher carrying capacity than single-deck buses. The BRT, with more double-deck buses, reduces the demand on private vehicles and thus reduces the possibility of road traffic crashes and the quantity of transport sector CO_2 emissions. Moreover, the population size also provides good support for public transport. It utilises the advantage of sufficiency in road networks in cities in Cluster B, as dedicated lanes are required for buses.

Although metro systems might not be economically viable for the cities in Cluster B, light rail may represent an initial urban rail transport system for them. According to the urban transport hierarchy, light rail is the second most desired transport means in terms of carrying capacity and environmental impact (Figure 7.1). In fact, among the 48 cities in this group, Dalian and Changchun already having light rail in operation. Moreover, the building of light rail may be regarded as preparation for the construction of a metro system, which requires a larger population size and higher income of citizens.

Currently, road crashes pose a serious challenge to cities in Cluster B. In order to reduce road fatalities, raising the safety standard of motor vehicles by using steel that is lighter but stronger in manufacturing is another choice available to cities in Cluster B. While citizens living in these cities have the highest proportion of expenditure on transport and communications, the governments can further support research and development in the area. In particular, road safety can be improved by producing safer public transport vehicles.

Cluster C

To deal with the problem of traffic congestion and pollution resulting from a high degree of motorisation, the government should emphasise more the importance of public transport, especially the metro systems. While all of the nine cities in Cluster C are currently operating metro systems, what the government should think of is how to expand the current railway network, increase the frequency of lines and reduce relevant pollution. The metro system strategy is recommended. The building, expansion and improvement of the metro system in these cities should be more carefully considered. Metro's huge carrying capacity and high accessibility can hopefully relieve the increase in private motor vehicles in cities in Cluster C. The strategy also alleviates the problems of traffic congestion, as well as pollution and traffic crashes. Given that the road area per capita is already very low, the strengthening of the metro system and alleviation of the rapid increase in motor vehicles represent two major directions for cities in the process of mobility transition.

The second strategy is to promote electric cars because cities in Cluster C are wealthier and rising vehicle ownership at the society level is almost inevitable. With the higher cost of electric vehicles, this strategy may not be economically feasible for citizens of cities in the other two clusters at a large scale. This strategy meets the heavy demand on private vehicles while minimising pollution. Considering the higher economic capacity of people and government's large input in scientific research, the promotion of electric cars, hybrid vehicles and an advanced internal combustion engine are viable for cities in Cluster C. At the same time, in order to suppress the increase in diesel or gasoline motor vehicles, the government might introduce the first registration tax for vehicles using diesel or LPG.

Summary

While the above strategies are discussed as being relatively distinct, they are not mutually exclusive. The promotion of cycling, for example, can be implemented in cities of all clusters, especially taking into consideration the geographical diversity within each city. Walking should be encouraged in all cities for short-distance mobility. The walking infrastructure needs to be improved and well-integrated with all of the strategies mentioned.

References

21st Yearly Session of the Conference of the Parties (COP21). (2015). *2015 United Nations Climate Change Conference*. Paris: United Nations Framework Convention on Climate Change.

Allport, R.J. (1990). The metro: Determining its viability. In M.J. Heraty (Ed.), *Developing World Transport* (pp. 64–69). London: Grosvenor Press International.

An, F. (2016). *China's NEV Policies and Market Development*. Presentation at the Industrial Upgrading and Economic Growth in China Conference, Ann Arbor, Michigan, 21 October 2016. Retrieved on 14 July 2017 from https://lsa.umich.edu/content/dam/lrccs-assets/lrccs-documents/Feng%20An%20-%20Notes%20-%202016%20Ross-LRCCS%20Conference.pdf.

An, F., & Sauer, A. (2004). *Comparison of Passenger Vehicle Fuel Economy and Greenhouse Gas Emission Standards around the World*. Pew Center on Global Climate Change. Retrieved 14 July 2017 from www.c2es.org/docUploads/Fuel%20Economy%20and%20GHG%20Standards_010605_110719.pdf.

Anonymous. (2015). *The Chinese Automotive Fuel Economy Policy*. Retrieved 10 January 2016 from www.globalfueleconomy.org/transport/gfei/autotool/case_studies/apacific/china/CHINA%20CASE%20STUDY.pdf.

Anonymous. (2017). *300,000 Tons of Scrapped Metal from Shared Bicycles Equivalent to Five Aircraft Carrier*. Retrieved 14 July 2017 from http://mp.weixin.qq.com/s/5heouOiD5EXvY1GHNhY_GA.

Austroads. (2015). *National Cycling Participation Survey*. Sydney: Austroads.

Bhattacharjee, S., & Goetz, A.R. (2012). Impact of light rail on traffic congestion in Denver. *Journal of Transport Geography*, *22*, 262–270. doi:10.1016/j.jtrangeo.2012.01.008.

Brader, C. (2009). Lagos BRT-Lite: Africa's first bus rapid transit scheme. *Lagos BRT-Lite Summary Evaluation Report*. Lagos: Integrated Transport Planning Ltd and IBIS Transport Consultants Ltd for LAMATA.

Chira-Chavala, T., Coifman, B., Porter, C. & Hansen, M. (1996). Light rail accident involvement and severity. *Transportation Research Record, 1521*, 147–155. doi:10.3141/1521-19.

Coates, G.J. (2013). The sustainable urban district of Vauban in Freiburg, Germany. *International Journal of Design and Nature and Ecodynamics, 8*, 265–286. doi:10. 2495/DNE-V8-N4-265-286.

Decker, K., Chin, J., Peng, A., Summers, C., Nguyen, G., Oberlander, A., ... Falck, R. (2017). *Conceptual Feasibility Study of the Hyperloop Vehicle for Next-Generation Transport* (art. no. AIAA 2017–0221). Paper presented at the AIAA SciTech Forum – 55th AIAA Aerospace Sciences Meeting, Grapevine, TX. Retrieved from https://ntrs. nasa.gov/archive/nasa/casi.ntrs.nasa.gov/20170001624.pdf.

Department of Energy (DOE), United States Government. (2014). *EV Everywhere Grand Challenge: Road to Success*. Retrieved from https://energy.gov/sites/prod/files/2014/02/ f8/eveverywhere_road_to_success.pdf.

Ding, Y., Han, W., Chai, Q., Yang, S. & Shen, W. (2013). Coal-based synthetic natural gas (SNG): A solution to China's energy security and CO_2 reduction? *Energy Policy, 55*, 445–453.

Egbue, O., Long, S. & Samaranayake, V.A. (2017). Mass deployment of sustainable transportation: Evaluation of factors that influence electric vehicle adoption. *Clean Technologies and Environmental Policy*. Advance online publication. doi:10.1007/ s10098-017-1375-4.

Ewing, R., & Cervero, R. (2010). Travel and the built environment. *Journal of the American Planning Association, 76*, 265–294. doi:10.1080/01944361003766766.

Farmer, S. (2011). Uneven public transportation development in neoliberalising Chicago, USA. *Environment and Planning A, 43*, 1154–1172. doi:10.1068/a43409.

Ferbrache, F., & Knowles, R.D. (2016). Guest editorial: Generating opportunities for city sustainability through investments in light rail systems: Introduction to the special section on light rail and urban sustainability. *Journal of Transport Geography, 54*, 369–372. doi:10.1016/j.jtrangeo.2016.06.004.

Fishman, E. (2016a). Cycling as transport. *Transport Reviews, 36*, 1–8. doi:10.1080/0144 1647.2015.1114271.

Fishman, E. (2016b). Bikeshare: A review of recent literature. *Transport Reviews, 36*, 92–113. doi:10.1080/01441647.2015.1033036.

Fishman, E., & Cherry, C. (2016). E-bikes in the mainstream: Reviewing a decade of research. *Transport Reviews, 36*, 72–91. doi:10.1080/01441647.2015.1069907.

Flyvbjerg, B., Bruzelius, N. & van Wee, B. (2008). Comparison of capital costs per route-kilometre in urban rail. *European Journal of Transport and Infrastructure Research, 8*, 17–30. Retrieved from https://d1rkab7tlqy5f1.cloudfront.net/TBM/Over%20faculteit/ Afdelingen/Engineering%20Systems%20and%20Services/EJTIR/Back%20issues/ 8.1/2008_01_02%20Comparison%20of%20capital%20costs%20per.pdf.

Fouracre, P., Dunkerley, C. & Gardner, G. (2003). Mass rapid transit systems for cities in the developing world. *Transport Reviews, 23*, 299–310. doi:10.1080/0144164032000083095.

Fyhri, A., Heinen, E., Fearnley, N. & Sundfør, H.B. (2017). A push to cycling: Exploring the e-bike's role in overcoming barriers to bicycle use with a survey and an intervention study. *International Journal of Sustainable Transportation, 11*, 681–695. doi:10.1 080/15568318.2017.1302526.

Goetz, A. (2013). Suburban sprawl or urban centres: Tensions and contradictions of smart growth approaches in Denver, Colorado. *Urban Studies*, *50*, 2178–2195. doi:10.1177/0042098013478238.

He, K., Huo, H., Zhang, Q., He, D., An, F., Wang, M. & Walsh, M.P. (2005). Oil consumption and CO_2 emissions in China's road transport: Current status, future trends, and policy implication. *Energy Policy*, *33*(12), 1499–1507.

Hidalgo, D., & Carrigan, A. (2010). *Modernising Public Transportation: Lessons Learned from Major Bus Improvements in Latin America and Asia*. Washington, D.C.: World Resources Institute. Retrieved from http://pdf.wri.org/modernizing_public_transportation.pdf.

Ho, T.K. (2015). Exporting railway technologies. In B.P.Y. Loo & C. Comtois (Eds.), *Sustainable Railway Futures: Issues and Challenges* (pp. 185–200). Surrey: Ashgate.

Intergovernmental Panel on Climate Change (IPCC). (2006). Volume 2 Energy. 2006 IPCC Guidelines for National Greenhouse Gas Inventories. Retrieved from www.ipcc-nggip.iges.or.jp/public/2006gl/vol2.html.

Jacobson, J., & Forsyth, A. (2008). Seven American TODs: Good practices for urban design in transit-oriented development projects. *Journal of Transport and Land Use*, *1*(2), 51–88. doi:10.5198/jtlu.v1i2.67.

James, B., Burke, M. & Yen, B.T.H. (2017). A critical appraisal of individualised marketing and travel blending interventions in Queensland and Western Australia from 1986–2011. *Travel Behaviour and Society*, *8*, 1–13. doi:10.1016/j.tbs.2017.03.002.

Jarzab, J.T., Lightbody, J. & Maeda, M. (2002). Characteristics of bus rapid transit projects: An overview. *Journal of Public Transportation*, *5*(2), 31–46. Retrieved from http://scholarcommons.usf.edu/cgi/viewcontent.cgi?article=1362&context=jpt.

Kolos, A., & Taczanowski, J. (2016). The feasibility of introducing light rail systems in medium-sized towns in Central Europe. *Journal of Transport Geography*, *54*, 400–413. doi:10.1016/j.jtrangeo.2016.02.006.

Larsen, J. (2017). The making of a pro-cycling city: Social practices and bicycle mobilities. *Environment and Planning A*, *49*, 876–892. doi:10.1177/0308518X16682732.

Levinson, H.S., Zimmerman, S., Clinger, J. & Rutherford, S.C. (2002). Bus rapid transit: An overview. *Journal of Public Transportation*, *5*(2), 1–30. Retrieved from http://scholarcommons.usf.edu/cgi/viewcontent.cgi?article=1361&context=jpt.

Levinson, H.S., Zimmerman, S., Clinger, J., & Gast, J. (2003). Bus rapid transit: Synthesis of case studies. *Transportation Research Record*, *1841*, 1–11. doi:10.3141/1841-01.

Li, L., & Loo, B.P.Y. (2016). Towards people-centered integrated transport: A case study of Shanghai Hongqiao Comprehensive Transport Hub. *Cities*, *58*, 50–58. doi:10.1016/j.cities.2016.05.003.

Li, W., Long, R. & Chen, H. (2016). Consumers' evaluation of national new energy vehicle policy in China: An analysis based on a four paradigm model. *Energy Policy*, *99*, 33–41. doi:10.1016/j.enpol.2016.09.050.

Loo, B.P.Y. (2009). Transport, urban. In R. Kitchin & N. Thrift (Eds.), *The International Encyclopaedia of Human Geography* (Volume 1, pp. 465–469). doi:10.1016/B978–008044910-4.01039-7.

Loo, B.P.Y. (2017a). *Final Report: Consultancy Services on Walkability in Pedestrian Planning and Enhancement of Pedestrian Network in Hong Kong* (PLB(Q)016/2015). Hong Kong: Institute of Transport Studies, The University of Hong Kong.

Loo, B.P.Y. (2017b). Realising car-free developments within compact cities. *Proceedings of the Institution of Civil Engineer – Municipal Engineer*. Advance online publication. doi:10.1680/jmuen.16.00060.

Loo, B.P.Y., & Cheng, A.C.H. (2010). Are there useful yardsticks of population size and income level for building metro systems? Some worldwide evidence. *Cities, 27,* 299–306. doi:10.1016/j.cities.2010.02.003.

Loo, B.P.Y., & Chow, A.S.Y. (2009). The relevance of transport-development strategies to understanding travel behaviour and transport sustainability in Hong Kong. *Asian Geographer, 26,* 67–82. doi:10.1080/10225706.2009.9684144.

Loo, B.P.Y., & du Verle, F. (2017). Transit-oriented development in future cities: Towards a two-level sustainable mobility strategy. *International Journal of Urban Sciences, 21*(Suppl. 1), 54–67. doi:10.1080/12265934.2016.1235488.

Loo, B.P.Y., & Lam, W.W.Y. (2012). Geographic accessibility around elderly health care facilities in Hong Kong: A micro-scale walkability assessment. *Environment and Planning B: Planning and Design, 39,* 629–646. doi:10.1068/b36146.

Loo, B.P.Y., & Li, D.Y.N. (2006). Developing metro systems in the People's Republic of China: Policy and gaps. *Transportation, 33,* 115–132. doi:10.1007/s11116-005-3046-2.

Loo, B.P.Y., & Li, L. (2012). Carbon dioxide emissions from passenger transport in China since 1949: Implications for developing sustainable transport. *Energy Policy, 50,* 464–476. doi:10.1016/j.enpol.2012.07.044.

Loo, B.P.Y., & Tsui, K.L. (2010). Bicycle crash casualties in a highly motorised city. *Accident Analysis and Prevention, 42,* 1902–1907. doi:10.1016/j.aap. 2010.05.011.

Loo, B.P.Y., Chen, C. & Chan, E.T.H. (2010). Rail-based transit-oriented development: Lessons from New York City and Hong Kong. *Landscape and Urban Planning, 97,* 202–212. doi:10.1016/j.landurbplan.2010.06.002.

Loo, B.P.Y., Cheng, A.H.T. & Nichols, S.L. (2017). Transit-oriented development on greenfield versus infill sites: Some lessons from Hong Kong. *Landscape and Urban Planning, 167,* 37–48. doi:10.1016/j.landurbplan.2017.05.013.

Loo, B.P.Y., Lam, W.W.Y., Mehandran, R. & Katagiri, K. (2017a). How is the neighborhood environment related to the health of seniors living in Hong Kong, Singapore, and Tokyo? Some insights for promoting aging in place. *Annals of the Association of American Geographers, 107,* 812–828. doi:10.1080/24694452.2016.1271306.

Loo, B.P.Y., Mehandran, R., Katagiri, K. & Lam, W.W.Y. (2017b). Walking, neighbourhood environment and quality of life among older people. *Current Opinion in Environmental Sustainability, 25,* 8–13. doi:10.1016/j.cosust.2017.02.005.

MacNeill, R.A., Kirkpatrick, S.W., Bocchieri, R.T. & Gough, G. (2015). *Development of a Prototype Retrofit Bumper for Improved Light Rail Vehicle Safety.* Paper presented at the 2015 Joint Rail Conference, JRC 2015, San Jose, CA. doi:10.1115/JRC2015-5810.

Massiani, J. (2015). Cost-benefit analysis of policies for the development of electric vehicles in Germany: Methods and results. *Transport Policy, 38,* 19–26. doi:10.1016/j.tranpol.2014.10.005.

Melton, N., Axsen, J. & Goldberg, S. (2017). Evaluating plug-in electric vehicle policies in the context of long-term greenhouse gas reduction goals: Comparing 10 Canadian provinces using the 'PEV policy report card'. *Energy Policy, 107,* 381–393. doi:10.1016/j.enpol.2017.04.052.

Metrobits.org. (2017). *Countries.* Retrieved from http://mic-ro.com/metro/selection.html.

MTR Corporation (MTRC). (2016). Historic patronage figures, 2015. *Patronage Updates.* Retrieved from www.mtr.com.hk/en/corporate/investor/patronage.php#search.

Mulley, C. (2017). Mobility as a Services (MaaS): Does it have critical mass? *Transport Reviews, 37,* 247–251. doi:10.1080/01441647.2017.1280932.

Naess, P. (2011). New urbanism or metropolitan-level centralisation? *Journal of Transport and Land Use*, *4*(1), 25–44. Retrieved from www.jtlu.org/index.php/jtlu/article/download/170/160.

National Bureau of Statistics of China. (2011). Energy. *China Statistical Yearbook 2011*. Retrieved from www.stats.gov.cn/tjsj/ndsj/2011/indexeh.htm.

National Bureau of Statistics of China. (2015). Energy. *China Statistical Yearbook 2015*. Retrieved from www.stats.gov.cn/tjsj/ndsj/2015/indexeh.htm.

Neaimeh, M., Salisbury, S.D., Hill, G.A., Blythe, P.T., Scoffield, D.R. & Francfort, J.E. (2017). Analysing the usage and evidencing the importance of fast chargers for the adoption of battery electric vehicles. *Energy Policy*, *108*, 474–486. doi:10.1016/j.enpol.2017.06.033.

Nieuwenhuijsen, M.J., & Khreis, H. (2016). Car free cities: Pathway to healthy urban living. *Environmental International*, *94*, 251–262. doi:10.1016/j.envint.2016.05.032.

Nikitas, A., & Karlsson, M. (2015). A worldwide state-of-the-art analysis for bus rapid transit: Looking for the success formula. *Journal of Public Transportation*, *18*(1), 1–33. Retrieved from http://scholarcommons.usf.edu/cgi/viewcontent.cgi?article=1023 &context=jpt.

OECD. (2001). *The Well-Being of Nations: The Role of Human and Social Capital*. Paris: OECD.

Olesen, M. (2014). Framing light rail projects: Case studies from Bergen, Angers and Bern. *Case Studies on Transport Policy*, *2*, 10–19. doi:10.1016/j.cstp.2013.12.002.

Olesen, M., & Lassen, C. (2016). Rationalities and materialities of light rail scapes. *Journal of Transport Geography*, *54*, 373–382. doi:10.1016/j.jtrangeo.2016.04.005.

Ou, X.M., Zhang, X.L. & Chang, S.Y. (2010). Alternative fuel buses currently in use in China: Life-cycle fossil energy use, GHG emissions and policy recommendations. *Energy Policy*, *38*, 406–418.

Popovich, N., Gordon, E., Shao, Z., Xing, Y., Wang, Y. & Handy, S. (2014). Experiences of electric bicycle users in the Sacramento, California area. *Travel Behaviour and Society*, *2*, 37–44. doi:10.1016/j.tbs.2013.10.006.

Porter, C.D., Hansen, M.M. & Gallardo, A. (1995). Cost of light rail collision accidents. *Transportation Research Record*, *1503*, 137–145. Retrieved from http://onlinepubs.trb.org/Onlinepubs/trr/1995/1503/1503-18.pdf.

Pucher, J., Dill, J. & Handy, S. (2010). Infrastructure, programs, and policies to increase bicycling: An international review. *Preventive Medicine*, *50*(Suppl.), S106–S125. doi:10.1016/j.ypmed.2009.07.028.

Quade, P., Douglas, L. & Cervero, R. (1996). *TCRP Report 16: Transit and Urban Form*. Washington, D.C.: Transportation Research Board, National Research Council.

Ransom, M.R., & Kelemen, T. (2016). The impact of light rail on congestion in Denver: A reappraisal. *Journal of Transport Geography*, *54*, 214–217. doi:10.1016/j.jtrangeo. 2016.06.009.

Reconnecting America. (2011). *2010 Inventory of TOD Programs*. Washington, D.C.: Reconnecting America.

Salon, D., Wu, J. & Shewmake, S. (2014). Impact of bus rapid transit and metro rail on property values in Guangzhou, China. *Transportation Research Record*, *2452*, 36–45. doi:10.3141/2452-05.

Sari, F. (2015). Public transit and labor market outcomes: Analysis of the connections in the French agglomeration of Bordeaux. *Transportation Research Part A: Policy and Practice*, *78*, 231–251. doi:10.1016/j.tra.2015.04.015.

Shao, Z., Gordon, E., Xing, Y., Wang, Y., Handy, S. & Sperling, D. (2012). *Can Electric 2-Wheelers Play a Substantial Role in Reducing CO2 Emissions?* (UCD-ITS-RR-12–04). Davis, CA: Institute of Transportation Studies, University of California, Davis.

Spinak, A., Chiu, D. & Casalegno, F. (2008). *Autolib' (Paris): Sustainability Innovation Inventory.* Retrieved 14 July 2017 from http://mobile.mit.edu/proj/connected-urban-development/files/cisco/autolib.pdf.

Victoria Transport Policy Institute. (2015). *Online TDM Encyclopedia.* Retrieved from www.vtpi.org/tdm.

Voelcker, J. (2011). One million plug-in cars by 2015? *IEEE Spectrum, 48*(4), 11–13. doi:10.1109/MSPEC.2011.5738384.

Walmsley, D.A. (1992). *Light Rail Accidents in Europe and North America* (TRL Report 335). Berkshire: Transport Research Laboratory.

Wang, Y., Sperling, D., Tal, G. & Fang, H. (2017). China's electric car surge. *Energy Policy, 102*, 486–490. doi:10.1016/j.enpol.2016.12.034.

Weinert, J., Ma, C., Yang, X. & Cherry, C. (2008). Electric two-wheelers in China: Effect on travel behavior, mode shift, and user safety perceptions in a medium-sized city. *Transportation Research Record, 2038*, 62–68. doi:10.3141/2038-08.

Wirasinghe, S.C., Kattan, L., Rahman, M.M., Hubbell, J., Thilakaratne, R. & Anowar, S. (2013). Bus rapid transit: A review. *International Journal of Urban Sciences, 17*, 1–31. doi:10.1080/12265934.2013.777514.

Xu, T., Zhang, M. & Aditjandra, P.T. (2016). The impact of urban rail transit on commercial property value: New evidence from Wuhan, China. *Transportation Research Part A: Policy and Practice, 91*, 223–235. doi:10.1016/j.tra.2016.06.026.

Yang, X., Jin, W., Jiang, H., Xie, Q., Shen, W. & Han, W. (2017). Car ownership policies in China: Preferences of residents and influence on the choice of electric cars. *Transport Policy, 58*, 62–71. doi:10.1016/j.tranpol.2017.04.010.

Yao, L., & Wu, C. (2012). Traffic safety for electric bike riders in China. *Transportation Research Record, 2314*, 49–56. doi:10.3141/2314-07.

Yao, S., & Loo, B.P.Y. (2016). Safety in numbers for cyclists beyond national-level and city-level data: A study on the non-linearity of risk within the city of Hong Kong. *Injury Prevention, 22*, 379–385. doi:10.1136/injuryprev-2016-041964.

Zhang, X., Rao, R., Xie, J. & Liang, Y. (2014). The current dilemma and future path of China's electric vehicles. *Sustainability, 6*, 1567–1593. doi:10.3390/su6031567.

Zhou, H.M. (2009). *Sustainable Transportation* (in Chinese). Wuhan: Wuhan Li Gong Da Xue Chu Ban She.

8   Incorporating the local context and modified sustainable transport strategies

The case study approach

While the initial sustainable transport strategies for the three different city clusters discussed in the previous chapter (Chapter 7) are helpful in eliminating highly irrelevant measures, such as the construction of expensive metro systems in cities with low income and population levels, the success of any sustainable transport strategy depends critically on a good understanding of the local contexts. Under market socialism, the importance of local government policies and existing travel patterns of local residents in specific cities will matter a lot. All in all, city governments always play a critical role in the development of transport systems by setting goals, formulating policies and supervising the implementation process. Hence, it is of vital importance to have a look into the governments' proposed policies in sustainable transport.

In order to have a better understanding of the local context of the three city clusters, Maoming, Changsha and Beijing were selected as case studies of Clusters A, B and C respectively. Table 8.1 summarises the major characteristics of the ten mobility drivers in these three case study cities. Since the aim is to recommend appropriate sustainable transport measures for the three city clusters, it is more appropriate that some local data be collected via fieldwork. Since the cities within the same city cluster face similar challenges in urban transport, information collected from fieldwork in the three cities and follow-up analysis may also apply to other members of the clusters.

Each fieldtrip was divided into a questionnaire survey and an observational survey. First, we conducted interviews with government officials from transport-related departments to get a better idea about the government's attitudes towards the suggested initial sustainable transport strategies for the city cluster, and other priorities or plans of the governments. Relevant local transport policies and strategies available were identified and studied before the fieldwork. The structured questionnaires were filled out in the form of personal face-to-face interviews. These questionnaires are shown in Appendices I to III. Each interview lasted around 45 to 60 minutes. Then, specific observational surveys were designed to gather more primary data regarding the development potential of the initial sustainable transport strategies. The locations of the observational surveys and the

Table 8.1 Characteristics of the case study cities by the ten mobility drivers, 2010

		Maoming (Guangdong)	Changsha (Hunan)	Beijing
Basic information	Area of municipality (km²)	11,458	11,819	16,801
	Population (thousand)	1,004	3,212	15,000
	Population density (people/km²)	1,148.74	3,349.32	1,230.82
	GDP (billion RMB)	46.62	290.07	1,170.71
	GDP per capita (RMB)	46,431	90,309	78,047
Motorisation	Total motor vehicles (10,000)	16.40	65.52	452.90
	Vehicles per thousand population	28.15	93.05	230.93
	Vehicles per km of road	10.51	42.80	214.50
Transport volume	Total freight volume (10,000 tonnes)	5,016	22,817	21,885
	Total passenger volume (10,000)	6,962	33,984	140,663
Sufficiency of road network	Road area per capita (m²)	4.85	11.26	6.26
Popularity of bus service	Number of bus passengers (10,000)	1,500	72,222	505,144
Electricity generation capacity	Total electricity consumption (10,000 kwh)	398,718	943,789	7,909,810
Availability of government support	Total government expenditure (RMB10,000)	487,471	2,815,100	26,119,405
	Proportion of expenditure on scientific research (%)	0.47	3.84	6.80
Citizens' willingness to pay for transportation	Proportion of citizens' consumption expenditure on transportation and communication (%)	10.53	16.54	17.30
Road safety	Road fatalities	266	239	974
	Road fatalities per million population	45.66	33.94	49.66
	Road fatalities per 10,000 vehicles	16.22	3.65	2.15

Source: Compiled by the author.

tailor-made survey field sheets were specially designed with regards to the readiness of the cities for the proposed strategies. More details are given below.

Maoming in Cluster A

Maoming is a city located in Guangdong province, south China. The area of the municipality is about 11,458 square kilometres. Its population has reached one million and the GDP was RMB46.62 billion in 2010. In other words, the population density and GDP per capita were at about 1,150 people per square kilometres and RMB46,000 per capita. These figures suggest that the city was the smallest in terms of population size and economic power when compared to the case studies of the other two city clusters. Maoming generally also has a lower level of motorisation with about 28 vehicles per thousand population and ten vehicles per kilometre of road. Nonetheless, its traffic fatalities were much higher than the other two case studies with about 46 road deaths per million population and 16 road deaths per 10,000 vehicles. Bus services and the road network remained rather undeveloped with only about 15 million bus passengers and less than five square metres of road area per capita. The city's total freight and passenger volumes were also rather low at about 50 million tonnes and 70 million passengers. The share of citizens' consumption expenditure on transport and communication was already over 10 per cent (10.53 per cent) by 2010, which was not much lower than the other two case study cities – 16.54 per cent and 17.30 per cent in Changsha and Beijing respectively. Last but not least, the electricity generation capacity was weak, and local government financial capability was also poor to support large-scale transport infrastructural projects or provide transport subsidies either to public transport companies or to the group of transport-disadvantaged citizens, such as the unemployed or the elderly, directly.

Local policies, decision-making and funding

According to the planning of Maoming's municipal government for the period 2012–2030, the goals of developing the transport system can be categorised into three aspects: inter-regional, regional and urban transport (Maoming Urban and Rural Planning Bureau & Maoming Transportation Bureau, 2013). For inter-regional transport, the goal is to develop Maoming as a major transport hub in western Guangdong. For regional transport, the goal is to reduce the travel time between Maoming and its surrounding counties and that the journeys should be within 30 minutes (the 'Thirty-minute Transport Circle'). For urban transport, the goals are to increase the proportion of public transport, enhance the efficiency of freight transport and develop a green transport system.

The Maoming government has three core philosophies regarding the development of its transport system, that is, to evolve the city into a transport hub, to expand transport capacity and to enhance transport quality. Based on these three core philosophies, the government developed 11 relevant strategies as shown in Table 8.2. The strategies evolve around developing into a regional hub for

Table 8.2 Maoming government's 11 transport development strategies up to 2030

1 Increasing the capacity of the port in handling freight
2 Becoming a regional hub for railway freight transport
3 Cooperating with Zhanjiang to build the new Guangdong International Airport
4 Increasing the coverage of the road network and better links for the urban area with other regions
5 Better coordinating the transition of passenger and freight transport
6 Enhancing the performance of the backbone road network such as separating passenger transport and freight transport
7 Focusing on the development of medium and large-scale public transport (introducing BRT and water bus service)
8 Upgrading the performance of buses through a more extensive route and more frequent service
9 Promoting 'Slow Transport' (walking and cycling) and enhancing their linkage with public transport
10 Improving parking facilities
11 Improving the efficiency of traffic management and regulation through the introduction of an Intelligent Transport System

Source: Compiled by the author.

railway freight transport, focusing on the development of medium- and large-scale public transport networks, improving parking facilities and improving the efficiency of traffic management.

In accordance with the above, a total of 80 projects have been proposed and the total estimated budget was around RMB80 billion. Some of the major projects include the Maoming-Zhanjiang Railway (Maoming Section), the Baotou-Maoming Expressway (Guangdong Section), the Maoming Public Transport Priority Project and nine Rapid Transit Routes.

Fieldwork findings

Cycling and BRT have been recommended for cities in Cluster A. The questionnaire was designed to understand more about the government's attitude and proposed policies vis-à-vis these two sustainable mobility strategies. The questionnaire used in Maoming is shown in Appendix 1. An interview with an official from the Maoming Traffic Management Bureau was conducted to accurately reflect the Maoming government's attitudes, philosophy and proposed policies towards developing sustainable mobility. The Bureau is in charge of formulating, implementing and supervising transport-related policies in the city.

The observational survey focused on the conditions and usage of cycling tracks and the popularity of cycling. Three major cycling tracks in Maoming

– Youcheng Road, Shuangshan Road and Wenming Road – were selected for the observation because they were proposed by the government as key areas for the enhancement of cycling-related facilities and would be part of the urban cycling network. Three major areas are observed. First, we observed the conditions of the cycle tracks to see whether they have the signs to indicate they are cycling tracks, signs of prohibiting other vehicles, and facilities preventing other vehicles from entering the tracks.

Second, a 30-minute observation was conducted to count the number of bicycles, e-bikes, motorcycles and cars passing through the observation points. The aim was to capture the utilisation rate of the bicycle tracks and to ascertain the potential for bicycles to play a bigger role in the city's transport system. However, it was also recognised that the unlawful use of bicycle tracks by motorcycles and private cars could severely jeopardise the attractiveness, if not safety, of using bicycles by the general public. Hence, these data were also collected.

Third, the bikes and e-bikes were further sub-divided into four groups: cyclists only, cyclists with passengers, cyclists with goods and cyclists with both passengers and goods. The intention was to understand the type and preferences (revealed preferences) of cyclists in the city using the existing cycle tracks.

Modified sustainable transport strategy

In this section, the initial sustainable transport strategy is modified based on the local context of the case study area. In particular, it is important to see whether the proposed strategies are in line with the local government's vision and directions for change (as revealed by the policy documents and questionnaire surveys), and the everyday life of local people (as captured by various observational surveys).

BRT

While BRT was the development direction for Maoming's bus service, the existing coverage and frequency of bus services are not mature enough to support the introduction of BRT. Before implementing BRT, the government would have to enhance the popularity and efficiency of bus services, which are currently underdeveloped.

There are two major challenges in developing BRT in Maoming. First, bus services faced fierce competition from other passenger modes. In particular, the cost of using motorcycles and private cars has been decreasing due to domestic automobile production. The number of motorcycles and private cars has been increasing rapidly and illegal parking was common. Second, due to the limited road resources in Maoming, it would be difficult to build or dedicate an exclusive lane for BRT.

If BRT can be successfully and efficiently implemented, the government expects that many benefits, including reducing people's reliance on private transport, increasing passenger transport efficiency, reducing transport sector CO_2 emissions, enhancing road safety and alleviating traffic congestion, could be realised. However, the difficulties mentioned above in developing BRT are still big obstacles for the government. In particular, the prevalence of motorcycle taxis in the city is expected to be a major obstacle for the large-scale introduction of BRT to replace this informal transport sector (Wu & Loo, 2016). While motorcycle taxi drivers were more likely to speed late at night or early in the morning, to allow passengers not to wear helmets, and to run a red light than non-occupational motorcyclists, replacing this informal transport sector in Maoming, as for many other informal transport modes in developing countries, would be difficult as a large number of stakeholders earn a living by offering such services on the one hand, and many people, especially low-income and disadvantaged groups, are highly reliant on their affordable and flexible services on the other (Guillen, Ishida & Okamoto, 2013).

Cycling

Although Maoming has cycle tracks along major roads, bicycles and e-bicycles are not popular. The use of cycle tracks by other vehicles, notably motorcycles and cars, is quite common. Figure 8.1 shows a typical situation. Table 8.3 shows the summary results of the observational survey on the three cycle tracks in

Figure 8.1 Cycle tracks used by other vehicles.
Source: The author.

Table 8.3 Summary of observational survey on three cycle tracks in Maoming, June 2013

	Shuangshan Road	Youcheng Road	Wenming Road	Average
Sign of cycle track	Yes	Yes	Yes	
Sign of prohibiting other vehicles	No	No	No	
Facilities preventing other vehicles from entering	No	Yes	No	
30-mins observation Starting time	21/06/2013, 3:30 p.m.	21/06/2013, 4:30 p.m.	21/06/2013, 5:30 p.m.	
Number of bikes (%)	65 (16.88)	76 (41.53)	212 (40.3)	117.67 (32.27)
Number of bikes with motor (%)	18 (4.68)	22 (12.02)	32 (6.08)	24 (6.58)
Number of motorcycles (%)	263 (68.31)	85 (46.45)	249 (47.34)	199 (54.57)
Number of cars (%)	39 (10.13)	0 (0)	33 (6.27)	24 (6.58)
Total	385	183	526	364.67

Source: The author.

Maoming. Table 8.4 further categorises the variables into 'cyclist only', 'cyclist with passenger(s)', 'cyclist with goods' and 'cyclist with both passenger(s) and goods'. Four problems are clear.

A THE LACK OF SIGNS AND FACILITIES PROHIBITING MOTORCYCLES AND CARS FROM ENTERING CYCLE TRACKS

With reference to Table 8.3, only one of the three surveyed cycle tracks has facilities preventing vehicles other than bicycles from entering and none of them has signs prohibiting other vehicles from using the cycle tracks. On Youcheng Road, iron pillars were in place at the entrance. Hence, no entry of cars was recorded. This demonstrates the necessity of building similar facilities on other cycle tracks to prevent their improper use. Since the iron pillars cannot prevent motorcycles from entering the cycle tracks, the government has to consider other solutions like strengthening the enforcement on cycle tracks and increasing fines for other vehicles using cycle tracks.

B THE FREQUENT USE OF CYCLE TRACKS BY MOTORCYCLES

Table 8.4 also shows that it is common for motorcycles to use cycle tracks in Maoming. Taking the average of the three cycle tracks, around 55 per cent of the recorded vehicles passing through the observation points were motorcycles while

Table 8.4 Characteristics of cyclists and motorcyclists on three cycle tracks in Maoming

		Shuangshan Road	Youcheng Road	Wenming Road	Average
Bikes	Cyclist only (%)	29 (44.62)	39 (51.32)	98 (46.23)	55.33 (47.02)
	With passengers (%)	8 (12.31)	11 (14.47)	27 (12.74)	15.33 (13.03)
	With goods (%)	23 (35.38)	18 (23.68)	54 (25.47)	31.67 (26.91)
	Passengers + goods (%)	5 (7.69)	8 (10.53)	33 (15.57)	15.33 (13.03)
	Total	65	76	212	117.67
Bikes with motor	Cyclist only (%)	7 (38.89)	7 (31.82)	15 (46.87)	9.67 (40.29)
	With passengers (%)	3 (16.67)	6 (27.27)	6 (18.75)	5 (20.83)
	With goods (%)	7 (38.89)	4 (18.18)	8 (25.00)	6.33 (26.38)
	Passengers + goods (%)	1 (5.56)	5 (22.73)	3 (9.38)	3 (12.50)
	Total	18	22	32	24
Motorcycles	Motorcyclist only (%)	175 (66.54)	38 (44.71)	129 (51.81)	114 (57.29)
	With passengers (%)	41 (15.59)	21 (24.71)	48 (19.28)	36.67 (18.43)
	With goods (%)	29 (11.03)	12 (14.12)	43 (17.27)	28 (14.07)
	Passengers + goods (%)	18 (6.84)	14 (16.47)	29 (11.65)	20.33 (10.22)
	Total	263	85	249	199

Source: The author.

only around 39 per cent were bicycles or e-bicycles. The data are consistent with the views collected at the questionnaire survey. The presence of faster-moving motorcycles and even cars on the cycle tracks would severely restrict the room for the further development of cycling in Maoming.

C THE MIX OF BICYCLES AND E-BICYCLES

While bicycles on average accounted for 32.27 per cent of the traffic volume, e-bicycles already accounted for 6.58 per cent. In this regard, the government should set up clear regulations to define the maximum speed that an e-bicycle can operate on cycle tracks in order to safeguard other users. Alternatively, the government may consider prohibiting e-bicycles with a power higher than a certain legal limit from using cycle tracks.

D THE HIGH FREQUENCY OF BICYCLES WITH PASSENGERS AND GOODS

Table 8.4 shows that more than half of the recorded bicycles and e-bicycles carried passengers and/or goods. This can be dangerous to the users of the cycle tracks as traffic accidents may be more likely to happen. Apart from restricting the number of motorcycles, the Maoming government should put more effort into ensuring that cyclists are aware of cycling safety and to avoid carrying heavy loads.

If the government would like to develop cycling on a large scale, it must enhance the popularity of cycling first, and must strictly prohibit the use of cycle tracks by motorcycles and cars. Even though the government has been providing bicycle-renting services to the public, we found that the bicycles on rent were mainly used by tourists.

The development of cycling as the major sustainable transport mode in the city was facing three major challenges. First, the number of existing cycling tracks was not adequate to cover most of the major roads and indeed some of them have even been re-converted to motorways in the past decade so as to cope with the rising number of motorcycles and private cars in the city. Second, there are inadequate parking facilities for bicycles and therefore many of them were found to be parked on pavements in Maoming. Lastly, the attractiveness of owning a bicycle or e-bicycle was low because the cost of riding motorcycles and private cars was getting lower. During our fieldwork and further research work, it seems that the motorcycle has already become a major mode of transport in Maoming. As described in Wu and Loo (2016), about 85.3 per cent of all registered motor vehicles in Maoming were motorcycles and this amounted to roughly 1.14 million registered motorcycles by the end of 2012 (Statistics Bureau of Maoming, 2013b). In the same year, the number of motorcycles per hundred families in Maoming was more than five times higher than the national average (110.00 vs. 20.27) (National Bureau of Statistics of China, 2014; Statistics Bureau of Maoming, 2013a). Figure 8.2 provides a snapshot of the abundance of motorcycles in the city taken in June, 2013. Motorcycle taxis have also become an informal urban sector that any attempt to control and regulate would

Figure 8.2 Popularity of motorcycles in Maoming.
Source: The author.

have to be conducted in a sensitive manner to avoid radical reactions from stake-holders (Wu & Loo, 2016).

While promoting cycling on a large scale can enhance people's environmental awareness and reduce traffic sector CO_2 emissions, it is unlikely to have an impact on people's reliance on motor vehicles and alleviate traffic congestion because the travelling distance of bicycles is limited, and people in Maoming today still treat cycling as an exercise more than a mode of transport.

Summary

Maoming's transport system was facing three major difficulties. First, the bus services were underdeveloped and the routes only covered parts of the urban area with low frequency. A major reason behind the poor bus services was insufficient funding from the government. Second, the number of motorcycles was overwhelming, resulting in around 90 per cent of the road fatalities for motorcycles (Wu & Loo, 2016). Third, parking spaces for cars and motorcycles were inadequate and illegal parking was common. One possible method to solve all three problems is to restrict the use of motorcycles. Once the number of motorcycles is under control, bus services will attract more passengers and the burden on parking spaces will be alleviated.

Changsha in Cluster B

Changsha is the capital city of Hunan province in central China. The area of the municipality is about 11,819 square kilometres, which is similar to Maoming. Nonetheless, its population size was much higher at about three million (nearly three times that of Maoming) and the GDP over RMB290 billion (over six times that of Maoming) in 2010. Hence, Changsha's population density and GDP per capita were much higher at about 3,349 people per square kilometre and RMB90,309 per capita. These figures suggest that the city had the highest population density and even GDP per capita, even when compared to Beijing in City Cluster C. Changsha, nonetheless, still had a low level of motorisation with about 93 vehicles per thousand population and 42 vehicles per kilometre of road. Hence, while its traffic fatalities per million population (33.94) did not look alarming, road safety was worse than in Beijing and a major concern with 3.65 road deaths per 10,000 vehicles. Bus services were relatively poorly developed despite a rather well-developed road network with only about 72 million bus passengers but more than 11 square metres of road area per capita. The road area per capita in Changsha was higher than in both Maoming and Beijing. The city's total freight volume was very high at about 228 million tonnes, reflecting the city's manufacturing production; yet, the total passenger volume was not particularly high at 339 million passengers. The share of citizens' consumption expenditure on transport and communication was nearly as high as Beijing at 16.54 per cent. The electricity generation capacity was not particularly strong, especially in view of its industrial base, at about nine billion kwh. Local government expenditure was about RMB28 billion per annum in 2010.

Local policies, decision-making and funding

According to the 12th Five-Year Plan for Economic and Social Development of Changsha prepared by the Changsha Government (Changsha Municipal Government, 2011), the overall target for the transport sector was to enhance the capacity and efficiency in carrying passengers and freight. In particular, the government proposed an increase in the total length of road networks to over 8,000 km, an increase in the proportion of public transport to 40 per cent, completion of the construction of the Changsha Metro Lines 1 and 2, and an increase in the coverage of bus stops to cover at least 70 per cent of the urban area.

As summarised in Table 8.5, the Changsha government's philosophies and strategies in developing the transport sector can be summarised as the 'four priorities'. First, the government proposed to increase the number of operating electric buses as well as to reduce the uneven distribution of bus services. Second, the government emphasised the importance of enhancing the performance of the transport system through increasing relevant infrastructure capacities and operation efficiency. Third, it is a priority for the government to promote low-carbon, high-efficiency and environmentally friendly transport systems. Finally, the

Table 8.5 Changsha government's 'four priorities' in developing transport up to 2015

Priority	Content
Bus service	Increase the number of operating electric buses and reduce the uneven distribution of the bus service
Efficiency of transport infrastructure	Enhance the performance of the transportation system by increasing the relevant infrastructure's capacity and operation efficiency
Sustainable transportation	Promoting low-carbon, high-efficiency and environmentally friendly transport system
Appropriate urban planning	Developing multi-urban centres instead of concentrating resources on a single centre; Speed up the outward expansion of the central business area, which is crowded with people and vehicles

Source: The author.

government stressed the importance of developing multi-urban centres instead of concentrating resources at a single centre.

Between 2011 and 2015, the Changsha government planned to invest RMB67 billion in building and improving transport infrastructure (Department of Transportation of Hunan Province, 2011). Some of the major projects included the construction of 48 km of expressways, completing the Changsha section of the Kunming-Shanghai high-speed railway and finishing off three new ports.

Fieldwork findings

The questionnaire in Changsha mainly focused on the development potential of both BRT and LRT. We interviewed the Changsha Municipal Bureau of Urban and Rural Planning, which is responsible for the future urban and rural development of Changsha including the transport system. Since BRT and LRT are prospective sustainable public transport modes that may be introduced in Changsha, the information gathered from the Bureau would be useful in understanding the development potential of and barriers to BRT and LRT locally.

The observational survey aimed at figuring out the development potential of BRT. Three government proposed BRT routes were chosen as the observation points. They are Central Renmin Road, Central Furong Road and West Jiefang Road. The three proposed BRT routes are all in the central urban area with high population flow and heavy traffic. BRT appeared to be a good choice with its high carrying capacity but there is a need to figure out the current bus service levels and its popularity which might show the potential of further developing the BRT system. If the bus service is already popular, the introduction of BRT will face less opposition and will probably further increase the efficiency of the bus system. Otherwise, the government may have to increase the attractiveness of buses first before implementing BRT. For the survey, data on the number of bus stops and bus routes on each road were gathered. Then, 30-minute observations at three bus stops located on the targeted roads were conducted to record more details like the route numbers of arriving buses, originating stations, destination stations, direction, arrival time, the number of passengers getting on, the number of passengers getting off and the bus departure time.

Modified sustainable transport strategy

To recall, the initial sustainable transport strategy for Cluster B cities includes BRT, particularly double-deck buses, and light rail. These leading sustainable transport modes were further investigated for their acceptability and feasibility in the fieldwork. Potential supporters and favourable factors, together with major obstacles, were also identified in the local context. Therefore, views from the local stakeholders were sought based on the initial sustainable transport strategy. The questionnaire used in Changsha is shown in Appendix 2.

BRT

From the questionnaire survey, the discussion of BRT in Changsha was still at an early stage. The government had identified several potential BRT routes without clearly defining the operating mechanism and the types of buses that would be used. Whether BRT can significantly enhance the performance of Changsha's transport system depends on the route arrangements and operation mechanism. The proposed BRT routes should be introduced on roads currently served by frequent bus services and with a large number of bus passengers. Furthermore, the system of allocating right of way to BRT routes (exclusively for buses or allowing a mixed usage with other vehicles) in different road sections during different periods was vitally important. While Changsha metro is still under construction, bus is the public transport that people heavily relied on. However, the existing bus routes are not extensive enough, and some urban areas are still uncovered. This has led to an increase in the use of private cars.

There are three major challenges with regard to the introduction of BRT. First, the total road area in Changsha is limited and it will be difficult to assign or build a dedicated BRT route (especially in busy areas). Second, it is difficult to change the land use of the built area within the urban district. However, it is known that the land use patterns near transit stations are important in influencing station patronage, and eventually affecting the success of developing TOD neighbourhoods, even within highly transit-dependent cities (Loo, Chen & Chan, 2010). Third, people are getting accustomed to the use of private cars and the introduction of BRT will not suddenly change their habits.

BRT would enhance the efficiency of public transport and road safety due to the large carrying capacity and the use of dedicated routes. However, the introduction of BRT would not help much in reducing people's reliance on private cars or alleviate traffic congestion if the proposed BRT routes only cover part of the urban areas. Nonetheless, should the BRT be able to connect people's homes with major destinations and, hence, result in significant travel time reductions, BRT could be attractive to many users. Moreover, a recent study by Ingvardson and Nielson (2017) reveals that the property value uplifts around BRT stops may be no less significant than more capital-intensive railway-based projects like light rail and metro systems.

The observational survey confirmed that Changsha has high potential for developing BRT further. Figure 8.3 shows a typical situation of a busy bus stop in Changsha. The large number of routes stopping at the bus station can be seen from the sign in the foreground. Table 8.6 presents the summary results of the observational survey. In particular, the three proposed BRT routes are well prepared for the introduction of BRT. There were on average 18 bus routes at each station and around 62 buses arriving at each of them every 30 minutes, revealing the popularity and intensity of existing bus services on the proposed BRT routes. The service frequency of the surveyed bus routes was high and the average interval between two arriving buses of the same route was only 5.77 minutes. The average number of bus passengers getting on and off the bus stops in 30 minutes was as high as 440, indicating that the customer base of current bus services in Changsha is huge. The existing large number of bus passengers will be beneficial to the introduction of BRT on the proposed routes.

Since the three proposed BRT routes have all shown impressive results regarding the popularity and intensity of existing bus services, they are ideal

Figure 8.3 A bus station in Changsha.
Source: The author.

Table 8.6 Observations along three proposed BRT routes in Changsha, June 2013

		West Jiefang Road	Central Furong Road	Central Renmin Road	Average
Number of bus routes		17	19	18	18
Number of bus stops		5	6	7	6
30-mins observation		Simenkou Station	Construction Bank Station	Geological Secondary School Station	Average
Starting time		19/06/2013, 2:55 p.m.	19/06/2013, 4:00 p.m.	19/06/2013, 5:27 p.m.	
Number of routes stopping here		15	10	11	12
Number of buses arriving		75	59	53	62.33
Average stopping time(s)		12	10	10	10.67
Number of passengers getting on	Total	267	149	326	247.33
	Mean	3.56	2.53	6.15	4.08
	Maximum	20	13	20	17.67
	Minimum	0	0	0	0
Number of passengers getting off	Total	296	122	160	192.67
	Mean	3.95	2.07	3.02	3.01
	Maximum	13	9	9	10.33
	Minimum	0	0	0	0
Number of passengers getting on and off	Total	563	271	486	440
	Mean	7.51	4.59	9.17	7.09
	Maximum	24	15	28	22.33
	Minimum	1	1	1	1
Service frequency (minutes between two arriving buses of the same route)	Average	6	5.08	6.22	5.77
	The most frequent route	2.73	2.73	4.29	3.25
	The least frequent route	15	10	10	11.67

Source: The author.

targets for the initial implementation of BRT in Changsha. However, as mentioned by the interviewees, the arrangement of the right of use of roads by different road users would be an important task for the government. Competing use of road space needs to be properly recognised by the government and be resolved with determination to allow dedicated BRT lanes so that the critical BRT success factor of travel time savings won't be compromised by traffic congestion caused by other vehicles.

LRT

Although the Changsha metro is still under construction, the government has already started the discussion on building a LRT. Figure 8.4 shows a picture of the Changsha metro under construction in 2013. The government was assessing the possibility of introducing LRT in the new urban district, Hexi, because the carrying capacity and environmental friendliness of LRT were attractive. The government would finance part of the development of the LRT.

There are three major challenges in introducing LRT. First, compared to BRT, it requires higher cost in construction, operation and maintenance. Second, junction points must be managed very carefully to ensure safety and to prevent collisions of LRT with other road traffic. Third, it is infeasible to introduce LRT

Figure 8.4 Metro line under construction in Changsha.
Source: The author.

to the built urban district as the land resources are limited and it is difficult to alter land use. Thus, the government can consider introducing LRT in a new urban district to avoid the difficulty of changing land use in a built-up area and it should be noted that the introduction of LRT may help to stimulate tourism in the new urban district. Within a new urban area where LRT is to be introduced, LRT is expected to reduce people's reliance on private cars significantly. In fact, new districts are likely to be necessary in Changsha with its population expected to increase by more than 50 per cent from 3.21 million in 2010 to 4.94 million in 2025. Hence, sustainable transport considerations should be given priority and fully integrated into the medium-term urban planning of Changsha to ensure that its rapid urbanisation will be sustainable.

Summary

Changsha's transport system is currently facing two major problems. The public transport system is not receiving enough attention and investment from the government such that the existing bus routes are not extensive enough to cover most areas of the urban district. Furthermore, the second issue is closely related to the first problem that people are overly reliant on private transport and the number of private cars has been increasing rapidly. In order to promote public transport, the rapid growth in private cars must be controlled. Changsha only has a few electric buses in operation but it would be infeasible to promote electric private cars at the current stage due to the immaturity of relevant technologies and insufficient charging stations. Since Changsha does not have much level land, it may also be difficult to promote cycling on a large scale.

Beijing in Cluster C

Beijing is the capital of the country, located in the North China Plain. The area of the municipality is about 16,801 square kilometres. Its population has reached 15 million and the GDP at 1,170.71 billion in 2010. In other words, the population density and GDP per capita were at about 1,230 people per square kilometre and RMB78,047 per capita (Beijing Municipal Bureau of Statistics, 2011). These figures suggest that the city, though being the second most populous in the entire country, had a rather concentrated population and economic pattern with a rather mountainous relief in the west. Beijing, however, has a very high level of motorisation with about 230 vehicles per thousand population (more than double that of Changsha and nearly ten times that of Maoming) and nearly 215 vehicles per kilometre of road. With the high motorisation rate, the road deaths per 10,000 vehicles were 2.15. When the population size is considered, its road safety problem was most pronounced with about 50 road deaths per million population. Its road network was not much higher than Maoming and much lower than Changsha, with about 6.26 square metres of road area per capita. Reflecting the importance of the city as the capital of the country, the total passenger volume in Beijing was very high at 140 million (more than four times that of Changsha) and bus passengers were also much larger at 505 million bus passengers per year. The city's total freight volume was 218.85 million tonnes, which was not as high as Changsha. The share of citizens' consumption expenditure on transport and communication was already the highest among the three cities studied, at 17.30 per cent. Both the electricity generation capacity and local government financial capability seem strong in Beijing.

Local policies, decision-making and funding

According to Beijing's Planning on Transport Development in the 12th Five-Year Plan Period (Beijing Municipal Commission of Transport & Beijing Municipal Commission of Development and Reform, 2012), the overall target for development in the transport sector in the 12th Five-Year Plan period was to ensure the smoothness and safety of the transport sector and to gradually alleviate the traffic congestion problems in the central urban area. In particular, the government proposed to increase the proportion of public transport in the central urban area to 50 per cent, increase the total road length to 21,500 km, increase the daily passenger volume of railways to over 12 million, reduce road fatalities per 10,000 vehicles to below 1.7 and reduce greenhouse gas emissions from vehicles by 10 per cent compared to the 11th Five-Year Plan period. Moreover, Beijing already has a BRT system in operation, though the scale was only limited and the locations were not at the CBD of the city. Figure 8.5 shows Line 2 of the BRT system in Beijing in June 2013.

Figure 8.5 Line 2 of the BRT system in Beijing.
Source: The author.

Table 8.7 lists the three core philosophies of the Beijing government in developing its transport system. They are people-centred, technology-based and green. People-centred refers to the building of a safe, convenient, fair and harmonious transport system. Technology-based means that the government is aiming to strive for technological breakthroughs in the transport sector. Green refers to the establishment of an environmentally friendly transport system compatible with its population size and the carrying capacity of the environment.

Between 2011 and 2015, the Beijing government proposed to invest RMB363.5 billion in enlarging and improving the transport system (Beijing Municipal Commission of Development and Reform, 2013). Some of the major transport infrastructural projects included the Beijing-Shenyang Passenger Railway Line (Beijing section) and Metro Lines 7, 10 and 14.

Fieldwork findings

The questionnaire in Beijing was mainly about the development prospects for electric cars and the metro system. The questionnaire used is shown in Appendix 3. We interviewed the Beijing Transportation Research Centre, which is an official research unit specialising in transport issues. Since the Centre is responsible for analysing Beijing's transport system and making recommendations to the municipal government, we obtained highly relevant data regarding the government's proposed policies in developing sustainable transport.

In Beijing, electric cars only formed a tiny proportion of the total vehicle population. The total number of electric vehicles in Beijing was around 100,000 in 2012 (planned to increase to 500,000 by 2015) which was less than 1 per cent of all vehicles. The promotion of electric cars in Beijing was only at an initial stage such that most of the electric cars were operating in the public sector, for

Table 8.7 Beijing government's philosophy in developing the city's transport system

Philosophy	Major content
People-based transport	• Safe, convenient, fair and harmonious transportation system • Address people's concern regarding transport safety
Technology-based transport	• Strive for technological breakthrough • Advanced transportation system supported by ICT, providing real-time information and business opportunities
Green transport	• Conserve energy and reduce emissions • Encourage road users to shift to more environmentally friendly means of transport • Encourage the production and use of vehicles with better energy efficiency and lower emissions rate • Establish an environmentally friendly transport system compatible with the population size and carrying capacity of the environment

Source: The author.

example electric buses, electric taxis and electric sanitation vehicles. The number of pure electric private cars was only around 100. In 2012, there were only 12 electric charging stations in Beijing. Most of them were located in the northern and southeastern districts. The inadequate number and uneven distribution of charging stations are potential barriers to the further development of electric cars in Beijing.

The observational survey conducted in Beijing aimed at figuring out the popularity of electric cars. Three electric car charging stations that are of relatively large scale in the urban district were chosen as the survey points. At each charging station, the number of charging slots was recorded. Then, a one-hour observation was conducted to record the number of electric vehicles entering the charging stations with a sub-division of four categories: electric cars, electric bikes, electric taxis and electric buses. Furthermore, the entry and exit time was recorded in order to calculate the average time spent for charging because the relatively long charging time for electric vehicles may be seen as a major barrier to potential buyers.

The metro is the backbone of Beijing's public transport system and will continue to enjoy top priority in Beijing's transport development. Due to the large population of Beijing, the existing metro service would have to be strengthened in order to meet the increasing demand. Therefore, new metro lines and stations are now under construction. The scale of the metro will continue to grow in order to be extensive enough to cover most of the urban areas.

However, there are two major challenges faced by Beijing metro. To begin with, although the cost of construction, operation and maintenance of the metro is mostly supported by the government, the funding has to go through a long and complicated approval procedure before the commencement of expansion projects. Due to the large amount of investment capital and low fares charged to passengers (fixed price at RMB2 in 2013), Beijing metro has always run on a deficit and receives around RMB10 billion from the government annually. Moreover, the metro has a limited capacity in transporting passengers during rush hours due to Beijing's large population. The metro operates at a two-minute interval during rush hours and it is technologically infeasible to further increase the service frequency. Possible solutions to further increase the popularity and efficiency of the metro would be to increase the coverage of metro stations and the number of routes, such as introducing urban-rural routes and adding new routes parallel to the existing ones along busy routes. Moreover, the train compartments used, even for the newly extended metro lines, were not of the large-capacity type to allow a significant upgrade of the overall capacity of its metro system.

The metro is efficient in reducing transport sector CO_2 emissions, as well as enhancing the capacity and efficiency of public transport. However, it does not help much in suppressing the rapid growth of private car ownership, nor in reducing people's reliance on private transport because the existing metro routes and stations are not extensive enough, causing inconvenience to some potential passengers.

The greatest challenge faced by Beijing's transport system is the city's over reliance on private cars running on diesel. The reasons behind this include limited service coverage of the metro, low attractiveness of electric vehicles (expensive and inadequate charging stations) and inadequate bus routes. Some possible solutions to reduce the number of diesel private cars are increasing parking fees, increasing fines for the violation of traffic regulations and imposing initial registration tax for diesel private vehicles. Expanding BRT might also be a good solution but the problem of limited road area would be a barrier to restricting further development.

Table 8.8 shows the usage rate of charging slots during the observation period and Table 8.9 shows the number and type of electric cars entering and exiting the charging stations during the one-hour observation. Although Beijing is one of the pioneers in supporting electric cars, the utilisation rates of the electric car charging points were disappointing.

Part of the problem may also be related to the lack of priority given to electric car charging facilities in land-use planning and planning requirements because all these stations were not located at easily accessible and prime sites in the city, where vehicle flows are high. Figure 8.6 shows the location of one of the stations, which was actually located beneath flyovers.

Figure 8.6 Location of an electric car-charging station in Beijing.
Source: The author.

Table 8.8 Usage rate of charging slots at three electric car-charging stations in Beijing, June 2013

	Hongyangqiao electric car charging station	Siyuanxiqiao electric car charging station	Huixinxiqiao electric car charging station	Average
Observation time	17/06/2013, 12:30 p.m.	17/06/2013, 2:30 p.m.	17/06/2013 5:00 p.m.	
Number of slots	34	46	44	41.33
Number of slots occupied (% of the total slots)	10 (29.41)	11 (23.91)	14 (31.82)	11.67 (28.24)
Number of vehicles charging – electric buses (% of the total vehicles charging)	3 (30.00)	2 (18.18)	2 (14.29)	2.33 (19.97)
Number of vehicles charging electric taxis (% of the total vehicles charging)	3 (30.00)	3 (27.27)	4 (28.57)	3.33 (28.53)
Number of vehicles charging electric sanitation vehicles (% of the total vehicles charging)	4 (40.00)	6 (54.55)	8 (57.14)	6 (51.41)

Source: The author.

Table 8.9 Vehicle characteristics at three electric car-charging stations in Beijing, June 2013

		Hongyanqiao electric car charging station	Siyuanxiqiao electric car charging station	Huixinxiqiao electric car charging station	Average
Observation time		17/06/2013, 12:45–1:45 p.m.	17/06/2013, 2:45–3:45 p.m.	17/06/2013 5:15–6:15 p.m.	
Number of electric cars entering	Electric private car (%)	0 (0)	0 (0)	0 (0)	0 (0)
	Electric bike (%)	0 (0)	0 (0)	0 (0)	0 (0)
	Electric taxi (%)	2 (33.33)	1 (20.00)	2 (33.33)	1.67 (29.45)
	Electric bus (%)	1 (16.67)	2 (40.00)	2 (33.33)	1.67 (29.45)
	Electric sanitation vehicles (%)	3 (50.00)	2 (40.00)	2 (33.33)	2.33 (41.09)
	Total	6	5	6	5.67
Number of electric cars exiting	Electric private car (%)	0 (0)	0 (0)	0 (0)	0 (0)
	Electric bike (%)	0 (0)	0 (0)	0 (0)	0 (0)
	Electric taxi (%)	1 (33.33)	1 (50.00)	0 (0)	0.67 (28.76)
	Electric bus (%)	1 (33.33)	0 (0)	1 (50.00)	0.67 (28.76)
	Electric sanitation vehicles (%)	1 (33.33)	1 (50.00)	1 (50.00)	1 (42.92)
	Total	3	2	2	2.33
Total number of electric cars entering and exiting	Electric private car (%)	0 (0)	0 (0)	0 (0)	0 (0)
	Electric bike (%)	0 (0)	0 (0)	0 (0)	0 (0)
	Electric taxi (%)	3 (33.33)	2 (28.57)	2 (25.00)	2.33 (29.13)
	Electric bus (%)	2 (22.22)	2 (28.57)	3 (37.50)	2.33 (29.13)
	Electric sanitation vehicles (%)	4 (44.44)	3 (42.86)	3 (37.50)	3.33 (41.63)
	Total	9	7	8	8

Source: The author.

Modified sustainable transport strategy

For cities in Cluster C, the initial sustainable transport strategy points to the building and extension of metro systems with high passenger carrying capacity and the conversion of the huge private vehicle fleet from using carbon-intensive fuels (largely diesel and petroleum) to low-carbon energy (especially electricity). Nonetheless, these spearheading sustainable transport modes are also the most demanding in terms of new investment in capital-intensive infrastructure and behavioural changes in travel patterns. Moreover, in view of the large number and diversity of people in these mega cities, the local context is particularly important in fine-tuning specific measures that can achieve sustainable transport goals without causing too much disturbance or social unrest.

Metro

While metro can have great potential in providing sustainable passenger transport for a capital and mega city like Beijing, its very limited capacity and limited extensions are major obstacles. An extension of the metro system in Beijing should consider creating and transforming the entire city structure with a connected railway network and new nodes around modern and high-capacity metro stations. The concept of TOD should be carefully considered to allow sufficient density of population and employment, wide diversity of land use and attractive urban design elements for developing new activity nodes along the railway lines, instead of retrofitting small stations and limited capacity railway stations in-between ring roads that fail to relieve the heavy road traffic congestion on the one hand and become overcrowded and unattractive to the users on the other hand. The 'pearl necklace' concept found in places such as Hong Kong and Amsterdam needs to be considered. There should be a better understanding that TOD is no longer just uniform, with a standardised development model such as the railway-cum-property development model of Hong Kong, and monotonous. There are different types of TOD that should be more fully explored to make the TOD neighbourhood attractive to the local residents on the one hand, and make the city more balanced on the other.

In Loo and du Verle (2017), for instance, five TOD types are discussed. With low-carbon transport as a fundamental policy guide, policy-makers and planners need to build upon but delve deeper into the general and broad principles of the 3Ds of density, diversity and design in TOD (Badoe & Miller, 2000; Bartholomew & Ewing, 2008; Boarnet & Crane, 2001; Cervero, 2002; Cervero & Kockelman, 1997; Ewing & Cervero, 2010; Frank & Pivo, 1994). In addition, governments also need to find better ways of describing and fostering different types of TOD neighbourhoods relevant to the local geographical context. In their study of 60 metro neighbourhoods and the matching 60 non-metro neighbourhoods in Hong Kong, Loo and du Verle (2017) have differentiated different TOD neighbourhoods by 20 variables directly relevant to the 3Ds. They range from population, employment, land use, housing type, household characteristics, transit accessibility and road density around each metro station. These variables are then analysed by the principal component analysis (PCA) to see whether there are common built environment characteristics underlying specific types of metro neighbourhoods, recognising that it is neither possible nor desirable to have uniformly high density, diversity and the same design in every TOD neighbourhood within a city.

The results of the PCA are shown in Table 8.10. Generally, five types of metro neighbourhood in Hong Kong could be identified. The five factors accounted for 63 per cent of the variance. The first factor explains more than 25 per cent of the variance. Each factor accounts for at least roughly 10 per cent of the variance. Yet, each factor includes more than one dimension of the 3D built environment variables. In other words, though the actual combination of variables differs, a combination of the density, diversity and design elements are common in characterising a metro neighbourhood type. Factor 1 mostly describes dense economic urban neighbourhoods – typically the central business district (CBD). Factor 2 areas have good station-neighbourhood integration. Factor 3 neighbourhoods are characterised by a great diversity of people and activity. Factor 4 are mostly residential neighbourhoods with large families. Finally, factor 5 areas are distinguished by good station design and integration with other transport networks. Each metro neighbourhood type is briefly described below.

The CBD-type TOD (factor 1) displays strong characteristics of high job density (DEN02), commercial development intensity (DEN04) and overall development intensity (DEN06). Belzer *et al.* (2011) found that high-density job clusters are the best way to increase transit use, especially if located around a transit station. Loutzenheiser (1997) also highlights that higher development intensity suggests less underutilised space for uses such as parking lots but higher accessibility for pedestrians. In terms of diversity, the CBD-type TOD has good provisions of other public transport services as well (DIV05). In terms of design, the CBD-type TOD has a higher number of road junctions (that is, smaller street blocks) (DSN01), denser street networks (DSN02) and a higher number of metro exits (DSN06). Handy (1996) has highlighted that dense and interconnected road networks can reduce travel distances within the network and hence increase the feasibility of walking in cities. Cervero (2009) also demonstrated that street density influences the likelihood of walking, with a dense street network considered as >0.25 km per km^2. In contrast, sparse curving streets forming loops and lollipops should be avoided (Ewing and Cervero, 2010). In the context of Hong Kong, a higher number of station exits (also serving as entrances) further characterised the CBD-type TOD. In fact, the number of exits gives us an idea of the degree of accessibility within the neighbourhood. A higher number of exits provides better direct accessibility to different parts of the neighbourhood and can offer alternative walking routes under bad weather, if all exits are connected without passing through the pay area of the metro system.

The integrated community-type TOD (factor 2) is characterised by high residential development intensity (DEN03), comprehensive development (DIV01),

Table 8.10 Five types of transit-oriented development (TOD) neighbourhoods in Hong Kong based on principal component analysis

	Factor					Communality extraction
	1: CBD-type TOD	2: Community-type TOD	3: Balanced-type TOD	4: Residential-type TOD	5: Station-type TOD	
DEN01: Population density	0.862					0.559
DEN02: Employment density		0.585				0.813
DEN03: Residential development intensity	0.687	-0.325				0.447
DEN04: Commercial development intensity	0.702					0.599
DEN05: Mixed commercial-residential development intensity				0.691		0.664
DEN06: Overall development intensity	0.837					0.721
DIV01: Comprehensive development		0.676				0.577
DIV02: Diversity of land uses	0.447		0.604			0.674
DIV03: Household size				0.798		0.746
DIV04: Diversity of housing types			0.696			0.581
DIV05: Levels of other public transit services	0.703					0.589
DIV06: Convenience of other public transit					0.712	0.646
DIV07: Income	-0.330		0.379	0.606		0.768
DSN01: Road connectivity	0.885					0.829
DSN02: Road density	0.733	0.323	0.311			0.794
DSN03: Open space	-0.312		0.728			0.636
DSN04: Covered walkway					0.595	0.430
DSN05: Expressways					-0.589	0.455
DSN06: Exit system	0.490	0.473				0.546
DSN07: Retail	–	0.682	–		0.372	0.608
Eigenvalues	5.058	2.125	2.020	1.877	1.602	12.682
% of variance	25.288	10.624	10.100	9.387	8.011	63.410

Source: Loo and du Verle (2017).

Notes
Extraction method: Principal Component Analysis.
Rotation method: Varimax with Kaiser Normalisation.
Rotation of the rotated Component Matrix converged in seven iterations.

dense street networks (DSN02) and a high number of metro exits (DSN06). The higher-density residential development and the mix of diverse activities under the zoning of comprehensive development area (CDA) encourage the flows of people throughout the day. Zhang (2007, p. 121), for instance, emphasised the importance of an 'integrated and synergetic development between land use and the transit system', not only to reduce the cost and risks of the development but also to increase the opportunities of better transit financing and ridership. Once again, a higher number of metro exits is a key feature of the community-type TOD.

For the balanced-type of TOD (factor 3), density variables are not as important. Instead, a great diversity of land uses (DIV02), housing type (DIV04) and good design elements like open space (DSN03) and dense street networks (DSN02) are key elements. Unlike DIV01, which only captures whether different types of land uses are present, DIV02 is calculated based on the balance of different land uses in the neighbourhood. An area with balanced land use creates more trip activities than a single-use-dominated area like office buildings (Loutzenheiser, 1997). Moreover, the balanced-type TOD has a higher ratio of public housing. Given the lack of detailed information on the occupation and other social status, DIV04 is a good proxy indicator of the diversity of the social strata living there as well. With appropriate design, parks and public places create attractive spaces for fostering a strong and healthy community, an important element of TOD. TOD neighbourhoods should not only be transit spaces but also living places for recreation and other purposes. Cervero *et al.* (2009) suggest that these open public spaces support and encourage physical activities. Moreover, the presence of open space also influences the willingness of residents to walk by creating a nicer environment in which to walk than the street next to vehicular traffic, and also by offering opportunities to pedestrians to rest, pause and orient themselves (Stonor *et al.*, 2003). Once again, the presence of dense street networks with high connectivity characterised this type of TOD.

High population density (DEN01), large family size (DIV03) and high household income (DIV07) are distinctive features of the residential-type TOD (factor 4). While population density has been the most commonly cited and is often mentioned first among all elements of TOD, it does not seem to be uniformly important in this study. People living in residential-type TODs tend to have larger families and have a higher household income. The metro system offers potential for each member of the bigger family to go to different destinations and to engage in different activities. The higher travel and other living expenses of larger households have probably been reflected in the higher median household income of the residents in this type of TOD neighbourhood.

Once again, density is not dominant in identifying the station-type TOD (factor 5). On the contrary, a short distance to other public modes (DIV06) and good design elements of the metro stations, including having at least one covered exit (DSN04), no expressways crossing through (DSN05) and retail activities within the station area (DSN07), seem to be important. While the unfavourable factor of snowfall in some temperate cities (Cervero *et al.*, 2009; Stonor *et al.*, 2003) is not present in Hong Kong, its sub-tropical climate poses challenges of high heat and heavy rainfall to road users during the summer months. An extended covered access to the metro station can be an important factor in encouraging people to walk and to use public transport. In some situations, the covered access is an extended covered walkway. In other situations, these metro exits are directly connected to indoor shopping malls, residential developments or other facilities. The negative factor loading of DSN05 confirms that express-ways are not good features of TOD. The higher traffic volume generates more air and noise pollution, and can represent major disincentives for people to walk and to use transit even if elevated walkways are provided. Finally, more retail activities also seem to be a distinct feature of this station-type of TOD.

Electric cars

The policy to use alternative-fuel vehicles in China and elsewhere needs to be put in the context of the growth of the entire vehicle fleet. As shown in the summary statistics, vehicle ownership in Beijing is very much out of line with the rest of China. Shanghai, for instance, has a level of vehicle ownership less than one third that of Beijing. In Beijing, until recently, there were no restric-tions on car purchase or use, but the numbers of new vehicles in Shanghai have been restricted by quotas and a bidding system.

Moreover, institutional cars constitute a large share of the vehicle fleet in Beijing. These vehicles, very often private vehicles and many of them luxury cars, belong to institutions, departments and bureaux at different levels from the central government to representatives of provincial and other local governments, as well as the vertically controlled bureaux of the central governments. Con-siderations for whether to own a car, what model to buy, what tank capacity, how many cars to own and car usage decisions, that is, whether to use a car for a particular trip, have not been driven by economic considerations such as costs or fuel efficiency because these decisions were all expenses of the institutions. The shift of these vehicles to electric cars perhaps will not make much sense with the provision of government subsidies, if people consider them unattractive on other grounds. The offer of tax incentives or tax breaks, as many other countries have adopted, may not be effective in Beijing.

However, the shift of institutional cars to an electric fleet can be more easily executed as the fleet is influenced directly by government policies. There has been, for instance, an announcement made by the Transport Ministry to add 200,000 buses and 100,000 taxis running on alternative fuels by 2020 in China. The opportunity for Beijing to be the pioneer ground for these experiments is much higher than other cities. Nonetheless, there should be an overall considera-tion of whether the shift can be more environmentally friendly with 'clean' elec-tricity. A policy to reduce the vehicle fleet size may instead be the ultimate policy goal to allow Beijing to become sustainable in urban transport.

Summary

Overall, it seems that Beijing's transport system is still primarily oriented towards automobiles with uncurbed solo-driving and the use of heavier vehicles (notably SUVs and other luxurious cars) over time. And, as observed by Hook and Replogle (1996), the rapid motorisation has not only led to the building of more and more ring roads around Beijing but also the replacement of tree-lined median strips to make way for additional road space. Nonetheless, it is recognised that the strong presence of the central government also means that 'major innovations can take place in a relatively short period of time' (Hickman & Banister, 2014, p. 220). The introduction of electronic road pricing, for example, has been discussed for a long time in the city. The push for electric cars may also take a sharp turn if the government introduces a strong policy to replace all institutional cars with electric ones.

References

Badoe, D.A., & Miller, E.J. (2000). Transportation-land-use interaction: Empirical findings in North America, and their implications for modeling. *Transportation Research Part D – Transport and Environment, 5*, 235–263. doi:10.1016/S1361-9209(99)00036-X.

Bartholomew, K., & Ewing, R. (2008). *Land Use-Transportation Scenario Planning in an Era of Global Climate Change*. Paper presented at the Transportation Research Board 87th Annual Meeting, Washington, D.C.

Beijing Municipal Bureau of Statistics. (2011). *Beijing Statistical Yearbook 2011*. Beijing: China Statistics Press.

Beijing Municipal Commission of Development and Reform. (2013). *Major Infrastructure Projects in 2013: Transport Sector*. Retrieved from http://project.bjpc.gov.cn/zdxm/download/2013zdlists.xls.

Beijing Municipal Commission of Transport & Beijing Municipal Commission of Development and Reform. (2012). *Beijing's Planning on Transportation Development in the 12th Five-Year Period*. Retrieved from www.bjpc.gov.cn/zwxx/ghjh/wngh/l25sq/2011 08/P020151222385396960265.doc.

Belzer, D., Srivastava, S., Wood, J. & Greenberg, E. (2011). *Transit-oriented Development (TOD) and Employment*. Oakland, CA: Center for Transit-Oriented Development.

Boarnet, M.G., & Crane, R. (2001). The influence of land use on travel behavior: Specification and estimation strategies. *Transportation Research Part A – Policy and Practice, 35*, 823–845. doi:10.1016/S0965-8564(00)00019-7.

Cervero, R. (2002). Built environments and mode choice: Toward a normative framework. *Transportation Research Part D: Transport and Environment, 7*, 265–284. doi:10.1016/S1361-9209(01)00024-4.

Cervero, R. (2009). Public transport and sustainable urbanism: Global lessons. In C. Curtis, J.L. Renne & L. Bertolini (Eds.), *Transit Oriented Development: Making It Happen* (pp. 23–35). Surrey: Ashgate.

Cervero, R., & Kockelman, K. (1997). Travel demand and the 3Ds: Density, diversity, and design. *Transportation Research Part D – Transport and Environment, 2*, 199–219. doi:10.1016/S1361-9209(97)00009-6.

Cervero, R., Sarmiento, O.L., Jacoby, E., Gomez, L.F. & Neiman, A. (2009). Influences of built environments on walking and cycling: Lessons from Bogota. *International Journal of Sustainable Transportation, 3*, 203–226. doi:10.1080/15568310802178314.

Changsha Municipal Government. (2011). *The 12th Five-Year Plan for Economic and Social Development of Changsha*. Retrieved from www.changsha.gov.cn/xxgk/szfxxg-kml/ghjh/qsfzgh/201108/t20110822_10921.html.

Department of Transportation of Hunan Province. (2011). *Chang Sha Shi 'Shi Er Wu' Jiao Tong Jian She Tou Ru 670 Yi Yuan* (Changsha invests 67 billion in transport sector for 12th Five-Year-Plan). Retrieved from www.its114.com/html/2012/xingyezhengce_0624/1944.html.

Ewing, R., & Cervero, R. (2010). Travel and the built environment: A meta-analysis. *Journal of the American Planning Association, 76*, 265–294. doi:10.1080/019443 61003766766.

Frank, L.D., & Pivo, G. (1994). Impacts of mixed use and density on utilisation of three modes of travel: Single-occupant vehicle, transit, and walking. *Transportation Research Record, 1466*, 44–52. Retrieved from http://onlinepubs.trb.org/Onlinepubs/trr/1994/1466/1466-07.pdf.

Guillen, M.D., Ishida, H. & Okamoto, N. (2013). Is the use of informal public transport modes in developing countries habitual? An empirical study in Davao City, Philippines. *Transport Policy, 26*, 31–42. doi:10.1016/j.tranpol.2012.03.008.

Handy, S.L. (1996). Methodologies for exploring the link between urban form and travel behavior. *Transportation Research Part D: Transport and Environment, 1*, 151–165. doi:10.1016/S1361-9209(96)00010-7.

Hickman, R., & Banister, D. (2014). *Transport, Climate Change and the City*. Oxon: Routledge.

Hook, W., & Replogle, M. (1996). Motorisation and non-motorised transport in Asia: Transport system evolution in China, Japan and Indonesia. *Land Use Policy, 13*, 69–84. doi:10.1016/0264-8377(95)00025-9.

Ingvardson, J.B., & Nielsen, O.A. (2017). Effects of new bus and rail rapid transit systems: An international review. *Transport Reviews*. Advance online publication. doi:10.1080/01441647.2017.1301594.

Loo, B.P.Y., & du Verle, F. (2017). Transit-oriented development in future cities: Towards a two-level sustainable mobility strategy. *International Journal of Urban Sciences, 21*(Suppl. 1), 54–67. doi:10.1080/12265934.2016.1235488.

Loo, B.P.Y., Chen, C. & Chan, E.T.H. (2010). Rail-based transit-oriented development: Lessons from New York City and Hong Kong. *Landscape and Urban Planning, 97*, 202–212. doi:10.1016/j.landurbplan.2010.06.002.

Loutzenheiser, D.R. (1997). Pedestrian access to transit: Model of walk trips and their design and urban form determinants around Bay Area Rapid Transit stations. *Transportation Research Record, 1604*, 40–49. doi:10.3141/1604-06.

Maoming Urban and Rural Planning Bureau & Maoming Transportation Bureau. (2013). *Comprehensive Planning on Maoming's Transportation System (2012–2030)*. Maoming: Maoming Urban and Rural Planning Bureau & Maoming Transportation Bureau.

National Bureau of Statistics of China. (2014). *China Statistical Yearbook 2013*. Beijing: China Statistics Press.

Statistics Bureau of Maoming. (2013a). *The Economic and Social Development Statistical Communique of Maoming in 2012*. Maoming: Statistics Bureau of Maoming.

Statistics Bureau of Maoming. (2013b). *2012 National Economy and Society Developed Statistical Bulletin in Maoming, China*. Maoming: Statistics Bureau of Maoming.

Stonor, T., Campos, M.B.D.A., Chiaradia, A., Takamatsu, S. & Smith, A. (2003). Towards a 'walkability index'. In Association for European Transport (Ed.), *Proceedings of the*

European Transport Conference (ETC) 2003. Strasbourg: Association for European Transport.

Wu, C.Y.H., & Loo, B.P.Y. (2016). Motorcycle safety among motorcycle taxi drivers and nonoccupational motorcyclists in developing countries: A case study of Maoming, south China. *Traffic Injury Prevention, 17*, 170–175. doi:10.1080/15389588.2015.10 48336.

Zhang, M. (2007). Chinese edition of transit-oriented development. *Transportation Research Record, 2038*, 120–127. doi:10.3141/2038-16.

9 Ways forward

Sustainable transport in smart cities

Ever since the 1990s, e-technologies, which essentially refer to the integration of advanced information and communication technologies (ICT) and various electronic devices (e-devices), have transformed people's everyday life and led to the emergence of e-society (Loo, 2012). All major spheres of a person's life, including the political, economic and social domains, are increasingly dependent on e-technologies. Nonetheless, it is clear that the progress of e-development varies in different countries based on the local geographical contexts. Geographical unevenness, therefore, remains at different spatial scales. In China, for example, remarkable progress in e-development has been achieved since 2004; yet, progress in different domains has been uneven both in space and in time (Loo & Wang, 2017). At the national level, e-government and e-networking have been spearheading changes, followed by e-commerce, with e-working then beginning to catching up (Loo & Wang, 2017). In the future, e-technologies still have huge potentials for further transforming and improving people's well-being worldwide, not only in the developed but also the developing countries. Furthermore, the advancement of technologies has led to new innovative applications that bring new opportunities, as well as challenges, to sustainable transport.

One of the new innovations has been the widespread use of the Internet of Things (IoT), formed by various types of electronic sensors connected through the Internet. The IoT has enabled the real-time transmission of not only spatial information (with the Global Positioning System, GPS) but also images (including two- and three-dimensional images) and videos (with a smooth broadcasting of reality) and different types of information collected by a whole range of affordable, reliable and durable sensors. With the IoT, the transport system can be transformed to achieve comprehensive sustainable transport goals. Using the four elements of transport as examples. Sensors can be installed in *ways* to minimise supporting infrastructure failures (such as heat stress on railway tracks), maximise flow efficiency (such as traffic signal optimisation) and enhance traffic safety (through timely identification and avoidance of potential conflicts and collisions). Sensors installed in *vehicles* can enhance public transport efficiency (particularly through real-time arrival information) and ensure optimal comfort and safety conditions inside the vehicles (with surveillance cameras, especially for women travelling alone, and advanced seat availability information). Sensors installed within goods vehicles are particularly useful for freight transport and logistics to ensure optimal in-vehicle conditions, like temperature and humidity controls for agricultural produce such as flowers and vegetables. Sensors installed in *terminals* would help vehicle fleet management and avoid dispatching vehicles unnecessarily, which can cause congestion and pollution. Sensors installed in *energy* may seem non-typical. Yet, this actually has one of the greatest application benefits through the smart electricity grid with an optimal use and control of the use of electrical appliances, including the charging of electric cars, at the optimal time for different facilities. With a smart electricity grid, it is possible to encourage a more even spread of electricity demand through shifting usage from the peak to the non-peak hours using price and other incentives.

Such advice or tips of optimisation, however, cannot just rely on the information collected from the sensors in a real-time manner. It is only through a careful analysis of the enormous amount of information repeatedly collected over time from all different types of sensors and transmitted via telecommunications that meaningful patterns can be identified for policy recommendations (Anda, Erath & Fourie, 2017). Imagine the spatial information of each smartphone user being transmitted through the mobile phone networks every five seconds (17,280 data points for each user each day). In a city like Hong Kong with nearly eight million mobile phone users, that would result in as many as 138.24 billion spatial locations in just one day for geo-validation even before any meaningful spatial analysis. Moreover, that is already independent of all the individual-level data of demographic and socio-economic variables, and the location-specific variables like stay duration and types of e-activities conducted on location. The number of data points can easily reach the trillions. These are therefore called big data. The applications of big data to improve the transport system for achieving comprehensive sustainable transport goals are enormous (de Gennaro, Paffumi & Martini, 2016; Cottill & Derrible, 2015).

Another new technological advancement is artificial intelligence (AI), as opposed to human intelligence, applied to various points of automation in the transport system. Based on patterns identified from the big data, real-time information (like obstacles and speed of nearby vehicles) collected by the IoT, AI algorithms based on the artificial neural network (ANN) and machine learning (Gazder & Ratrout, 2015), various types of automation have been actively researched both in laboratories (with prototypes) and for real-life applications (currently still on a limited scale, like Google's automated vehicles). Automated vehicles, for instance, hold particularly great promise for improvements in road safety, and has proven to be possible, for example, by avoiding poor decisions, such as lane-changing that might result in a traffic collision. Generally, autonomous vehicles refer to vehicles that do not need a driver to actively drive, control and park them. A driver's seat and the manual driving option may or may not be present. The latter are also known as driverless vehicles. In other words, autonomous vehicles are not merely vehicles installed with computer-assisted driving systems or vehicles with cruise or 'auto-pilot' options that are designed to help drivers in specific circumstances, like driving on expressways or parking. Very often, human beings are prone to fatigue, errors of judgement and irregularities/inconsistencies due to physical conditions and/or psychological emotions. Simply by avoiding various human errors in driving, thousands of lives can potentially be saved each year; and traffic injuries can also be dramatically reduced (Huang & Song, 2003; Winkle, 2016; Zhao *et al.*, 2017). The use of autonomous vehicles, however, not only has potential for improving road safety but also for making private vehicles more accessible to the non-driving licence-holding segments of the population.

However, whether autonomous vehicles are in line with the sustainable transport strategy is uncertain. Table 9.1 shows some of the potential negative externalities associated with the wide use of autonomous vehicles. One crucial point is whether the wide array of autonomous vehicles will actually lead to more vehicle-kilometres travelled, more vehicles on the road, more traffic congestion, more consumption on resources (including in the manufacturing of more vehicles) and the building of more roads. In addition, the tendency of autonomous

Table 9.1 Potential negative externalities associated with the wide use of autonomous vehicles

Possible unintended transport consequences	Further 'knock-on' effects
Longer vehicle-km	• More roads/infrastructure • More traffic congestion • Especially during peak hours • Especially at CBD • Consumption of energy (electricity has to be generated)
More vehicles	• Energy and materials used in the production of automobiles • The 'sky-rocketing' of the vehicle fleet • More frequent change of vehicles and upgrading (e.g. the habit of changing smartphones) • The 'cascading' of used vehicles (now from developed to developing countries) • Danger of the mixed used of autonomous cars (including second-hand ones) and non-autonomous cars in developing countries
Even more automobile-dependent lifestyle	• Lack of physical exercise • Making more trips a possibility • Making longer trips a possibility • Making trips at any time a greater possibility • No thinking about public transport, cycling and walking as alternatives

Source: The author.

vehicles to further spur an automobile-dependent lifestyle, which, in turn, is associated with physical inactivity (and hence obesity) and a lack of interaction with other people in society (and hence social isolation), needs to be carefully guarded. In addition, there is a fear of the degradation of human motor skills to synthesise information (especially spatial information), analyse it and make decisions. As autonomous vehicles become more readily available, people are less likely to think twice before making a trip and making a decision to use a private car, rather than using public transport, cycling or walking. This 'easy' and 'ready to drive' mentality can be associated with all the negative externalities that may overwhelm or counter-balance any benefits that are achieved through the social benefits of autonomous vehicles, if not also other efforts towards making comprehensive sustainable transport.

All in all, the challenge is to make sure that our behavioural responses do not overwhelm or counter-balance the potential environmental, economic and social gains in sustainability brought about by autonomous vehicles. We need to study more carefully the nature and extent of behavioural changes and adaptations with the availability of autonomous vehicles. These are words of caution that autonomous vehicles may bring about changes that conflict with the other sustainable transport initiatives. Similarly, measures need to be in place to ensure that the use of electric vehicles really contributes to comprehensive transport sustainability. The use of more electric vehicles without a corresponding decline in diesel and petroleum cars, the environmentally polluting ways that used electric batteries are dumped/recycled, and the ways that electricity is generated need to be properly dealt with before the huge potential for electric vehicles to become a backbone of sustainable road transport can be realised.

Like all new innovations, the introduction of autonomous vehicles will trigger changes in the four elements of the transport system. For *vehicles*, there is a need for drastic changes in the automobile manufacturing industries from design to manufacturing and marketing. Each autonomous vehicle has to be equipped with not only computer-controlled steering, braking and acceleration systems but also the supporting sensors (for sensing the surrounding) and the communication systems (for supporting vehicle-to-vehicle and vehicle-to-infrastructure communication). For *ways*, demands on the road infrastructure will range from making lanes and other road markings more 'readable' to autonomous vehicles under different weather and lighting conditions, to the installation of beacons and sensors to effectively communicate with autonomous vehicles driving on the road. The constant consumption of *energy* to support the autonomous driving system and the big risk of an energy disruption/failure affecting road safety means that it is likely that more energy will be required to support an autonomous vehicle than otherwise. The use of electricity and alternative fuels will make autonomous vehicles less polluting on the roads. However, once again, the sources of electricity and the ways of extracting alternative fuels are key areas to look out for, which may offset hard-won gains in saving non-renewable energy. Moreover, the energy charging points may need to be re-allocated for an efficient refuelling system because the entire temporal and spatial patterns of vehicular flows within cities may change with the wide use of autonomous vehicles. For *terminals*, will autonomous vehicles ever be parked? Theoretically, they can be 'sent' to be on the road at all times without needing a driver. Moreover, with car-sharing, autonomous vehicles are also likely to be more fully utilised serving users whose travel needs (including time and destinations) are complementary but who may not know each other. What will be the total area required for parking in a city? Where should parking areas be located? What type of parking facilities will be the most efficient with autonomous vehicles (for example, there would no longer be a need for drivers to reach the car parks to drop and pick up their cars)? These are all crucial and important questions for researchers interested in sustainable transport transition to ponder.

From the user's perspective, various smartphone applications (apps) have proven to facilitate sustainable transport behavioural changes. Various types of vehicle sharing, especially car and bicycle sharing, have applied IoT and been introduced in different parts of the world. Since it began operations from its inception in 2012, the bicycle-sharing system in Sao Paulo, Brazil, reduced 837.26 tonnes of carbon dioxide emissions by 2 April 2017 (Bikesampa, 2017). Figure 9.1 is a photograph taken during my fieldwork in 2014 that references an impressive initiative to close part of the major roads and expressways for bicycles on weekends in Sao Paulo, Brazil. The continuous bicycle tracks allow bicyclists to reach almost any destination downtown and to the nearby suburb and rural areas for leisure and recreation. However, prior registration with shared-bicycle schemes through joining 'clubs' and with local transport authorities for access codes or devices can deter casual cyclists or tourists (including domestic tourists in large countries like Brazil, China and India) from using the service.

The use of e-technologies, particularly with a mobile app and related e-networking and e-commerce sites, can overcome these barriers. A case in point is the flourishing of bicycle rentals in major Chinese cities like Shenzhen and Guangzhou. In Shenzhen alone, there are three popular bicycle-sharing systems. With the relevant smartphone app and WeChat's 'wallet' function (WeChat is currently the most popular social networking platform in mainland China), anyone (including non-locals) can use a shared bicycle on the roadside by scanning the QR code at the back of the bicycle and using the WeChat 'wallet' to pay. Figure 9.2 shows a shared bicycle in Shenzhen, China. As of 2017, the cost is as low as RMB50 cents per half-an-hour in the city. The user-friendly apps and software allow for the much wider use of bicycle rentals after 2015. Similar technologies can be applied to encourage a more healthy and sustainable transport mode of walking in cities. Comprehensive all-in-one apps that advise users not just about different driving routes but also public transit services and walking paths should be developed. When all information is integrated, a smart sustainable transport app should be able to advise its user to get off a bus or the metro earlier or later by one stop and to advise a pedestrian route, depending on the time of day (for example, along a bright street, which may be of use for a woman travelling alone) and individual preferences

Figure 9.1 Conviva in Sao Paulo, Brazil.
Source: The author.

Figure 9.2 A shared bicycle in Shenzhen, China.
Source: The author.

(like avoiding stairs, which would be helpful for a parent travelling with a baby in a pram) based on the number of steps taken by that user earlier on that day (for example, via a pedometer app).

The above is sometimes called smart transport, and is just one of the initiatives of a smart city. In fact, there is much synergy with the development of smart transport and other initiatives like smart homes, smart buildings and a smart grid. The idea of smart city infrastructure is best summarised by the United Nations (United Nations, 2016), as shown in Figure 9.3. After reviewing 116

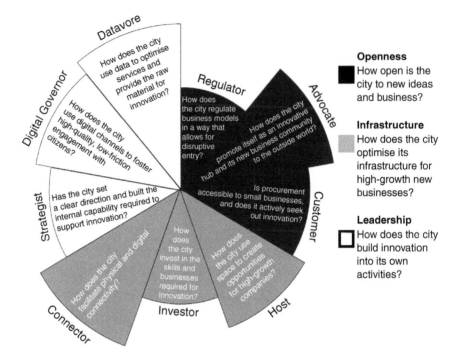

The figure contains the following labels and text:

Datavore — How does the city use data to optimise services and provide the raw material for innovation?

Digital Governor — How does the city use digital channels to foster high-quality, low-friction engagement with citizens?

Regulator — How does the city regulate business models in a way that allows for disruptive entry?

Advocate — How does the city promote itself as an innovative hub and its new business community to the outside world?

Strategist — Has the city set a clear direction and built the internal capability required to support innovation?

Customer — Is procurement accessible to small businesses, and does it actively seek out innovation?

Connector — How does the city facilitate physical and digital connectivity?

Investor — How does the city invest in the skills and businesses required for innovation?

Host — How does the city use space to create opportunities for high-growth companies?

Openness
How open is the city to new ideas and business?

Infrastructure
How does the city optimise its infrastructure for high-growth new businesses?

Leadership
How does the city build innovation into its own activities?

Figure 9.3 Smart city and infrastructure.

Source: Modified from United Nations (2016). Adapted from *Issues Paper on Smart Cities and Infrastructure*, by UNCTAD secretariat, ©2016, United Nations. Modified with the permission of the United Nations.

definitions, the International Telecommunication Union (ITU, 2014) has suggested that the definition of a smart sustainable city as:

> an innovative city that uses information and communication technologies (ICTs) and other means to improve quality of life, efficiency of urban operation and services, and competitiveness, while ensuring that it meets the needs of present and future generations with respect to economic, social and environmental aspects.

When the hardware of infrastructure is considered, the major components are smart buildings, smart mobility, smart energy, smart water, smart waste management, smart health and smart digital layers. While all these components are important, the development of smart applications that ensure the city's optimal use of resources and improves performance through the data generated from these smart infrastructure elements remains challenging.

Importance of governance

In a similar vein, sustainable transport, being built upon the concept of comprehensive sustainability, essentially covers many different aspects of a society and touches upon different government policies. In cities, sustainable transport involves at least several ministries or bureaux including those in charge of the environment, transportation, land development and urban planning. While recognising multiple stakeholders, a sustainable transport strategy needs to have a champion or lead agency responsible for the overall policy formulation, goal-setting, measure package, implementation and evaluation to ensure that the society can benefit as much as possible from the strategy. Without such a champion, the efforts can become piecemeal and the lack of coordination will not only become ineffective and inefficient but also give rise to highly undesirable side effects (like worsened road safety with many bicycle injury and fatalities) and contradictory outcomes (like the promotion of electric or low-emission cars giving rise to a sharp increase in overall car usage and, in turn, traffic congestion).

The example of electric cars is indeed a very good example to illustrate the potential problem of uncoordinated sustainable transport measures. In cities, the environmental protection departments responsible for ensuring overall air quality, especially by the roadside, often advocate the use of electric or low-emission cars. Financial incentives like a reduction in vehicle registration tax for the purchase of these alternative fuel vehicles are typically introduced. While the success of the tax reduction or exemption scheme is often measured by the total number of low-emission vehicles purchased and used in the city, the reduction of vehicles using petroleum or diesel often has not been set as an accompanying target to be achieved through such a scheme. As a result, the total number of alternative fuel vehicles may have increased dramatically in a city without necessarily any concurrent reduction in the number of petroleum or diesel vehicles. Indeed, the total vehicle fleet in the city may have increased dramatically, leading to more severe traffic congestion and even worsened air quality (from the petroleum or diesel vehicles travelling much slower on roads due to the increased traffic congestion) (refer to Figure 2.2 on vehicular speed and pollution). Should better coordination between the environmental protection and transport authorities be achieved, the real policy goal should be a shift of the city's entire vehicle fleet from petroleum or diesel-based vehicles to alternative fuel vehicles, that is, a percentage change or qualitative transformation, rather than the absolute number of electric vehicles in the city alone.

Another typical example is the implementation of TOD with the 'rail-cum-property' model (Tang & Lo, 2015) leading to the gentrification of local neighbourhoods and the displacement of low-income residents or small local shops from the transit neighbourhood. The unintended consequence of this sustainable transport strategy must be carefully monitored and counter-balanced by measures, such as the building of public housing in transit neighbourhoods to ensure mixed neighbourhoods and that low-income households are not displaced. Social equity (an important dimension of comprehensive sustainability) needs to be more seriously considered at the planning level, using indirect measures like effective land-use controls or direct measures like the building of public or affordable housing by the government.

As all sustainable transport strategies must be geared towards the movement of people and goods, the transport ministry or bureau is in a very good position to lead the initiatives with the support of the other ministries and bureaux. Visionary strategic policy documents on sustainable transport must be developed with a sufficiently long time horizon – at least 10–20 years – for deliberation in the local community and for all different responsible parties to get involved and know their respective roles in the sustainable transport strategy. In this light, publicity and education are required, especially for the younger generations, in order to adopt a lifestyle that is both smart and sustainable.

Last but not least, the sustainable transport strategy needs to be followed through at different spatial levels and different levels of government, from the national and provincial to city/county levels. Certain strategies, like the promotion of walkability, need to be implemented primarily at the district/local street level, seeing through all the aspects of micro-scale walkability assessments of comfort, convenience and safety for each road crossing and walkway (Loo & Lam, 2012). Yet, higher-level interventions also need to be implemented through, for example, making walking a priority in the transport system, promulgating walkability guidelines, and walkability audits as mandatory in the planning of new settlements and in fixing existing infrastructure, especially in downtown areas. Such need for multi-level or regional-local planning coordination is also crucial for the building of strategic railways across regions within a country and even countries across continents. For the former, the building of the high-speed railways (HSR) in the UK is a perfect example. The complexity of the politics involved has been discussed in Chapman (2015). For the latter, the building of intercontinental railways linking Asia and Europe under the grand 'belt and road initiative' has just started (Li & Loo, 2016a). All sustainable mobility strategies should be carefully thought through at different spatial levels.

Local participation

Nowadays, the general public has an increasing expectation to be able to express their opinions on public policies. Furthermore, sustainable transport strategies are just general directions that suggest the major pillars or anchors of the entire transport system. Nonetheless, the specific measures can vary substantially. The implementation of transit-oriented development (TOD), for example, may adopt the railway-operator-led rail-cum-property development model as exemplified in the case of Hong Kong, or the government-led planning model with specifications on the land use pattern and density mix. Whether the former or the latter is more appropriate for a specific local context is arguably best decided with inputs from the local residents.

The views of the general public, however, have to be taken and analysed by professionals. Typically, the general public won't be a single voice. Divergence of opinions in a local community is more the norm than the exception. It is suggested that the approach should not be simply taking the 'majority' view of the general public or conducting a poll to direct the sustainable transport strategies but to listen to the concerns of the local community about particular sustainable transport strategies and to see if there are ways to address these concerns without jeopardising the proposed general directions. There is a need to work together with the advocacy groups to mobilise the general public to support the various initiatives. It is important not to simply ignore the concerns while pursuing the sustainable transport strategies. This will in turn lead to the reversal of the policy/strategy at the next election or change of government officer in the medium to long term.

The next point is perhaps to undertake public participation and engagement by stage. At each stage, there should be different foci. It is important not to turn over the decision of the previous stage easily at the next stage. In other words, there should be sequential and logical steps, as in the scientific method. Unless there are very strong reasons, previous decisions or the general directions should not be challenged or revisited. Or else the society will suffer from not experiencing the benefits of the sustainable transport strategies sooner. Moreover, the sustainable transport strategies will remain on the drawing board and government agenda, with the efforts of professionals and government officials spent on the one hand and the resources of government spent on the other, without any citizen or the society benefiting directly.

Finally, it should be emphasised that fine tuning is possible and necessary. No matter how successful a sustainable transport strategy is when it was first introduced, the associated measures must be reviewed critically every five to six years. The most important reason being that the society changes. As the measures are implemented, people's travel behaviour will change. For instance, should subsidies be given to transit users when a new rail line is opened? The success of the rail line in the first few years may mean that the total number of transit users will become too high (with more people moving to live in TOD neighbourhoods and more businesses relocated there as well) but that the line might become financially viable without government subsidy. The amount of money spent on subsidies can be used in other sustainable transport measures like the extension and enhancements of pedestrian walkways instead. In this regard, a stable agency to oversee the entire sustainable transport strategy is necessary.

The two levels of internal and external movements

While this book so far has focused a lot on transport in cities without differentiating between intra- and inter-city movements, the actual policy packages to be developed under a holistic sustainable transport strategy need to look more closely into the nature of the movements. For passenger transport, a people-oriented and place-based approach in formulating the sustainable transport strategy is necessary.

Governments should endeavour to move beyond simply pledging to reduce carbon emissions to a specific level by a certain year but to adopt a life-cycle approach in guiding the planning and development of future cities. The built environment should be understood both at the neighbourhood and city scales. There may need to be a shift in the transport system with a different balance of transport modes. Moreover, the correct type and mix of transport modes should be provided with respect to where people are and their activities take place.

For intra-city movements, the potential key role of TOD in creating local communities that are economically sustainable with strong public transit patronage, healthy with easily walking and cycling, and attractive with good urban planning and design features like greenery and vibrancy, should be carefully examined. For inter-city movements, integrated transport with seamless intermodal transfers (Li & Loo, 2016b) and station–neighbourhood integration (Rodrigue, 2015) would enable a fast and pleasant passenger experience without compromising the comprehensive transport principles. Through integrated transport, a two-level sustainable transport strategy can be developed based primarily on heterogeneous TOD neighbourhoods supported by different forms of public transport to support both the internal and external movements of people (Loo & du Verle, 2017). In particular, the details are important and governments should endeavour to move beyond simply making low-carbon transport modes available but also make them attractive to people from all walks of life. Furthermore, as argued by Bertolini (2007), cities evolve gradually over time (some over centuries), reflecting both the physical and human (such as political, economic and cultural factors) geography of the localities. While no sustainable transport policy and strategy is likely to work if there is no wide public acceptance, many of the policies and strategies need to be considered together and implemented holistically for real changes to happen. It is not desirable, and not possible, to isolate any single cause for more sustainable travel behaviour to take place. In this regard, the issue of residential self-selection is logical because people naturally choose to live in areas that fit their lifestyle, within constraints. Nonetheless, this does not make TOD less important or relevant. The missions of providing people who prefer public transport (already) with more choices and more attractive choices, and of getting people who are sceptical of the use of public transport to get out of their cars (more often) by creating attractive TOD all point in the same direction. The case study of Hong Kong is particularly revealing in that people living in the city are generally more used to using public transit and have a similar culture and value systems. Nonetheless, people living in TOD neighbourhoods still have higher public transport shares, when compared to those living in other non-TOD neighbourhoods (Loo & du Verle, 2017). Though TOD may not be the major (certainly not the only) reason for people's travel preferences (and changes, if any), its key value actually lies in providing people with more travel options – real and attractive choices – over the use of private cars for different trip purposes and length.

Another major aspect of TOD to be further investigated and fostered in future cities is the recognition of the value of the many co-benefits associated with

TOD. Co-benefits are defined as both direct and indirect benefits beyond traditional transport impacts measured by the increased public transport usage, reduced automobile usage, and various emissions and congestion benefits resulting directly from 'less cars on the street'. Examples of key TOD co-benefits include improved liveability, quality of life, social equity and public health (Cutts *et al.*, 2009; de Nezelle *et al.*, 2011; Litman, 2006). The co-benefits associated with the 'Three Ds' of TODs are numerous. Density, for instance, is conducive to increased social interactions, the provision of more neighbourhood lower-order facilities, and generating the labour pooling effects for spatial agglomeration to happen. Diversity is conducive to higher vibrancy at street level, less crime, more non-local residents. Design is conducive to more physical exercise, better public health conditions, fewer traffic injuries and better quality of life. All these 'intangible' values beyond the metro patronage and carbon reduction should be properly reflected in the whole planning process. For municipality governments and policy-makers, the co-benefits of TOD beyond the transport realm have to be recognised in planning future cities. As a future research direction, more efforts should be devoted to developing practical guidelines and manuals for implementing TOD at the neighbourhood level by taking into account other good urban planning and design principles, relevant local contexts and stakeholders' views.

Towards a holistic sustainable transport plan

Last but not least, there is a need to 'connect the dots'. While the focus of this book is on transportation, an essential point that anyone interested in unsustainable transport and its transition must recognise is that transport is actually part of people's everyday life. Solutions to unsustainable transport problems do not lie in the transport sector alone. Very often, one hears comments that 'there is a simple solution within the transport system'. Transport engineers may argue that a technological solution, such as zero-emission vehicles, will be able to decarbonise transport, making any significant modal shift or curb to urban sprawl unnecessary. Theoretically, the provision of sufficient economic incentives and penalties can eliminate all negative transport externalities, like traffic congestion, without government interventions. The introduction of congestion pricing, for example, can reduce car usage on the one hand and internalise the external costs of congestion on the other. None of these parochial approaches, however, will be able to address the whole series of unsustainable transport problems listed in Table 1.1. Moreover, repercussions on the other dimensions of comprehensive sustainability (Figure 2.1) are not fully considered. For instance, the replacement of even 100 per cent of all vehicles by 'zero-emission' vehicles will drastically reduce transport carbon emissions but will not address the widespread traffic congestion that wastes millions of hours among drivers (and passengers) sitting in their vehicles. The latter is likely to get worse as people will no longer have to worry that their driving will generate transport carbon emissions. In societies where electricity is still largely generated based on coal and other fossil fuels/non-renewable energy, the carbon emissions have simply shifted to the energy sector. The above already ignores the energy used to produce the batteries, as well as the recycling issues. Similarly, the economists' approach of asking users to pay for their negative externalities may sound great in theory. Nonetheless, trips made by disadvantaged groups, for example, the elderly to health care facilities, the unemployed to find jobs, and children to go to school, are all driven out. There is a key problem of social equity, if the road charging scheme is not carefully designed to address the associated issues, for example, through the dedicated use of the funding obtained from the road charges to improve public transit and walkability within the city. Therefore, a holistic sustainable transport plan that takes into account different aspects of people's everyday life and comprehensive sustainability is advocated. Figure 9.4 is a schematic representation of the holistic sustainable transport plan. Efforts in all five transformations will not only ensure that the chance and speed of addressing the unsustainable transport problems be maximised through complementary measures but also maximise the chance of gaining general public support for the sustainable transport plan. The five transformations are elaborated below.

City transformation

A city's transport system will not be sustainable if things that people need on a daily basis (for example, jobs for workers and schools for children) continue to

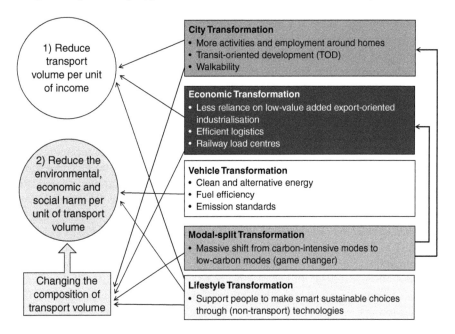

Figure 9.4 A holistic sustainable transport plan and the five transformations.

Source: The author.

be located in large patches of homogenous land use separated by long distances and expressways only (Loo & Chow, 2011). Appropriate regional and local planning that takes people's transport needs into account when deciding where to put different land uses is highly necessary.

In support of the spearheading sustainable transport modes and strategies (identified in Chapter 7 and further fine-tuned in Chapter 8), there needs to be appropriate land use and planning measures within a city. Promoting TOD around the spearheading transport modes, such as metro, light rail and BRT, has to be done. To recall, TOD is a healthy and vibrant community concept centred around a public transit stop, where the surrounding neighbourhood is economically vibrant, socially diverse and walkable. The main planning and land use interventions often revolve around the three Ds of increasing density, diversity and design (Loo & du Verle, 2017). Although there have been many additional refinements, the three Ds remain the most fundamental (Cervero & Kockelman, 1997). In fact, many of the additional dimensions, such as 'destinations', can be incorporated into the three Ds. Generally, a good design already takes into account the actual needs and preferences of the people, diversity ensures that there are a range of activities for people in place, and the density ensures that there are sufficient people flowing through.

Improving walkability may require some additional elaboration. There is a need to focus sharply on the pedestrian experience. Putting 'pedestrians first' means that the car-oriented approach in urban and transport planning has to be changed. Nowadays, wide two-way trunk roads, with six to eight lanes each way, are built in downtown areas to satisfy the car users and ease traffic congestion. As a result, pedestrians are often completely 'driven out' or forbidden to use the road at grade and are forced to go over purpose-built pedestrian flyovers or subways with minimal shade and comfort. The purpose was to eliminate vehicular delays caused by pedestrian 'interference'. Where an elevator is not available, either a series of long staircases or a long ramp is built to allow pedestrians to cross such wide road junctions. It is not hard to imagine the resulting extra effort and stress for pedestrians, especially vulnerable ones like pregnant women, simply to cross the road, especially in difficult weather conditions like heavy rain and hot sun. In contrast to a driver stepping on the accelerator to go up a slope, a pedestrian has to use physical energy to do so. Does this make good sense? This is a fundamental question to ask for transport policy-makers and planners. Planning for pedestrians needs to consider the comfort, convenience and safety dimensions (Loo & Lam, 2012). Attractions and activities in a city can be created through careful land-use zoning and coordination; and these activity nodes need to be carefully connected by well-planned and pleasant pedestrian walkways. Where an elevated pedestrian walkway system is available, the addition of new links should consider factors other than just street-level walkability, such as network connectivity and characteristics of the users (Loo, 2017).

In addition, there is indeed much synergy in the promotion of TOD and walkability. As shown in Table 9.2, residents living in the metro neighbourhoods in Hong Kong are not only using the metro more frequently but walking more

Table 9.2 Modal shares of residents living in different metro and non-metro neighbourhoods in Hong Kong

Transport mode (%)	Metro neighbourhoods (n = 60)		Non-metro neighbourhoods (n = 60)		All neighbourhoods (n = 120)	
	2001	2011	2001	2011	2001	2011
Single-mode only						
• Walking	26.3	23.0	20.6	20.5	23.5	22.0
• Metro	9.9	10.0	2.5	2.4	6.2	6.3
• Bus	10.3	13.8	14.2	13.1	12.3	13.5
• Minibus	3.9	5.2	4.2	8.1	4.0	6.7
• Private car	4.8	8.4	12.0	14.0	8.4	11.3
Multi-mode involving a trip leg of:						
• Walking	31.5	47.7	28.9	37.8	30.2	43.1
• Metro	22.5	40.4	14.8	23.3	18.7	32.2
• Bus	13.2	16.5	18.3	24.2	15.7	20.3

Source: Loo and du Verle (2017). Copyright obtained from Taylor and Francis.

Note
Modal shares do not add up to 100 per cent because not all modes are listed and multimodal trips are also counted. For a multimodal trip involving metro as the first leg and bus as the second leg, it is counted under both transport modes.

consistently than their counterparts living in non-metro neighbourhoods. The differences are statistically significant (Loo & du Verle, 2017). More effort should be made to promote synergy for the first and the last mile of using public transport by walking.

Economic transformation

Economic transformation is particularly important when considering freight transport. Although this book is primarily concerned with people, the movement of goods to satisfy human needs and as an economic sector in supporting people's livelihoods is always relevant. Given that China's economic growth in the last three decades has been so heavily dependent on export-oriented low-value-added industrialisation, the growth of road freight turnover relying on goods vehicles was almost inevitable. If this experience is to be repeated in other developing countries, the impacts on the environment and safety will be enormous. Goods vehicles in developing countries, especially in poor rural areas, tend to be highly polluting and some not even road worthy. The development of an efficient and sustainable inland port distribution system needs to be in place to support developing countries' industrialisation through railway containerisation (Loo and Liu, 2005). Local logistics systems need to be efficient to avoid unnecessary repeated and unnecessary freight transport.

Vehicle transformation

Vehicles here refer to all means of conveyance of different modes. In other words, they refer to airplanes for air transport, locomotives and compartments for rail transport, vehicles for road transport, various types of shipping vessels for water transport, and pipelines for pipeline transport. The transition from carbon-intensive and non-renewable fuels (notably diesel and petroleum) to alternative low-carbon and renewable energy needs to be accelerated. Electricity may be an option in the longer term. Other options include biofuels (including vegetable oil, biodiesel and bioethanol), ethers, alcohol (including methanol and ethanol) and other gaseous fuels (such as natural gas, LPG and hydrogen) (Li & Loo, 2014). These alternative vehicles need to be actively supported not only in terms of the technologies that can use them more efficiently in transport (for instance, solar energy is known to be highly inefficient for propelling vehicles) and the distribution system of transporting and storing these fuels safely and efficiently, but also the recharging system, that is, making it convenient for vehicles to be recharged without making additional trips or long detours, which would again add to the total transport volume in the society.

Modal-split transformation

This transformation is particularly relevant to cities that are highly dependent on road transport. For passengers, the emphasis should be to make the unsustainable transport modes (such as the carbon-intensive modes) more expensive and inconvenient to use, and the sustainable transport modes (such as the low carbon-intensive modes of public transport and the active transport modes of walking and cycling) more available, affordable and attractive. Cities should provide a range of transport modes to cater for people's diverse needs and preferences. It is not sufficient for a few enthusiasts (such as bus fans) or advocates (such as cycling groups) to change to public transit or use active transport. The majority of the population need to be using these sustainable transport modes for the spearheading modes (see Chapter 8) to become real 'game changers' in the unsustainable transport transition. In this regard, government policies are instrumental in bringing about the modal-split transformation.

Lifestyle transformation

Every individual in a society makes decisions in order to fulfil one's obligations and inspirations. However, these decisions do have implications on other human beings. The collective human decisions in turn affect nature and the urban environment. A higher awareness of the environmental, economic and social externalities that our travel decisions generate is necessary. Perhaps, the best way to achieve this is through educating the younger generation; this would be much more effective than trying to convince existing drivers to use public transport. It is high time we educate the next generation on the importance of physical exercise, the benefits of cycling and walking, the joy of making trips together with fellow peers on public transport, and to use private vehicles sensibly and only in a discretionary manner. There is a need for us to 'think twice before making a trip'. When a trip has to be made, transport modes other than driving should be taken into consideration. Thus, spearheading sustainable transport modes need to be well-developed and integrated to form the backbone of the local transport system. These sustainable transport modes should be make as widely available, affordable and attractive as possible. It is also important to think about closer and/or alternative destinations that would allow the best use of a trip, for example, as in trip chaining.

Through the implementation of a holistic sustainable transport plan, specific measures can be developed based on the local context. The above are the major components and directions that all cities should seriously consider for addressing unsustainable transport problems and the transition required.

Reflections on unsustainable transport globally

The analytical framework in this book is to urge and facilitate developing countries to realistically consider strategies to overcome unsustainable transport, taking into consideration country-specific conditions like population size, economic capability, transport performance and supporting infrastructure. As shown in Figure 9.5, although the geographical contexts, values, local constraints and priorities of different countries will inevitably differ, countries should share the same goal of comprehensive sustainability. Following the research design laid out in Figure 1.1,

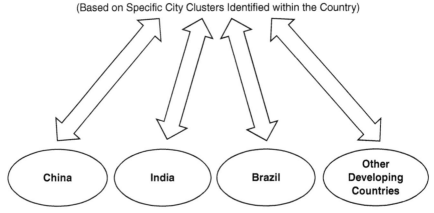

Emerging Solutions for Sustainable Urban Transport
(Based on Specific City Clusters Identified within the Country)

China   India   Brazil   Other Developing Countries

Different Contexts, Different Values, Different Constraints/Priorities, Same Goal of Comprehensive Sustainability

Figure 9.5 The analytical framework beyond China.
Source: The author.

there are three major steps or stages that another country, such as India or Brazil, can undertake. Stage 1 is international benchmarking (Stage 1), in order to really appreciate the relative strengths and weaknesses of the current transport situation in the country. India, for example, may have the advantage of high average passenger loads for vehicles on its roads. Brazil, on the other hand, has a rich source of alternative fuels, such as ethanol fuel, which provides opportunities not just for the wider adoption of existing models of alternative fuel vehicles but also new innovations in automobile production using environmentally friendly fuels and technology.

Stage 2 is an analysis of national geographical diversities with respect to sustainable mobility, the grouping of city clusters and some initial sustainable mobility strategies that could be advanced for detailed study. This analysis would help countries to understand that any sustainable transport strategy should be realistically evaluated in groups of cities rather than as a uniform bundle of strategies suitable for all cities within the country. It is clear that the sustainable transport strategies for Mumbai and Bhubaneswar in India would not be the same, though the goal of making public transport attractive to the local people would be shared.

Stage 3 involves a reality check and the refinement of local sustainable transport strategies by the local governments. Even for cities within the same cluster, local history, sentiments and other factors like existing local infrastructure will make certain sustainable transport measures unrealistic or undesirable for delivering the sustainable transport promise. A practical way to evaluate the initial sustainable transport strategy is through a critical examination of the four different elements of the local transport system (Figure 2.3) in order to identify the opportunities and constraints. What are the most 'ready' and biggest opportunities for 'quick wins'? What are the 'hardest' and most obvious constraints that would mean a consensus is unlikely to be reached in the local society?

In an e-society, where people's mind set and lifestyles have already fully embraced information and communication technologies (Loo, 2012), these opportunities and constraints may not be limited to the hardware, including the transport network, vehicular fleet, the other infrastructure and other physical objects like smart phones, but the software, especially mobile applications and intelligent transport systems. While smart city initiatives are launched in many cities in developed countries, these opportunities should not be considered as appropriate only for the developed world. Many cities in developing countries, including China and India, have been by-passing fixed-line phone installations and taking up mobile telecommunications directly with the latest 3G and 4G technology (Loo & Ngan, 2012). Smart mobile applications (apps) can therefore be developed to advise people on real-time transit information, cycling routes and pedestrian paths. One major direction should be to facilitate people to make more sustainable travel choices like using the mass transit, cycling and walking. Moreover, people's actual travel behaviour can be captured and understood through big data for mapping the sustainable transport opportunities and challenges ahead.

Once again (as stated in Chapter 1), the distinction between developed and developing countries is rather general and conceptual, suggesting similar basic economic conditions (United Nations, 2014) rather than the specific and statistical, and also implying a uniform group of developing countries and a modernisation paradigm that they will 'naturally' or 'inevitably' follow the same development path as developed countries (Rostow, 1990). The alternative terms high-income, middle-income and low-income countries seem no less 'arbitrary' and equally subject to challenges of generalisation. Hence, some precautionary notes on the interpretation of terms and rationale for the choice of words are reiterated in these concluding remarks. In contrast to developed countries, which generally have more mature economies with higher income, developing countries typically face tougher economic conditions of low income and have not fully undergone the processes of industrialisation, urbanisation and motorisation. There is no proposition that developing countries must follow in the footsteps of the developed countries in completing the modernisation (including industrialisation, urbanisation and motorisation) process. Instead, each developing country is seen as capable of breaking new paths (not only different from the developed countries but also different from other developing countries) in achieving economic growth and satisfying the needs of its population. Against this background, this book sets out to examine the issues, problems and solutions of unsustainable transport in developing countries, especially in China. The overall approach is to find ways to overcome the unsustainable transport trends. While it is recognised that there is no 'magic bullet' that can take a country with persistent, if not accelerating, unsustainable transport trends over the last few decades (especially during a period of rapid economic growth) to sustainable transport within a short time span such as the next decade, it is believed that a transition in the direction of sustainable transport is possible if the right sets of measures and strategies are put in place and sustained efforts are made to reverse the high reliance on private automobiles and fossil fuels, and the enormous negative transport externalities of pollution, congestion and fatalities. Instead, the positive role of transport in fulfilling people's basic needs and various other needs, desires and aspirations for national identity, economic development, social objectives and personal wellbeing should be strengthened.

References

Anda, C., Erath, A. & Fourie, P.J. (2017). Transport modelling in the age of big data. *International Journal of Urban Sciences*, 21(Suppl. 1), 19–42. doi:10.1080/12265934.2017.1281150.

Bertolini, L. (2007). Evolutionary urban transportation planning: An exploration. *Environment and Planning A*, 39, 1998–2019. doi:10.1068/a38350.

Bikesampa. (2017). *Bikesampa*. Retrieved from https://bikesampa.tembici.com.br/.

Cervero, R., & Kockelman, K. (1997). Travel demand and the 3Ds: Density, diversity, and design. *Transportation Research Part D – Transport and Environment*, 2, 199–219. doi:10.1016/S1361-9209(97)00009-6.

Chapman, D. (2015). The rise of localism in railway infrastructural development. In B.P.Y. Loo & C. Comtois (Eds.), *Sustainable Railway Futures: Issues and Challenges* (pp. 145–166). Surrey: Ashgate.

Cottrill, C.D., & Derrible, S. (2015). Leveraging big data for the development of transport sustainability indicators. *Journal of Urban Technology*, *22*, 45–64. doi:10.1080/10630 732.2014.942094.

Cutts, B.B., Darby, K.J., Boone, C.G. & Brewis, A. (2009). City structure, obesity, and environmental justice: An integrated analysis of physical and social barriers to walkable streets and park access. *Social Science & Medicine*, *69*, 1314–1322. doi:10.1016/j. socscimed.2009.08.020.

de Gennaro, M., Paffumi, E. & Martini, G. (2016). Big data for supporting low-carbon road transport policies in Europe: Applications, challenges and opportunities. *Big Data Research*, *6*, 11–25. doi:10.1016/j.bdr.2016.04.003.

de Nazelle, A., Nieuwenhuijsen, M.J., Anto, J.M., Brauer, M., Briggs, D., Braun-Fahrlander, C., ... Lebret, E. (2011). Improving health through policies that promote active travel: A review of evidence to support integrated health impact assessment. *Environment International*, *37*, 766–777. doi:10.1016/j.envint.2011.02.003.

Gazder, U., & Ratrout, N.T. (2015). A new logit-artificial neural network ensemble for mode choice modeling: A case study for border transport. *Journal of Advanced Transportation*, *49*, 855–866. doi:10.1002/atr.1306.

Huang, L., & Song, R. (2003). Safety and reliability analysis of automated vehicle driving systems. In IEEE (Ed.), *Proceedings of the 2003 IEEE International Conference on Intelligent Transportation Systems* (Volume 1, pp. 21–26). doi:10.1109/ITSC.2003. 1251913.

International Telecommunication Union (ITU). (2014). *Smart Sustainable Cities: An Analysis of Definitions. Technical Report of the Focus Group on Smart Sustainable Cities – Working Group 1*. Retrieved from www.itu.int/en/ITU-T/focusgroups/ssc/ Documents/Approved_Deliverables/TR-Definitions.docx.

Li, L., & Loo, B.P.Y. (2014). Alternative and transitional energy sources for urban transportation. *Current Sustainable/Renewable Energy Reports*, *1*, 19–26. doi:10.1007/ s40518-014-0005-6.

Li, L., & Loo, B.P.Y. (2016a). Carbon dioxide emissions from urban transport in China: Geographical characteristics and future challenges. *Geographical Research* (in Chinese), *25*, 1230–1242. Retrieved from www.dlyj.ac.cn/EN/10.11821/dlyj201607002.

Li, L., & Loo, B.P.Y. (2016b). Towards people-centered integrated transport: A case study of Shanghai Hongqiao Comprehensive Transport Hub. *Cities*, *58*, 50–58. doi:10.1016/j.cities.2016.05.003.

Litman, T. (2006). *Rail Transit in America: A Comprehensive Evaluation of Benefits*. Victoria, BC: Victoria Transport Policy Institute.

Loo, B.P.Y. (2012). *The E-society*. New York, NY: Nova Science.

Loo, B.P.Y. (2017). *Final Report: Consultancy Services on Walkability in Pedestrian Planning and Enhancement of Pedestrian Network in Hong Kong* (PLB(Q)016/2015). Hong Kong: Institute of Transport Studies, The University of Hong Kong.

Loo, B.P.Y., & Chow, A.S.Y. (2011). Jobs-housing balance in an era of population decentralisation: An analytical framework and a case study. *Journal of Transport Geography*, *19*, 552–562. doi:10.1016/j.jtrangeo.2010.06.004.

Loo, B.P.Y., & du Verle, F. (2017). Transit-oriented development in future cities: Towards a two-level sustainable mobility strategy. *International Journal of Urban Sciences*, *21*(Suppl. 1), 54–67. doi:10.1080/12265934.2016.1235488.

Loo, B.P.Y., & Lam, W.W.Y. (2012). Geographic accessibility around elderly health care facilities in Hong Kong: A micro-scale walkability assessment. *Environment and Planning B: Planning and Design, 39*, 629–646. doi:10.1068/b36146.

Loo, B.P.Y., & Liu, K. (2005). A geographical analysis of potential railway load centers in China. *Professional Geographer, 57*, 558–579. doi:10.1111/j.1467-9272.2005.00499.x.

Loo, B.P.Y., & Ngan, Y.L. (2012). Developing mobile telecommunications to narrow digital divide in developing countries? Some lessons from China. *Telecommunications Policy, 36*, 888–900. doi:10.1016/j.telpol.2012.07.015.

Loo, B.P.Y., & Wang, B. (2017). Progress of e-development in China since 1998. *Telecommunications Policy*. Advance online publication. doi:10.1016/j.telpol.2017.03.001.

Rodrigue, J.-P. (2015). Structuring effects of rail terminals. In B.P.Y. Loo & C. Comtois (Eds.), *Sustainable Railway Futures: Issues and Challenges* (pp. 23–38). Surrey: Ashgate.

Rostow, W.W. (1990). *The Stages of Economic Growth: A Non-Communist Manifesto.* Cambridge: Cambridge University Press.

Tang, S., & Lo, H.K. (2015). Property models for financing railway investment. In B.P.Y. Loo & C. Comtois (Eds.), *Sustainable Railway Futures: Issues and Challenges* (pp. 219–231). Surrey: Ashgate.

United Nations. (2014). *World Economic Situation and Prospects 2014*. Retrieved from http://unctad.org/en/PublicationsLibrary/wesp2014_en.pdf.

United Nations. (2016). *Smart Cities and Infrastructure*. Commission on Science and Technology for Development, United Nations Economic and Social Council (E/CN.16/2016/2). Retrieved from http://unctad.org/meetings/en/SessionalDocuments/ecn 162016d2_en.pdf.

Winkle, T. (2016). Safety benefits of automated vehicles: Extended findings from accident research for development, validation and testing. In M. Maurer, J.C. Gerdes, B. Lenz & H. Winner (Eds.), *Autonomous Driving: Technical, Legal and Social Aspects* (pp. 335–364). doi:10.1007/978-3-662-48847-8_17.

Zhao, D., Lam, H., Peng, H., Bao, S., LeBlanc, D.J., Nobukawa, K. & Pan, C.S. (2017). Accelerated evaluation of automated vehicles safety in lane-change scenarios based on importance sampling techniques. *IEEE Transactions on Intelligent Transportation Systems, 18*, 595–607. doi:10.1109/TITS.2016.2582208.

Appendix 1

Guided questions used in the fieldwork in Maoming

Part 1 Bus rapid transit (BRT)

1 Maoming has planned several routes for BRT in its 12th Five-Year Plan. How would you predict BRT's effectiveness in the following perspectives? 5 being the highest and 1 being the lowest.

	1	2	3	4	5
a Reduce people's reliance on private cars	☐	☐	☐	☐	☐
b Increase transport volume and efficiency	☐	☐	☐	☐	☐
c Reduce transport sector CO_2 emissions	☐	☐	☐	☐	☐
d Alleviate traffic congestion	☐	☐	☐	☐	☐
e Enhance road safety	☐	☐	☐	☐	☐

2 What is the greatest challenge in developing BRT?

_____

_____

3 In order to realise the full benefits of BRT, how would the government plan in terms of basic infrastructure, vehicle specifications, route design and service management?

_____

_____

4 Will BRT be one of the priorities in Maoming's future planning on the urban transport system? What possible benefits do you expect from it?

_____

_____

Part 2 Cycling

5 Maoming has proposed 'Slow Transport' (Cycling + Walking) in its 12th Five-Year Plan. What are the reasons behind this? What possible benefits to the transport system do you expect by promoting cycling widely?

_____

_____

6 In terms of cycling tracks, bike parking facilities and other relevant equipment, does the government have plans to better prepare Maoming for the widespread promotion of cycling?

_____

_____

7 What are the challenges in the widespread promotion of cycling?

_____

_____

8 How would you comment on the effectiveness of promoting cycling in the following aspects? 5 being the highest and 1 being the lowest.

	1	2	3	4	5
a Reduce people's reliance on motor vehicles	☐	☐	☐	☐	☐
b Reduce transport sector CO_2 emissions	☐	☐	☐	☐	☐
c Alleviate traffic congestion	☐	☐	☐	☐	☐
d Increase people's environmental awareness	☐	☐	☐	☐	☐
e Reduce road fatalities	☐	☐	☐	☐	☐

Part 3 Sustainable transportation system

9 What is the biggest challenge in Maoming's transport system? Are there any urgent issues that need to be dealt with immediately?

_____

_____

10 Apart from promoting BRT and cycling, what else do you think would be effective in achieving a sustainable transport system in Maoming?

_____

_____

11 Based on the projection of the United Nations, Maoming's population and economy will undergo rapid growth up to 2030 and this will place a burden on its transport system. How will the government deal with it?

_____

_____

12 Any other opinions?

_____

_____

Appendix 2

Guided questions used in the fieldwork in Changsha

Part 1 Bus rapid transit (BRT)

1 Do you think the introduction of BRT can help to advance Changsha's sustainable transport? Does the government have any plan for it?

_____

_____

2 How would you comment on the role of buses in Changsha's transport system? If it is changed to a BRT system, will Changsha benefit from this? How?

_____

_____

3 What is the greatest foreseeable challenge if Changsha decides to introduce BRT?

_____

_____

4 If Changsha introduces BRT, how will you predict its effectiveness in the following aspects? 5 being the highest and 1 being the lowest

	1	2	3	4	5
a Reduce people's reliance on private cars	☐	☐	☐	☐	☐
b Increase transport volume and efficiency	☐	☐	☐	☐	☐
c Reduce transport sector CO_2 emissions	☐	☐	☐	☐	☐
d Alleviate traffic congestion	☐	☐	☐	☐	☐
e Enhance road safety	☐	☐	☐	☐	☐

Part 2 Light rail transit (LRT)

5   While Changsha Metro is under construction, does the government plan to build LRT as well? How would you comment on the desirability and feasibility of LRT in the city?

_____

_____

6   With the rapid growth of the population and the economy, the burden on Changsha's transport system will also increase. Do you consider the introduction of LRT to be an effective solution?

_____

_____

7   If Changsha introduces LRT, how will you predict its effectiveness in following aspects? 5 being the highest and 1 being the lowest.

		1	2	3	4	5
a	Reduce people's reliance on private cars	☐	☐	☐	☐	☐
b	Increase transport volume and efficiency	☐	☐	☐	☐	☐
c	Reduce transport sector CO_2 emissions	☐	☐	☐	☐	☐
d	Alleviate traffic congestion	☐	☐	☐	☐	☐
e	Enhance road safety	☐	☐	☐	☐	☐

8   What is the general attitude of citizens towards urban rail transit? Do you think that LRT will become one of the major transport means if it is introduced?

_____

_____

9   What will be the greatest challenge if Changsha decides to introduce LRT?

_____

_____

Part 3 Sustainable transportation system

10   What is the biggest challenge in Changsha's transport system? Are there any urgent issues that need to be dealt with immediately?

_____

_____

11 Apart from promoting BRT and LRT, what else do you think would be effective in achieving a sustainable transport system in Changsha?

_____

_____

12 With the population expansion and economic growth, the number of motor vehicles in Changsha has been rising sharply. How will the government deal with the associated problems such as air pollution and traffic congestion?

_____

_____

13 What will the government do to enhance road safety which is one of the key elements of sustainable transport?

_____

_____

14 Any other opinions?

_____

_____

Appendix 3

Guided questions used in the fieldwork in Beijing

Part 1 Electric cars

1 How would you comment on the effectiveness of electric cars in the following aspects? 5 being the highest and 1 being the lowest.

		1	2	3	4	5
a	Reducing CO_2 emissions from vehicles	☐	☐	☐	☐	☐
b	Reducing the number of diesel vehicles	☐	☐	☐	☐	☐
c	Increasing citizen's environmental awareness	☐	☐	☐	☐	☐
d	Advancing sustainable transportation	☐	☐	☐	☐	☐

2 What is the biggest challenge faced by Beijing in widely promoting electric cars?

_____

_____

3 Following Question 2, does the government have any solutions to deal with it?

_____

_____

4 What is the current percentage share of electric cars in the total motor vehicle fleet of Beijing? Has the government set up any specified goal?

_____

_____

5 In supporting research and development, and the practical application of electric cars, what are the government's current and future plans?

_____

_____

6   How many plug-in facilities for electric cars does Beijing currently have? How are they distributed?

_____

_____

Part 2   Metro

7   How would you comment on the effectiveness of metro in following aspects? 5 being the highest and 1 being the lowest.

	1	2	3	4	5
a Alleviate traffic congestion	☐	☐	☐	☐	☐
b Encourage the use of public transport and reduce reliance on private cars	☐	☐	☐	☐	☐
c Suppress the rapid increase of vehicles	☐	☐	☐	☐	☐
d Reduce transport sector CO_2 emissions	☐	☐	☐	☐	☐
e Increase passenger volume	☐	☐	☐	☐	☐
f Increase transport efficiency	☐	☐	☐	☐	☐

8   Are there any challenges faced by Beijing Metro in terms of operation and expansion?

_____

_____

9   Following Question 8, if yes, does the government have any solutions to deal with it (them)?

_____

_____

10   Apart from the extension of current lines and the construction of new lines, are there other possible methods to further boost the efficiency of the metro service?

_____

_____

11   In the future planning of Beijing's transport system, what will be the role of the metro system?

_____

_____

Part 3 Sustainable transportation system

12 What is the biggest challenge faced by Beijing's transportation system? Are there any urgent issues that need to be dealt with immediately?

_____

_____

13 Apart from promoting electric cars and expanding the metro network, what else do you think would be effective in achieving a sustainable transport system in Beijing?

_____

_____

14 Will the building of a sustainable transport system be one of the focal points in the future urban planning of Beijing?

_____

_____

_____

15 Any other opinions?

_____

_____

Index

Taylor & Francis eBooks

Helping you to choose the right eBooks for your Library

Add Routledge titles to your library's digital collection today. Taylor and Francis ebooks contains over 50,000 titles in the Humanities, Social Sciences, Behavioural Sciences, Built Environment and Law.

Choose from a range of subject packages or create your own!

Benefits for you

» Free MARC records
» COUNTER-compliant usage statistics
» Flexible purchase and pricing options
» All titles DRM-free.

REQUEST YOUR **FREE** INSTITUTIONAL TRIAL TODAY

Free Trials Available
We offer free trials to qualifying academic, corporate and government customers.

Benefits for your user

» Off-site, anytime access via Athens or referring URL
» Print or copy pages or chapters
» Full content search
» Bookmark, highlight and annotate text
» Access to thousands of pages of quality research at the click of a button.

eCollections – Choose from over 30 subject eCollections, including:

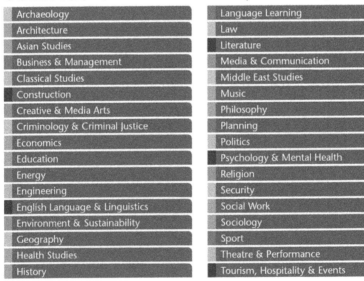

Archaeology	Language Learning
Architecture	Law
Asian Studies	Literature
Business & Management	Media & Communication
Classical Studies	Middle East Studies
Construction	Music
Creative & Media Arts	Philosophy
Criminology & Criminal Justice	Planning
Economics	Politics
Education	Psychology & Mental Health
Energy	Religion
Engineering	Security
English Language & Linguistics	Social Work
Environment & Sustainability	Sociology
Geography	Sport
Health Studies	Theatre & Performance
History	Tourism, Hospitality & Events

For more information, pricing enquiries or to order a free trial, please contact your local sales team:
www.tandfebooks.com/page/sales

Routledge
Taylor & Francis Group

The home of
Routledge books

www.tandfebooks.com

For Product Safety Concerns and Information please contact our EU
representative GPSR@taylorandfrancis.com
Taylor & Francis Verlag GmbH, Kaufingerstraße 24, 80331 München, Germany

www.ingramcontent.com/pod-product-compliance
Ingram Content Group UK Ltd.
Pitfield, Milton Keynes, MK11 3LW, UK
UKHW021001180425
457613UK00019B/776

* 9 7 8 0 3 6 7 8 7 4 1 6 2 *